Pedagogy, Image Practices, and Contested Corporealities

Edited by
Sarah Brophy and Janice Hladki

Routledge
Taylor & Francis Group
LONDON AND NEW YORK

First published 2015 by Routledge

2 Park Square, Milton Park, Abingdon, Oxfordshire OX14 4RN
711 Third Avenue, New York, NY 10017

Routledge is an imprint of the Taylor & Francis Group, an informa business

First issued in paperback 2018

British Library Cataloguing in Publication Data
A catalogue record for this book is available from the British Library

ISBN 13: 978-1-138-78768-1 (hbk)
ISBN 13: 978-1-138-37931-2 (pbk)

Typeset in Palatino
by RefineCatch Limited, Bungay, Suffolk

Publisher's Note
The publisher accepts responsibility for any inconsistencies that may have arisen during the conversion of this book from journal articles to book chapters, namely the possible inclusion of journal terminology.

Disclaimer
Every effort has been made to contact copyright holders for their permission to reprint material in this book. The publishers would be grateful to hear from any copyright holder who is not here acknowledged and will undertake to rectify any errors or omissions in future editions of this book.

Contents

Citation Information vii
Notes on Contributors ix

1. Introduction: Pedagogy, Image Practices, and Contested Corporealities 1
Sarah Brophy and Janice Hladki

2. The Ends of the Body as Pedagogic Possibility 8
Tanya Titchkosky

3. Why Do Dolls Die? The Power of Passivity and the Embodied Interplay Between Disability and Sex Dolls 20
Eunjung Kim

4. Augmented Spirit/Extreme Embodiment: A Mapped Landscape of Vent Life 33
Katerie Gladdys and Deshae E. Lott

5. The Reworking of Spatial Attribution: People with Intellectual Disabilities and the Micropolitics of Dissensus 49
Ann Fudge Schormans and Adrienne Chambon

6. The Narrator Witness: Dis/Connections Between Disability and Death 62
Nicole Markotić

7. Crip Excess, Art, and Politics: A Conversation with Robert McRuer 74
Danielle Peers, Melisa Brittain, and Robert McRuer

8. *The Specials* Meet the Lady Boys of Bangkok: Sexual and Gender Transgression and Smashing Intellectual Disability 82
Michael Gill

9. Intimate Borders: The Ethics of Human Organ Transplantation in Contemporary Film 96
Donna McCormack

10. "The Most Famous Brain in the World": Performance and Pedagogy on an Amnesiac's Brain 110
Katherine W. Sweaney

11. Ending Fat Stigma: *Precious*, Visual Culture, and Anti-Obesity in the "Fat Moment" 123
Scott Stoneman

12. Afterword: The End of Contested Corporealities 134
Robert McRuer

Index 139

Citation Information

The chapters in this book were originally published in *The Review of Education, Pedagogy, and Cultural Studies*, volume 34, issue 3–4 (July 2012). When citing this material, please use the original page numbering for each article, as follows:

Chapter 1
Introduction: Pedagogy, Image Practices, and Contested Corporealities
Sarah Brophy and Janice Hladki
The Review of Education, Pedagogy, and Cultural Studies, volume 34, issue 3–4 (July 2012) pp. 75–81

Chapter 2
The Ends of the Body as Pedagogic Possibility
Tanya Titchkosky
The Review of Education, Pedagogy, and Cultural Studies, volume 34, issue 3–4 (July 2012) pp. 82–93

Chapter 3
Why Do Dolls Die? The Power of Passivity and the Embodied Interplay Between Disability and Sex Dolls
Eunjung Kim
The Review of Education, Pedagogy, and Cultural Studies, volume 34, issue 3–4 (July 2012) pp. 94–106

Chapter 4
Augmented Spirit/Extreme Embodiment: A Mapped Landscape of Vent Life
Katerie Gladdys and Deshae E. Lott
The Review of Education, Pedagogy, and Cultural Studies, volume 34, issue 3–4 (July 2012) pp. 107–122

Chapter 5
The Reworking of Spatial Attribution: People with Intellectual Disabilities and the Micropolitics of Dissensus
Ann Fudge Schormans and Adrienne Chambon
The Review of Education, Pedagogy, and Cultural Studies, volume 34, issue 3–4 (July 2012) pp. 123–135

Chapter 6
The Narrator Witness: Dis/Connections Between Disability and Death
Nicole Markotić
The Review of Education, Pedagogy, and Cultural Studies, volume 34, issue 3–4 (July 2012) pp. 136–147

Chapter 7
Crip Excess, Art, and Politics: A Conversation with Robert McRuer
Danielle Peers, Melisa Brittain, and Robert McRuer
The Review of Education, Pedagogy, and Cultural Studies, volume 34, issue 3–4 (July 2012) pp. 148–155

Chapter 8
The Specials *Meet the Lady Boys of Bangkok: Sexual and Gender Transgression and Smashing Intellectual Disability*
Michael Gill
The Review of Education, Pedagogy, and Cultural Studies, volume 34, issue 3–4 (July 2012) pp. 156–169

Chapter 9
Intimate Borders: The Ethics of Human Organ Transplantation in Contemporary Film
Donna McCormack
The Review of Education, Pedagogy, and Cultural Studies, volume 34, issue 3–4 (July 2012) pp. 170–183

Chapter 10
"The Most Famous Brain in the World": Performance and Pedagogy on an Amnesiac's Brain
Katherine W. Sweaney
The Review of Education, Pedagogy, and Cultural Studies, volume 34, issue 3–4 (July 2012) pp. 184–196

Chapter 11
Ending Fat Stigma: Precious, *Visual Culture, and Anti-Obesity in the "Fat Moment"*
Scott Stoneman
The Review of Education, Pedagogy, and Cultural Studies, volume 34, issue 3–4 (July 2012) pp. 197–207

Chapter 12
Afterword: The End of Contested Corporealities
Robert McRuer
The Review of Education, Pedagogy, and Cultural Studies, volume 34, issue 3–4 (July 2012) pp. 208–211

Please direct any queries you may have about the citations to clsuk.permissions@cengage.com

Notes on Contributors

Melisa Brittain teaches Critical Theory and English Literature at the University of Alberta, Canada, and Athabasca University, Canada, has published on representations of interracial desire in war coverage and feminist fiction, and has presented on drag-kinging and activist video art. Co-founder of KingCrip Productions, she co-directed, edited, and produced *G.I.M.P. Boot Camp* (8 min., 2008); *And the Rest is Drag* (32 min., 2009); and *Bill 44: Smaller Classes, Smaller Minds* (5 min., 2009). Most recently, she made *Elephant in the Room* (4 min., 2012) with Lucas Crawford; this video provokes viewers to reflect on their own investments in slender culture and self-shaming.

Sarah Brophy is Associate Professor of English and Cultural Studies at McMaster University, Canada. Her research explores representations of sexuality, reproduction, and illness, bringing together theoretical frameworks drawn from several areas: testimony, witnessing, and autobiography; affect and intimacy; theories of gender and sexuality; critical race studies; postcolonialism; and cultural studies. She is the author of *Witnessing AIDS: Writing, Testimony, and the Work of Mourning* (2004) and of essays in *End of Empire and the English Novel Since 1945, Contemporary Women's Writing, PMLA, Literature and Medicine, scrutiny2,* and *Teaching Life-Writing Texts (MLA Options for Teaching)*. She and Janice Hladki co-edited the interdisciplinary book, *Embodied Politics in Visual Autobiography* (2014), which examines the cultural politics of health, disability, and the body in forms such as photography, video art, graphic memoir, film, body art and performance, and digital media.

Adrienne Chambon is Professor at the Factor-Inwentash Faculty of Social Work at the University of Toronto, Canada. She has been inquiring into destabilizing narratives of self and institution through a Foucauldian perspective (as co-editor of *Reading Foucault for Social Work*, 1999), using the arts and, most recently, drawing on historical archives. She publishes in interdisciplinary venues.

Michael Gill is Assistant Professor in Residence in the Women's Studies Program at the University of Connecticut, USA. His essays appear in *Disability and Society, Disability Studies Quarterly,* and *Sexuality Research and Social Policy.* He is working on a book that explores the sexual rights of individuals with intellectual disabilities.

Katerie Gladdys is Assistant Professor in Art and Technology in the School of Art and Art History at the University of Florida, USA. She examines place, marginalized landscapes, sustainability, mapping, consumption, food, agriculture, and disability by creating installations, interactive sculpture, video, and relational performances. Recent partners in collaboration include the University of Florida's Office of Sustainability and Institute of Food and Agricultural Sciences' Center for Public Issues and Education and the Gainesville community. In 2010, she received the University of Florida's College of Fine Art Graduate Mentor Award. Her creative work has been exhibited in national and international juried venues, including in the United Kingdom, Canada, Germany, Spain, and Croatia. She has an MFA in New Media and an MA in Teaching English to Speakers of Other Languages.

Janice Hladki is Associate Professor of Theatre and Film Studies in McMaster University's School of the Arts. Her interdisciplinary research engages with critical and political issues in media, art, and culture, and draws from approaches in disability, gender, sexuality, indigenous, and cultural studies. Recent publications include the exhibition book, *Fierce: Women's Hot-Blooded Film/Video* (2010), and essays in *Feminist Media Studies, International Journal of Qualitative Studies in Education*, and *ARIEL: A Review of International English Literature.* She has created over 40 works in theatre, performance art, and video art and curated a number of exhibitions including *Fierce* (2010–2011) and, with Sarah Brophy, *Scrapes: Unruly Embodiments in Video Art* (2010–2011). She and Sarah Brophy co-edited the interdisciplinary book, *Embodied Politics in Visual Autobiography* (2014), which examines the cultural politics of health, disability, and the body in forms such as photography, video art, graphic memoir, film, body art and performance, and digital media.

Eunjung Kim is Assistant Professor of Gender and Women's Studies at the University of Wisconsin, Madison, USA. She is a member of the Disability Studies Cluster and is affiliated with the Centers for East Asian Studies and Visual Cultures. Her research interests include historical and cultural factors that shape disabled women's experiences in South Korea; the politics of cultural representations of disability, gender, and sexuality; transnational disability studies theories; and asexuality representations.

Deshae E. Lott teaches at Louisiana State University, Shreveport, USA. She previously taught at Texas A&M University, where she won multiple teaching awards, and the University of Illinois at Springfield, where she worked among the online-instruction pioneers. Spirituality and living with a disability both infuse Lott's professional scholarship as well as her personal essays and poetry. In 2011, Lott received for one of her essays an EXCEL Gold Medal from Association Media and Publishing. Lott also started in 2007 a foundation whose Outreach Program awards scholarships and quality-of-life grants to individuals with severe physical disabilities. Learn more at www.deshae.net.

Nicole Markotić is Professor of Creative Writing, Disability Studies, and Children's Literature at the University of Windsor, Canada. She has written five books: *Connect the Dots* (1994), *Minotaurs & Other Alphabets* (2011), *Yellow*

Pages (2002), *Scrapbook of My Years as a Zealot* (2008), and *Bent at the Spine* (2012). She has co-edited (with Sally Chivers) the anthology, *The Problem Body: Projecting Disability on Film* (2010), and has edited a special disability issue for the *Canadian Journal of Film Studies*. Recent articles include "Leading with Your Head" (co-written with Robert McRuer) in *Sex and Disability*, and "The Body in Pieces: Lacan and the Unified Fragmentary" in *Open Letter*.

Donna McCormack is a Research Fellow at the Helsinki Collegium for Advanced Studies, Finland, where she is working on a monograph entitled *Recycling Global Life: Human Organ Transplantation in Contemporary Visual and Literary Texts, 1978–2010*. She is also transforming her doctoral thesis into a monograph, to be published with Continuum Press, entitled *Queer Postcolonial Narratives and the Ethics of Witnessing*. She has published and forthcoming articles in the *Journal of West Indian Literature*, the *Journal of Literary and Disability Studies*, the *Journal of Transatlantic Studies*, the *Journal of the History of Sexuality*, and the *Journal of Lesbian Studies*.

Robert McRuer is Professor of English and Chair of the Department of English at The George Washington University, USA. He is the author of *Crip Theory: Cultural Signs of Queerness and Disability* (2006), *The Queer Renaissance: Contemporary American Literature and the Reinvention of Lesbian and Gay Identities* (1997), and co-editor (with Anna Mollow) of *Sex and Disability* (2012). His articles have appeared in *Radical History Review*, *Genders*, *GLQ: A Journal of Lesbian and Gay Studies*, *Journal of Literary and Cultural Disability Studies*, and many other locations.

Danielle Peers is a PhD student in the Faculty of Physical Education & Recreation at the University of Alberta, Canada, where she studies the relationship between disability sport and social justice movements. She is also a video artist and a former Paralympic athlete. Danielle thanks the Vanier Canada Scholarship and the Trudeau Foundation for their generous support.

Ann Fudge Schormans is Assistant Professor at the School of Social Work at McMaster University, Canada. Rooted in her personal and social work practice history with people with intellectual and developmental disabilities, her work has focused on questions related to (self)representation and (self)advocacy and on how the arts can be used as a means of facilitating voice and social activism.

Scott Stoneman is a PhD candidate in the Department of English and Cultural Studies at McMaster University, Canada. His research on topics including the cultural politics of childhood obesity, globalization, and discourses of pedagogy and the spectacle has appeared in the journals *InTensions*, *Politics and Culture*, and *The Review of Education, Pedagogy, and Cultural Studies*. He is currently completing his thesis on how concepts of youth, population, and culture are mobilized through representations of the contemporary obesity crisis.

Katherine W. Sweaney is a PhD candidate in Northwestern University's Interdisciplinary Theatre and Drama program. Her work focuses on intersections between performance and science, especially concerning anatomical representation. A dramaturge and a graduate affiliate of Northwestern's Science and Human Culture program, she received her BA in Literature–Theatre from Reed College in 2006.

Tanya Titchkosky is Associate Professor and Associate Chair and Graduate Coordinator at the Ontario Institute for Studies in Education at the University of Toronto, Canada, in the Department of Sociology and Equity Studies in Education. She is the author of three books *The Question of Access: Disability, Space, Meaning* (2011), *Reading and Writing Disability Differently: The Textured Life of Embodiment* (2007), and *Disability, Self, and Society* (2003) and the co-editor, (with Rod Michalko) of *Rethinking Normalcy: A Disability Studies Reader* (2009). Her research interests include disability studies, interpretive methods of social inquiry, feminist and phenomenological theories of the body, sociology of knowledge, contemporary social theory, and the meaning of access.

Introduction: Pedagogy, Image Practices, and Contested Corporealities[1]

Sarah Brophy and Janice Hladki

Democracy is no longer a given; it is an interrogation. There is not one democracy, but multiple democracies; there is not one form of documentary, but multiple documentary practices. Coupling these new documentaries with a notion of democracies requires a new cartography, one that is almost three-dimensional—like a hologram—composed of mobile, endlessly morphing layers of nation, borders, spaces, technologies, access, identities, transnationals, and pirates, where each layer is not parallel to any other, but all the layers are always in fact in relationships of varying impact and influence.

—Patricia Zimmermann (2000, 24)

This conjunction of affect and critical awareness may be understood to constitute the basis of an empathy grounded not in affinity (feeling for another insofar as we can imagine being that other) but on a feeling for another that entails an encounter with something irreducible and different [...].

—Jill Bennett (2005, 10)

This special issue began as a series of questions about the representation of health and bodies in visual culture: How do forms of visual culture provoke new ways of imagining trauma and illness, the representation of disenfranchised subjects, and the mediation of bodies by technologies? These questions generated two specific projects: our international conference, "Health, Embodiment, and Visual Culture: Engaging Publics and Pedagogies," held at McMaster University in 2010, and this journal issue, which features a selection of the exciting research presented at that conference.

Our first thoughts about the conference were broadly shaped by concerns in Visual Culture Studies, a field that explores how individuals and groups visually represent human life and the social sphere, how spectators respond to visual forms, and how visual culture shapes everyday life. We sought to facilitate conversations about why and how modern human culture visualizes experience to such a great extent. As our epigraph from Patricia Zimmermann (2000) emphasizes, a multi-dimensional understanding of the relationships between visuality and democracy informed our conference design. Endeavoring to map what

Zimmerman describes as a new visual-democratic "cartography," we solicited papers addressing a broad range of media and political urgencies, and we encouraged the participation of activists, artists, and academics. Throughout this process, we paid particular attention to how visual culture—and the affective operations of art in particular—can contend with normative forms of sense-making about embodiment. Following Jill Bennett (2005), we attended to how and when contemporary visual culture generates unsettled forms of communication, empathy, and politics, thereby inviting ongoing contestation.

Collaboration is integral to our research methodology, and, from the beginning, we saw the conference as an occasion to engage students in creative, critical, materially grounded thought. In turn, the contributions of students, both graduate and undergraduate, became crucial to designing the program and to mounting an event that would be as accessible as possible for delegates with disabilities. We are deeply grateful to the core organizing committee members, Melissa Carroll, Emily Hill, Dilia Narduzzi, Sarah Trimble, and PhebeAnn Wolframe, for the thoughtfulness, critical reflexivity, energy, political savvy, focus, and practical skills that they brought to the conference project at every stage. Later on, Jessie Travis performed stellar work as our Volunteer Coordinator: She and Emily Hill collaborated with the Office of Human Rights and Equity Services at McMaster to develop and facilitate a workshop for undergraduate volunteers on accessibility goals, practices, and services for the conference. We extend particular thanks to Emily Hill and Sarah Trimble, who worked closely with us not only during the many months of conference planning and throughout the conference, but also in the development stages of this special issue. The conference would not have flowed as smoothly as it did without the high turnout of students from our graduate and undergraduate programs to assist with registration, accessibility, and navigating the campus. The organizing committee and the volunteers helped to create a stimulating and hospitable environment, and we hope that the students learned as much as we did, not only about visual culture, health, embodiment, disability provisions, and the logistics of conference organizing, but also about the joys, challenges, and political possibilities of working collaboratively.

In the early planning stages, we were energized by exchanges with students about potential organizing ideas and ultimately decided on technologies, cultural production, disability, and affect as the conference thematics. With the theme of "Technologies," the conference recognized pressing public debates about bodily interactions with "old" and "new" technologies, the visual surveillance of bodies, and the implications of imaging practices for wellness, identity, and community. The idea of "Cultural Production" was resonant for the timeliness of its focus on a range of modalities, including film, video art, photography, performance, and digital arts. With this theme, the conference also emphasized political cultural practices, particularly as they have been developed by and about specific bodies—including persons with disabilities and Indigenous peoples—and in terms of diaspora, transnationalism, and biological citizenship. Developments in the growing field of Disability Cultural Studies are profoundly re-shaping understandings of normalcy, diverse embodiments, wellness, and representations of the body. In relation to the theme of "Disability" for the conference, the recent work of Robert McRuer (2006) and Rosemarie Garland-Thomson (2009) exemplifies these provocations in relation to visual culture practices. Finally, Critical Affect Studies is an exciting new field of Humanities research that investigates art and culture by focusing on the imbrication of bodies, intimacy, sensation, shame, and ethical relations (Ahmed 2006, 2010; Berlant 1997, 2011; Ngai 2005). Central questions for the fourth theme, "Affect," included what does it means to "see" and respond to visual culture and how is empathy generated by representations in visual practices of testimony and witnessing (Bennett 2005; Cartwright 2008)?

Papers at the conference engaged with technologies, cultural production, disability, and affect in a range of ways: always compelling, often surprising. The lively and innovative program included research on images of pain, blind photography in Mexico, representations of intersexuality, cinematic depictions of madness, the teaching of documentaries about sex work and violence, trauma in art installation, disability in reality TV, human rights brochures in Israel, the *Body Worlds* exhibition, race and gender in birth control commercials, and representations of Aboriginal women's bodies. In developing this special issue of the *Review*, we sought to echo the interdisciplinary and international focus of the conference and to develop its engagement with a range of visual artifacts.

Articles in this special double issue advance critical perspectives on visual culture's constitution of the "human" and regulation of citizenship possibilities. In "Why Do Dolls Die? The Power of Passivity and the Embodied Interplay Between Disability and Sex Dolls," Eunjung Kim reads life-size dolls in contemporary art films as uncanny manifestations of the material objecthood of human bodies. Kim argues for a critical practice of de/familiarization in which acts of caring for radically passive bodies can emerge as both erotic and beautiful. Nicole Markotić critiques the prioritizing of death as the most desirable, logical outcome in biopics of disability, showing how genre norms and assumptions about virile masculinity work together to reinforce the association of disability with impairment and unliveability. And, situating his discussion of biological citizenship at the intersection of fat studies and critical race studies, Scott Stoneman, a graduate plenary panel member at the conference, discusses the body politics of the film *Precious*. The often contemptuous reception of Gabrielle Sidibe's performance in the lead role of *Precious* reveals both fat stigma and racism, leading Stoneman to connect fat disgust directed at the body of an African American single mother with histories of race oppression in the United States and their ongoing impact on education, citizenship, and reproduction. Resonating with Kim's and Markotić's critical investigations of disability and passivity, Stoneman's critical take on anti-fat rhetoric as a pernicious "norm of civility" that defines biological citizenship (Rose 1999, 69; 2006) underscores the urgent need to interrogate the injustices of what Robert Crawford (2006) calls "healthism" as it is articulated in relation to multiple modes of embodied difference.

In our co-curated exhibition, scheduled to coincide with the conference, we also explored questions about the regulation of citizenship, particularly for Indigenous, trans, and HIV/AIDS activist subjects, and about the performance of the human in, for example, representations of disability dance, scarred bodies, and human/animal relations. Generously funded and hosted by the McMaster

Museum of Art, the exhibition, *Scrapes: Unruly Embodiments in Video Art*, presented contemporary video art that mobilizes bodies as sites of political, social, and cultural investigation. We imagined the idea of scraping as an agitation, capturing how the artworks "scrape"—uncover, and make trouble for—the regulatory mechanisms regarding the organization of normalcy as shaped by gender, race, disability, and sexuality. By establishing the Museum space as our conference hub, *Scrapes* facilitated remarkable opportunities. Three of the exhibition artists—John Greyson, Deirdre Logue, and Allyson Mitchell—"toured" the show with the conference delegates by discussing the aesthetic and philosophical interrelationship of the artworks. And renowned Anishinaabe multidisciplinary artist Rebecca Belmore offered a plenary performance piece addressing colonial legacies, embodiment, and the economics of the art world.

Many of the articles in this special double issue relate closely to the exhibition's concern with "bodies in commotion": unruly embodiments that transgress and transform. For example, Danielle Peers, Melisa Brittain, and Robert McRuer discuss the significance of crip possibilities in art and academia and elaborate on how McRuer's writing about queer crip cultural practice/theory/activism generates vital ways to understand crip and queer excess and creativity "between movements, across bodies and borders" (this issue, 154). Lending further dimension to this conversation about inventiveness, Katerie Gladdys and Deshae E. Lott contribute an article about their collaborative art installation, *Augmented Spirit: Extreme Embodiment*, a critical, lyrical investigation of the life of a mechanical-ventilator-dependent individual. The authors' installation and article argue for a complex recognition of the "creative process" (this issue, 109) that shapes vent-user Lott's experience at the interface of body and machine. Although the *Augmented Spirit* project and the interview with McRuer both meditate on ways of disrupting "dominant cultural narratives on disability and its accompanying apparatuses" (Gladdys and Lott this issue, 108), Katherine W. Sweaney's article on the online anatomization of an amnesiac's brain in the context of Project H.M. reminds us that there are high stakes for medicine and science in the public display of producing knowledge of bodies and embodiment. Sweaney shows that even creative and innovative projects are at risk of being folded into long-standing Western narratives of science's masterful visioning of bodily interiors—a mastery that, so caught up in displaying its own penetrative powers, tends to produce "humanity" as an abstract universal.

Two articles in the special issue engage with popular film and televisual representations of transnational circuits of embodied exchange. Michael Gill considers episodes of the British web-based RTV program, *The Specials*, where young men labeled as intellectually disabled fashion their erotic self-understandings as they discuss and appreciate an ensemble of Thai *kathoey* performers. Focusing on a different dynamic of exchange—the global politics of organ transplantation—Donna McCormack critically examines three feature films that mediate the attendant questions of community, ethics, and mobility. These two articles suggest that self-definition and, indeed, survival are contingent on how we constitute our relation to "others." Taking Judith Butler's body of work as a shared touchstone (1993, 2004a, 2004b), Gill and McCormack reflect on how such ethical questions suffuse popular media representations of health, disability, embodiment, and citizenship, suggesting, in turn, that fantasies of hospitable embodied encounters (Ahmed 2000; Derrida 2001)—that is, of an enlivening reciprocity—are a charged, persistent, and contradictory preoccupation within contemporary popular media.

Two keynote speakers from the conference, Tanya Titchkosky and Robert McRuer, contribute, respectively, an opening article and an Afterword to this special issue. These renowned Disability Studies scholars provide an insightful framing and contextualization for the other articles. Titchkosky's article, "The Ends of the Body as Pedagogic Possibility," posits that the concept of "ends" can help us to understand the edges that define normalcy/abnormalcy, inclusion/exclusion, and presence/absence. Titchkosky examines representations of disability in two cultural texts for how they rethink assumptions about disability as an individual impairment and as a threat to life and personhood. Committed to a method of "beginning in the middle of things" (this issue, 84) and to understanding bodies deemed as ends or "limits" as powerfully educational about what constitutes "the human," Titchkosky echoes feminist scholars' emphasis on the pedagogical potential of the limit moment and its tensions—a moment that becomes an opportunity to interrogate epistemological assumptions and to generate new questions (Visweswaran 1994). Also raising questions about inclusion/exclusion and agency, Ann Fudge Schormans and Adrienne Chambon examine how image-making by persons with intellectual disabilities can interrupt regulatory discourses of normalization and the organization of ableist-defined social space. Their article explores the pedagogical potential of an arts inquiry project that involved the re-working of photographs of and by people with intellectual disabilities "to trouble non-disabled knowing" (this issue, 125). Linking Titchkosky's questions about disability as a limit/end—and as an embodiment to be ended—to Fudge Schormans and Chambon's exploration of non-limiting spaces for people labeled intellectually disabled and, indeed, to all the articles, McRuer offers a reflective Afterword, "The End of Contested Corporealities." He explores how the research in this special issue underlines the possibilities and impossibilities for visual representational practices to configure non-normative spaces. As McRuer points out, attempting and/or achieving "otherwise" considerations of the end of the body is a fragile project: Strategies that can interrupt and transform the normative constitution of disability in visual culture require, he maintains, a commitment to collaborative labor and resistance, representations of crip excess, creative risk, and a concentration on intersubjective relations.

Our initial discussions about the possibility of collaborating to organize a scholarly conference began in the early months of 2009. Now, in 2012, this project reaches a conclusion—or, perhaps, a new beginning, as readers engage with the authors' work and the research extends to other audiences. We are struck by how "spaces" shape our practices and research activities: the intellectual and embodied spaces of the conference; the spaces of representation, politics, and pedagogy that the articles engage as they discuss sites of visual culture and embodied life; and the spaces of future circulation and mobilization of the articles. We are especially pleased to present the dialogues and debates flowing from the conference in *The Review of Education, Pedagogy, and Cultural Studies.* With its emphasis on the analysis of power and meaning in a range of pedagogical contexts, this journal affords a space for the recognition of cultural and pedagogical complication and for an understanding of pedagogy as a political and ethical cultural practice (Giroux 2006). In a recent issue of this journal, Alex Means (2011) draws from Jacques Rancière's understanding of education and citizenship to suggest that "education is a question" and "an indeterminate process of attention and exploration" (29). In another *Review* article, Penelope Rossiter (2012) insists on the importance of the immeasurable pedagogical event or space to resist "the calculable, the verifiable, and the attribution of comparative value" in university governance (69). These thoughts on the purpose and process of pedagogy, its space of query and accountability, intersect with ideas highlighted in our epigraphs: the simultaneous grounding and ungrounding of visual culture politics, and the imperative of encountering the "irreducible." We might also consider Michel Foucault's concept of heterotopic space (1970), which surfaces in a number of the articles, as a framing reflection on these ideas, whereby cultural, pedagogical, visual, and corporeal spaces can be understood as sites of "crisis": transgressing boundaries of thought and interrogating the possibilities and limits of the knowable.

NOTE

1. Sarah Trimble provided an invaluable contribution, assisting us with editing as we developed the final manuscript of this double issue. We are grateful for her finesse and generosity. Many thanks, too, to Susan Searls Giroux, the Managing Editor of *The Review of Education, Pedagogy, and Cultural Studies*, for her guidance and patience. Janice and Sarah thank each other for the learning and pleasure generated by this collaborative endeavor. This research was supported by the John Douglas Taylor Conference fund in the Department of English and Cultural Studies at McMaster University and by the Social Sciences and Humanities Research Council of Canada through their Aid to Research Workshops and Conferences in Canada program.

REFERENCES

Ahmed, S. (2000). *Strange Encounters: Embodied Others in Postcoloniality*. New York: Routledge.

Ahmed, S. (2006). *Queer Phenomenology: Orientations, Objects, Others*. Durham, NC: Duke University Press.

Ahmed, S. (2010). *The Promise of Happiness*. Durham, NC: Duke University Press.

Berlant, L. (1997). *The Queen of America Goes to Washington: Essays on Sex and Citizenship*. Durham, NC: Duke University Press.

Berlant, L. (2011). *Cruel Optimism*. Durham, NC: Duke University Press.

Bennett, J. (2005). *Empathic Vision: Affect, Trauma, and Contemporary Art*. Stanford, CA: Stanford University Press. Used with permission from Stanford University Press.

Butler, J. (1993). *Bodies that Matter: On the Discursive Limits of 'Sex'*. New York: Routledge.

Butler, J. (2004a). *Precarious Life: The Powers of Mourning and Violence*. London: Verso.

Butler, J. (2004b). *Undoing Gender*. New York: Routledge.

Cartwright, L. (2008). *Moral Spectatorship: Technologies of Voice and Affect in Postwar Representations of the Child*. Durham, NC: Duke University Press.

Crawford, R. (2006). Health as a Meaningful Social Practice. *Health, 10*, 401–420.

Derrida, J. (2001). *On Cosmopolitanism and Forgiveness*. London: Routledge.

Foucault, M. (1970). *The Order of Things: An Archeology of the Human Sciences*. New York: Pantheon.

Fudge Schormans, A. and Chambon, A. (this issue). The Reworking of Spatial Attribution: People with Intellectual Disabilities and the Micropolitics of Dissensus. *The Review of Education, Pedagogy & Cultural Studies, 34*(3–4), 123–135.

Garland-Thomson, R. (2009). *Staring: How We Look*. Oxford, UK: Oxford University Press.

Giroux, H. (2006). *The Giroux Reader*. Ed. Christopher G. Robbins. Boulder, CO: Paradigm.

Gladdys, K. and Lott, D. E. (this issue). Augmented Spirit/Extreme Embodiment: A Mapped Landscape of Vent Life. *The Review of Education, Pedagogy & Cultural Studies, 34*(3–4), 107–122.

McRuer, R. (2006). *Crip Theory: Cultural Signs of Queerness and Disability*. New York: NYU Press.

Means, A. (2011). Jacques Rancière, Education, and the Art of Citizenship. *Review of Education, Pedagogy, and Cultural Studies, 33*(1), 28–47.

Ngai, S. (2005). *Ugly Feelings*. Cambridge, MA: Harvard University Press.

Peers, D., Brittain, M., and McRuer, R. (this issue). Crip Excess, Art, and Politics: A Conversation with Robert McRuer. *The Review of Education, Pedagogy & Cultural Studies, 34*(3–4), 148–155.

Rose, N. (1999). *Powers of Freedom: Reframing Political Thought*. Cambridge, UK: Cambridge University Press.

Rose, N. (2006). *The Politics of Life Itself: Biomedicine, Power, and Subjectivity in the Twenty-First Century*. Princeton, NJ: Princeton University Press.

Rossiter, P. (2012). Cultural Studies, Pedagogy, and Response-Ability. *Review of Education, Pedagogy, and Cultural Studies, 34*(1–2), 61–70.

Titchkosky, T. (this issue). The Ends of the Body as Pedagogic Possibility. *The Review of Education, Pedagogy & Cultural Studies, 34*(3–4), 82–93.

Visweswaran, K. (1994). *Fictions of Feminist Ethnography*. Minneapolis: University of Minnesota Press.

Zimmermann, P. (2000). *States of Emergency: Documentaries, Wars, Democracies*. Minneapolis: University of Minnesota Press.

The Ends of the Body as Pedagogic Possibility

Tanya Titchkosky

Critical projects such as feminist research, gender and queer theory, and cultural and critical race studies share an interest in questioning how certain people are regarded as on the edge of all that counts as human. Disability studies shares this interest as well; it explores how disabled people figure on the edge of the ordinary orders of daily life, including education, work, leisure, and love, and it studies how such exclusion is normalized. The case of normalized exclusion is poignant. In relation to disability, there are millions of people in Canada who find themselves with unequal access to education, under-employed, unemployed, or excluded from housing, leisure, politics, transportation, services, and other support systems (Government of Canada 2009). Yet, this state of affairs, shared by more than one billion disabled people around the world (World Health Organization 2011, 7), rarely takes shape as a non-individualized social issue because it often appears as though impairment itself leads naturally to limited inclusion. As a way to denaturalize processes of cultural exclusion, this article addresses representations of disability in order to explore how the edges of human inclusion are constituted and normalized.

Disability-exclusion is normalized through an array of cultural processes that make "disability" represent limit without possibility. Disability is made to serve as a signifier of an end without appreciable difference and without future (Campbell 2009; Hughes 2007; Titchkosky 2011). Blindness, for example, is not imagined as a way to perceive differently but, instead, as "not seeing"; wheelchair use is typically regarded as "confinement," not as moving differently; and differences in learning and emotions are imagined as an inability to think, learn, remember, or as a lack of control, as *un*-predictability. Within Western cultures, disability is typically taken for granted as the end of an expected form of functionality, voided of normalcy, and transposed into the end of human legitimacy. Such an interpretive process easily gives way, both figuratively and literally, to treating disability as a stage *par excellence* for end-of-life dramas and debates. These common interpretive moves are as dangerous as they are perplexing.

In contrast, approaches to disability that do not deny it *as* a "location of culture" (Bhabha 1994) teach us that the tie between "end" and "disability" is neither natural nor essential, that bodily impairments are inhabited by interpretations that could be (and sometimes are) otherwise. Our interpretive relations, both disabled and non-disabled, to embodiment do the work of transforming *vital* lived-differences or impairments into nothing but ends, and these interpretive relations make it seem normal to imagine disability as a limit without possibility. Even if a naturalized connection between disability and end is assumed, that assumption is formed within cultural processes of narrating bodies in the round of daily life. From this cultural understanding of the perception of human limits, some questions arise. For example, when people who do not understand themselves as representing the ends of the body regard those who are taken for granted as the opposite, what goes on? How are humans-as-ends used to sustain the sense of embodied differences as inherently divisive, and what are the consequences for conceptions of the human? Insofar as the meaning of disability is *made* through our interpretive relations to embodiment, it is critical to consider the way we relate to "discovering" the body in the shape of an "end" so as to learn something from interpretive relations to disability about the constitution of the edges of humanity.

From a cultural conception of disability, I address two narrative representations of disability as a way to explore how the ends of the body are made and noticed, and how their meaning is sustained. My two examples are Peter Singer's (2008) interactions with and obituary for Harriet McBryde Johnson and Audre Lorde's 1984 essay, "Eye to Eye," in which she writes of her blind and Black existence as this ends up encapsulated by a racist gaze that regards her as "probably simple, too" (148). I explore these two narratives for their pedagogic possibilities insofar as they offer different ways of representing and thus engaging the ends of the body. But first, a few words about interpretive methods.

METHODS OF PROCEEDING WITH DANGEROUS DIVIDES

A ubiquitous way to handle the no-end/end body debates in the realm of disability, including in disability studies, is through person-first linguistic schemes that take "disability" as a limit (an end) understood as distinct and separate from "persons," which is taken to mean potentiality. Since at least the 1981 International Year of Disabled Persons, there has been a global move by the majority of national governments, the UN's World Health Organization, and by some disability groups to use language that attempts a separation between "people" and their "impairments." Person-first language schemes suggest that while disability may be the end of the normative body, personhood represents no end of possibilities. The belief is that, by separating ends from the possibility of life conceived of in the shape of the generic "human," people can find some liberty from the stigmatization and devaluation that typically accompany impairment and other embodied differences.

Yet, this process of separation has done little to address the fact that the category of disability maintains the legal and bureaucratic mechanisms whereby people *are* stripped of their human rights, a stripping connected to medical, legal, and everyday ways of justifying the ending of participatory possibilities, as well as the ending of some lives. Separating ends (disability) from life (personhood) also does not acknowledge that disability *is lived* and is lived as something other than a negative add-on to personhood, or even a detractor from personhood. Moreover, insofar as it excludes embodiment, this process of separation makes use of an abstract conception of personhood and can thus bar learning about human embodiment. Rather than disregarding the ambiguity that intersects disability and person, human and body, my analysis proceeds by engaging this complexity as a pedagogic possibility. While it is undoubtedly true that disability intersects race, class, and gender, my point is to emphasize how interpretations of "human" intersect with the types we are already taken to be.

Questioning the cultural processes that shore up the capacity to divide ends (disability) from no-ends (person) requires a method of inquiry that can re-inhabit the desire that aims to make such a divide in the first place (cf. Bhabha 1994; Weiss 2008). Unless we address the making of this divide, which is, after all, as cultural as the production of the categories "person" and "disability," there is little possibility of change. Addressing the divide means exploring how we live with conceptions of ends in relation to no-ends, both as these relations are ambiguously narrated in everyday life and as they serve the pedagogical function of orienting all involved (cf. Ahmed 2006; Weber 1947, 88). Thus, even narratives that enact the degradation and disqualification of disabled people can serve here as the site from which inquiry can and should proceed.

I am methodologically committed to beginning in the middle of things (Titchkosky 2003, 209). After all, people do not merely sit on the edge of human identities; we inhabit them, and they inhabit us. Granting that human identity is not well understood in essentialist terms, as it neither inheres within itself nor only in the act of recognition of its ends, allows us to examine how the meaning of "human" is unstably forged in the midst of how we speak about ourselves and others as disabled. The ways that we understand our interrelations reside in what is said about disability; how we understand our interrelations has much to do with how we identify and make separations, and so make the meaning of people. Talking about a body's ends in the midst of life is one such interrelation from which there is much to learn. I turn now to a story of Peter Singer's narration of Harriet McBryde Johnson that provides us with the possibility of addressing this between-ness.

A STORY OF ENDS

Peter Singer, a Princeton philosophy professor specializing in bioethics, has worked to address the right to life for animals while arguing against the same right for those people who may not qualify as human because their disability is taken as an end devoid of life possibilities. Singer has argued that the life of "infants with disabilities" is a questionable one that does not yet share with other infants or animals the right to life (Kuhse and Singer 1985, 217). He suggests that parents should "decide, in consultation with their doctors, to end the life of a baby when the child has disabilities so serious that the family believes this will be best for the child or for the family as a whole" (Singer 2008, MM34). For Singer, departures from normalcy are not expected and, in this sense, represent ends; where normal expectations meet their ends is a condition (disability) that makes one's status as "person" questionable.

Disability, according to Singer, may not afford the human in question the complex form of future-oriented consciousness that is reflective of ordinary relations to common values and normal expectations. He writes:

> To have a child with Down syndrome is to have a very different experience from having a normal child. It can still be a warm and loving experience, but we must have lowered expectations of our child's abilities. We cannot expect a child with Down syndrome to play the guitar, to develop an appreciation of science fiction, to learn a foreign language, to chat with us about the latest Woody Allen movie, or to be a respectable athlete, basketballer or tennis player. (Singer 2001, 228)

There are many issues here: Among these is that Singer is empirically incorrect. That Singer generalizes from one condition (Down syndrome) to a multiplicity of life activities and trajectories is yet another issue. That he seemingly already knows "parents' expectations" of their children (high or low), and knows them in simplified terms (tennis or guitar), is still another set of issues. Finally, that he holds that a departure from normal expectations should be used to shore up the distinction between human and disability, where the latter category can disqualify one from participation in the former, is a significant ethical issue that leaves "normal expectations" an unexamined but forceful power.

For more than a decade, Singer has been invited by various North American universities to speak publically on, among other things, his conception of disability as an end devoid of possibility. People in the disability movement, such as those involved in *Not Dead Yet*, have tried to resist and disrupt this public display of disability degradation, a display for which Singer is paid. One way this redress has taken place is through *Not Dead Yet*'s support for Harriet McBryde Johnson (1957–2008)—a lawyer, skilled debater, and notable author writing on disability as a lived experience—to engage in public debate with Singer. Many of Johnson's writings advocate, not the right to life, but the right to live outside of institutions, or what she called the "Disability Gulag." For example,

> I talked up the need for comprehensive civil rights legislation. Extend Section 504's principles to all levels of government and the private sector.
>
> It'll never happen, people said. The civil rights era has passed.
>
> We got civil rights legislation—the Americans With Disabilities Act—in 1990. It's a fluke, people said. It won't be enforced.
>
> In 1995, the United States Court of Appeals for the Third Circuit ruled that the A.D.A. bans segregation. Needless isolation of people with disabilities in institutions is segregation. That's a liberal circuit, people said. The Supreme Court will reverse.
>
> In 1999, the Supreme Court, in Olmstead v. L.C., affirmed that needless institutional confinement violates the A.D.A.
>
> Fine, but it's just words on paper, people said. The financing still drives us into institutions. (Johnson 2003, 8)

It is important to note that Johnson's aim to "shift from care and protection to rights and equality for people with disabilities" (1) is pursued from a form of embodiment that Singer's ethics would understand as better off dead.

The story of the encounter between Johnson and Singer is both nuanced and complex. I turn now to the consideration of a single example that vividly represents how the end/no-end relation is accomplished.

An Obituary

Following her death in 2008, Peter Singer wrote Harriet McBryde Johnson's obituary for the *New York Times*, entitled, "Happy Nevertheless." Singer begins:

> I met Harriet McBryde Johnson in the spring of 2001, when I was giving a lecture at the College of Charleston. Her brand of Southern etiquette prescribed that if you're not prepared to shoot on sight, you have to be prepared to shake hands, so when I held out mine, she reached up from her powered wheelchair and took it with the three working fingers on her right hand. She added that she was attending my lecture as a supporter of Not Dead Yet, the disability rights organization that a year and a half earlier blockaded Princeton University's Nassau Hall in protest against my appointment as a professor of bioethics. I told her I looked forward to an interesting exchange. (Singer 2008, MM34)

If we grant that everyday incidents that bring the question of the meaning of "human" to mind involve a complicated form of consciousness, then this obituary, this cultural artifact, has much to teach us about the interpretive maneuvers that course through our unexamined relations to embodiment. Disability signifiers—power wheelchair, three working fingers, descriptions of sitting and reaching—are the narrative details that lend sense to the act of describing one person's handshake as signifying the strength of Southern etiquette while, at the same time, narrating one's own handshake in terms of an unremarkable normalcy: "I held out mine." Singer uses bodily differences to introduce the reader to the end of Johnson's life, leading, here, to a depiction of disability as an end overcome by culture; the life of Southern etiquette seems to make three working fingers rise to a handshake that, while customary, is marked as out-of-the-ordinary.

Turning to narrate his own work and the genesis of his and Johnson's debates about death and disability, Singer goes on to write of one particular encounter in 2002, when he had invited Johnson to his large undergraduate class:

> After she spoke, I arranged for her to have dinner with a group of undergraduates who met regularly to discuss ethical questions. I sat on her right, and she occasionally asked me to move things to where she could reach them. At one point her right elbow slipped out from under her, and as she was not able to move it back, she asked me to grasp her wrist and pull it forward. I did so, and she could then again reach her food with her fork. *I thought nothing of the incident*, but when she told some of her friends in the disability movement about it, they were appalled that she had called on me to help her. I'm pleased that she had no difficulty with it. It suggests that she saw me not simply as "the enemy" but as a person with whom it was possible to have some forms of human interaction. (Singer 2008, MM34, emphasis added)

"I thought nothing of the incident," says Singer, while seeming surprised that others did. Those who did think about it include Harriet McBryde Johnson, who wrote of it in her book, *Too Late to Die Young* (2005), and in articles such as "Unspeakable Conversations" (2003); disability activists and scholars involved with *Not Dead Yet* (2011); and Johnson's friends, who were appalled, as Singer notes, also thought of it. Still, Singer is thinking about something. He remembers this incident. Johnson's elbow slips and Singer is asked by Johnson to "grasp her wrist and pull it forward"—perhaps a common occurrence for Johnson, but certainly not for Singer. He notes a slip and a touch that constitute an incident which, for him, is "nothing" to think about. Singer writes that he responded to Johnson's request and that her friends from the disability movement were "appalled," and through this entangled set of bodily responses Singer comes to feel less like an enemy. He does think about being seen as a person—at least as this pertains to his own personhood. Even for Singer, then, the body does "not end at the skin" (Haraway 1991, 178): The grasp and pull of another person's wrist in order to move an elbow back onto the table during dinner is explicitly dismissed, even as Singer is implicitly engaged by thinking about what constitutes friendly and hostile relations to disabled and non-disabled forms of embodiment.

Singer's narrative frames him as a participant in a departure from normal role expectations, a departure that engages him in a form of bodily consciousness that is not included as an expected part of ordinary life. He participates in the version of disability that he encourages parents to decide against and, in so doing, disability comes alive as something other than a living death. Still, what sort of life does Singer find? Singer grasped and pulled Johnson's wrist while noting that she could again reach her food with her fork. Having accompanied Johnson on a departure from routine expectations about eating, Singer wishes to think nothing of it. Instead, he focuses on a return to normalcy, a return to the taken-for-granted where the more familiar expectations of eating become the story: She could "again reach her food with her fork." The significance of a complex lived encounter that has created something other than the reproduction of normalcy is now narrated through a functionalist reduction. This reduction heralds a return to eating with a fork as the end of which Singer *is* thinking. In this way, a vapid functionalism is the generative ground of Singer's interest in disability, which still fits unproblematically with his explicitly eugenicist orientation toward disability.

In Singer's account, the extraordinary touch and interconnectedness of embodied beings in the act of eating is replaced by the explicit consciousness of functionality—a reaching body, holding a fork, feeding oneself on the fabled island of independence. The fable is re-achieved when Singer's story of the face-to-face remains within the normative confines and takes for granted the material reality of the table, the makers of forks and food, the built environment, the service industry, as well as his own interaction with others at the table. That which actually occurs between Peter Singer and Harriet McBryde Johnson—food, fork, table, touch, pull, and reach, all animated by differing conceptions of disability—is articulated as nothing to think about. The reader is being taught how to attend to the value of functionality by dismissing the "difference that disability makes" (Michalko 2002). Instead of the messy intermingling of embodied movements and meanings, Singer tries to give the reader one body that ends at the skin meeting another, and all else is framed as but an incident better left un-thought. In this moment, Singer's obituary offers a conception of equality that is dis-embodied—unless and until disability is made to appear again.

The need not to think does, nonetheless, lead to some important thoughts. Any sense of other lives being produced by this story and consumed with every fork ful of food is re-focused by a functionalist gaze that encapsulates the body in such a way that Singer can find *his* humanity. Singer suggests he feels pleasure in a sense of recognition that "she saw me not simply as 'the enemy' but as a person with whom it was possible to have some forms of human interaction." Through the movement of self and other, between slipped elbows and reclaimed forks, an interpretive relation to the body arises that offers Singer a sense of himself as something other than an enemy because he is touched by the possibility of being engaged as human. That Singer knows that his other could have seen him simply as the enemy but now also sees the possibility of human interaction with him, implies that arguing against Singer, or on behalf of disability-as-life, represents yet another form of estrangement in the realm of humanity that he understands McBryde-Johnson to be bridging.[1] Faced with a life that Singer has trouble understanding as worthwhile, he finds self-recognition, and disability-experience offers Singer exactly what he denies about disability-experience: that this is a place of and for humanity.

It is not that Singer found a lost status as human when called upon to move Johnson's elbow back to the table. Rather, he came to the table already human. The same was true when Singer shook hands with Johnson. His humanity is not discovered; it is enacted and achieved between himself and McBryde Johnson. That is, humanity is achieved through interactional work that makes use of typically unexamined conceptions such as those involved in delineating the ends of the body as the non-human. This, too, is something to think about.

SPACES BETWEEN US

Narrating the end of the body as though disconnected from possibility requires interpretive work within interactional scenes not necessarily of our own choosing. It requires not thinking about how one's taken-for-granted sense of being human is achieved through the interpretive activity of somehow regarding an other's life as nothing but limit (cf. Butler 1997). Moreover, the inescapably intermeshed nature of the body—its slips, touches, and pulls, and the basic quest to matter to and for each other—requires work in order to think "nothing of it." This work can entail emptying some people of possibility by making their embodiment an "incident"—a thing, a condition, an episode—taken as a limit; an incident treated as blocking engagement or as in need of transcendence. It requires interpretive work to think nothing of how limits are always part of the grounds of proceeding, how they stage life possibilities. It also takes work to engage another as lifeless and to make it appear as if engagement—for example, shaking three working fingers—is disconnected from the human activity of meaning making. Finally, it takes work to garner a sense of one's own humanity from those regarded as not quite human (Goodley 2007).

Now, it is true that Singer narrates his embodied interactions with Johnson in what is "just" an obituary, and perhaps one that was even hastily written.

Moreover, it is an obituary written by a bioethicist philosopher participating in a particular tradition, and who might not grasp that his descriptions do something more than reflect an "objective state of affairs," as obituaries are normally imagined to do (Couser 2012, 31). Whatever Singer may say of his intentions, his story of a life in death, an obituary, is sensible enough to be requested, written, edited, published, distributed, and read within a system of economic exchange. The act of describing a first encounter, a handshake, an elbow slipping, and the pulling of another's wrist, describing both his thought and unthought encounters with the deceased, provides us with a sense of what is possible to say. Texts are cultural artifacts representing the "say-able" (Titchkosky 2011, 73). Thus, we can read Singer's obituary as a cultural depiction of existing cultural understandings of body-as-function that reflects understandings of humanity and its others.

Some bodies are described as impediments that must be gotten out of the way. Nonetheless, the body exceeds its encapsulation, not only by the skin, but also by the routine narrative schema of "being in the way." Though greetings, sitting at tables, and sharing a meal typically require and expect a "non-impaired carnality" (Paterson and Hughes 1999, 607), Singer's obituary nonetheless reflects the unexpected ways that we do join and relate to the *table*, understood here as a metaphoric expression of situations that lie between us, and from which we both make and glean our orientations. Considering what lies between us, suggests Sara Ahmed (2006), requires a focus on the table—the social space and surface of gathering—as that which *"affects what we do"* (43, emphasis added). The metaphor of the table offers a way of focusing on the grounds of stories. It is the space between us that allows for a consideration of "how things come to matter . . . through and in the labor of others," and how things that matter come to make an appearance (44). This is how we are *an effect of the tables between us.* Disability and non-disability can be read as such effects, and, given this, an analysis of Singer's obituary (or any articulation of bodies) teaches us that embodiment is separate neither from others nor from personhood but is, instead, that intermeshed place where the meaning of human is made, unmade, and remade.

To focus on the space between ends and no-ends, or between limit and possibility, is not to deny the power of acts of identification but, rather, to re-focus us on the space between identified subjects, where the meaning of persons consists of embodied interpretations of our interwoven existence. Our interests and, indeed, the very meaning of people come from the tables,[2] the spaces, between us. If we think nothing of what lies between our encounters with others, we might not come to know about the actual work we are involved in, work that makes up the meaning of people. True enough, as the saying goes, "stuff happens": elbows slip, tables appear, dinner invitations occur, and people also disappear. "Stuff happens" because of the particular tables we find between us, and how we orient ourselves to this in-between *makes the difference.* The study of how we notice and make difference is critical (cf. Michalko 2002; Walcott 2011) and, for this reason, I turn now to the work of Audre Lorde, who brings us face to face with the social accomplishment of difference.

NARRATIVE BEGINNINGS

Addressing how bodies appear in the spaces of racism, Audre Lorde offers another way to narrate bodies encapsulated by a taken-for-granted sense of ends without possibility. Unlike Singer, Lorde does not assume the good of functional versions of embodiment, so turning to her work allows us to continue to develop this analysis and question the meaning of limits and the production of the "human" that occurs between us as we speak of bodies.

In "Eye to Eye" (1984), Lorde tells a series of stories from her adult perspective about being seen as a child on the street, in the bus, at the library, and in the doctor's office. She narrates the act of being recognized as a black girl in these ordinary scenes of daily life—recognized through contempt, downcast eyes, leers, and eyes of hate, all of which force a sense of limitation on her. As we uncovered in Singer's descriptions of Johnson, Lorde, too, uncovers the ways in which any relation of recognition is simultaneously the medium of our making. In Ahmed's terms, finding herself at various tables made through the labor of racism, Lorde offers a reading of how her sense of self is the effect of these tables and reveals the look of a racist gaze.

Describing what is perhaps one of her first memories of her movement toward legal blindness, Lorde writes:

> My three-year-old eyes ache from the machinery used to test them. My forehead is sore. I have been poked and prodded in the eyes and stared into all morning. I huddle into the tall metal and leather chair, frightened and miserable and wanting my mother. On the other side of the eye clinic's examining room, a group of young white men in white coats discuss my peculiar eyes. Only one voice remains in my memory. "From the looks of her she's probably simple, too." They all laugh. One of them comes over to me, enunciating slowly and carefully, "OK, girly, go wait outside now." He pats me on the cheek. I am grateful for the absence of harshness. (148)

Peculiar eyes, probably simple, certainly black—these remembered judgments, while delivered without harshness, still signify limits, ends. These recollected voices and memories suffused with severe social judgment mark not only the literal end of interaction, as in "Ok, girly, go wait outside now," but also painful ends; her sore forehead and eyes, her sore body and flesh, and emotions ending up as painful memories, including one memory in particular: "she's probably simple, too." Lorde narrates a sense of herself as a child imbued with limits, without possibilities, leaving her grateful for the mere absence of harshness.

Still, the reader can notice that both how Lorde is seen and how she perceives this seeing are lifted toward us, thereby achieving something other than a reproduction of the same. Disability, for example, is the injustice delivered by the racist gaze: "by the looks of her" (the *look* of her eyes, the *look* of her mind) she is "simple" (disabled). But for Lorde to craft this story, the functionality of the racist gaze achieved through unquestioned able-ism cannot be assumed; it is, instead, represented as a question that Lorde's life embodies, and becomes a story of ends for readers to consider. We are offered the possibility of perceiving the limiting ways a racist scopic regime makes belonging and worth appear through a moment of radical disqualification. The white men in white coats can now share a laugh of mutual self-recognition; whatever the other *is*, they see that *it* is not them. They laugh. The voice that says, "she's probably simple too," wraps together blackness and blindness as ends meeting in what is today, as it was then, a significant form of cultural disqualification: cognitive differences. Lorde's narrative teeters on the edge of representing cognitive differences as a form of disability as beneath contempt, as an end without possibility. But Lorde joins neither in the laughter nor in her own dismissal. And, so, there is more.

Lorde characterizes her eyes as peculiar, as something of interest to others, something to be brought to eye clinics and poked and prodded, and involved in the work of keeping her separated from her mother. She characterizes her eyes as signs of further troubles, such as interactions with white men in white coats who leave behind bad memories; and all this becomes, for Lorde, something to think about, to recall. Along with her eyes so, too, does looking become something to think about. In Rod Michalko's (1998) words, "blindness is a reflexive phenomenon insofar as the *living* of blindness reflects a conception of what it is" (156). As the title of the essay, "Eye to Eye," suggests, the incident that was one of Lorde's many memories of childhood reveals not only how her eyes appear as blind to the White men in white coats, but also how such looks form a sense of her blindness and blackness. Those others who are "in the know" are those who make *simple* pronouncements on the look of her.

By depicting how others saw her, Lorde narrates how these others see. Between white and black, men and girl, doctor and patient, sighted and blind, smart and simple lies a perceptual field that Lorde brings to our attention. Recall that, in Singer's text, we encounter a disability narrative that assumes the normative ground of unquestioned versions of functionality that tells the story of difference and the body's end *as end*. The field of functionality that organizes Singer's perception of disability is reproduced, but he does not bring it to his own or to our attention. Through Lorde's text, we encounter a story that does draw attention to the ground of perception itself, and to the social fact that what lies between us are the grounds that organize our perceptions of self and other. Lorde's narration of the end of the body as the mere absence of harshness is done in such a way as to show that her body's appearance is generated from all that lies between see-ers and the seen, knowers and the "simply" known. Attending to what lies between the perception of human limits and possibilities, such as oppressive power relations, allows us to learn about the social character of perception instead of re-enacting the ground of perception as if it is natural or unquestionably good.

"They all laugh. Ok, girly go wait outside now." The laugh of the look that can see only limit and thus disability-as-disqualification is a pleasure produced by an unquestioned certainty that there is no life "in" disability. This is a linear pleasure that proceeds as though eyes merely see things and as though perception is not organized on the basis of the cultural grounds of power. The sort of vision that can see disability as nothing but an end to, at best, be laughed off, entails deploying a gaze that will not address how all perception is in fact formed "eye to eye." It is not a question of seeing or not seeing, nor of "color blindness"; instead, Lorde draws out for our consideration the perceptual ground framing the possibility and limits of sight itself. There is no end to the degradation heaped on Lorde as a young, black, legally blind girl, but her narration opens up the possibility that "simple, too" *is not in* individuals. The meaning of bodies, minds and senses are formed from our relations—from the in-betweens of histories, politics, and cultures through and against which we perceive each other.

Again, we learn that humanity is not discovered, but achieved through the taken-for-granted grounds of its assumed presence or absence. Once recognized as limit and at the end of what counts as human, disability is emptied of life and its grounding as a cultural (not natural) production is obscured. Lorde "eyeballs" this in a narrative that refuses to reproduce blackness, mental differences, or disabilities as unquestioned forms of disqualification but, instead, shows embodiment as a productive scene through which the ends of the body become a starting place for learning about the meanings of "human." Evaluations of bodies are places to reconsider how we make up the meaning of human limits and possibilities. Making lives on the edges of humanity requires the positing of some lives as almost limitless (normal lives?); that is, it privileges those who believe that they can simply look and know, despite the fact that "eyes do not allow for such a vision" (Michalko 1998, 155). Lorde shows the limits of the endless belief that people can know merely by the look of things, and she questions perception itself since how things look is already framed by an intermeshed racist-able-ism. The beliefs that eyes know, that functionality is obvious, certain, and good, or that the meaning of the being of the other is an end without possibility are dangerous not only because they risk reproducing more of the same, but also because they sacrifice awareness of their own grounds of possibility. But Lorde engages in the riskiness of representing knowledge as it is produced and situated between self and other; she risks the status quo, the taken-for-granted certainty of daily life.

Considering articulations of the body's ends makes it possible to learn that we are not alone in our bodies, and to know that behind what seems like the simple and obvious effect of impairment, there are powerful social delineations of the "human" tied to the cultural production of normalcy and difference. Narratives of the body's ends can teach us that in exploring everyday moments of what appear to be simple ends, we can (re)establish a relation to the body that does not leave off at the skin, that need not be stuck in a vapid functionalism, and that can re-think the ground of perception itself. Ultimately, this means that uncovering interpretive relations to embodiment is a complex scene of pedagogic possibility—one where we might learn how to ask new questions of our ordinary cultural narrations of the end/no-end dialectic of embodied existence.

NOTES

1. Thanks to Brandy Jensen for helping me develop this point and for her editorial assistance. Thanks also to Rod Michalko for his editorial assistance. Thanks, too, for the creative inspiration and careful editorial work of Janice Hladki and Sarah Brophy with editorial assistance from Sarah Trimble.
2. The table can be read as a metaphoric rendering of Homi K. Bhabha's (1994) "third space," a kind of between-ness, or interpretive sociology's concept of "social orientation," all of which point us toward the importance of attempting to inhabit the spaces between what otherwise seem like clear divisions or dichotomies, including black/white, man/woman, abled/disabled, and self/other.

These dichotomies seem to shore up the idea that *possibility* can be split from *limit; whereas theorizing needs to draw out their lived embodied connection.* Tables, put into Gail Weiss's (2008) terms, represent "narrative possibility" as well as "narrative limit" (64); affecting the sort of work we can do, tables allow for certain messages, as well as their sacrifices and secrets, to be revealed. For a discussion of between-ness directly related to disability, see my "Betwixt and Between: Disability is No-Thing" (Titchkosky 2003).

REFERENCES

Ahmed, S. (2006). *Queer Phenomenology: Orientations, Objects, Others.* Durham, NC: Duke University Press.

Bhabha, H. K. (1994). *The Location of Culture.* New York: Routledge Classic.

Butler, J. (1997). *The Psychic Life of Power: Theories in Subjection.* Stanford, CA: Stanford University Press.

Campbell, F. K. (2009). *Contours of Ableism: The Production of Disability and Abledness.* Basingstoke, UK: Palgrave MacMillan.

Couser, T. (2012). *Memoir: An Introduction.* New York: Oxford University Press.

Goodley, D. (2007). Towards Socially Just Pedagogies: Deleuzoguattarian Critical Disability Studies. *International Journal of Inclusive Education, 11*(3), 317–334.

Government of Canada. (2009). *Advancing the Inclusion of People with Disabilities: 2009 Federal Disability Report.* Gatineau, Canada: Human Resources and Skills Development. www.hrsdc.gc.ca/publicationsCanada (accessed May 2011).

Haraway, D. (1991). *Simians, Cyborgs and Women: The Reinvention of Nature.* New York: Routledge.

Hughes, B. (2007). Being Disabled: Towards a Critical Social Ontology for Disability Studies. *Disability & Society*, 22(7), 673–684.

Johnson, H. M. (2003, November 23). The Disability Gulag. *The New York Times Magazine.* http://www.nytimes.com/2003/11/23/magazine/the-disability-gulag.html?src=pm (accessed January 10, 2012).

Kuhse, H. and Singer, P. (1985). *Should the Baby Live?* Oxford, UK: Clarendon Press.

Lorde, A. (1984). Eye to Eye: Black Women, Hatred, and Anger. In A. Lorde (Ed.), *Sister Outsider: Essays and Speeches* (pp. 145–175). Freedom, CA: The Crossing Press.

Michalko, R. (1998). *The Mystery of the Eye and the Shadow of Blindness.* Toronto: University of Toronto Press.

Michalko, R. (2002). *The Difference of Disability.* Philadelphia: Temple University Press.

Not Dead Yet. (2011). NDY Fact Sheet Library: Pete Singer. http://www.notdeadyet.org/docs/singer.html (accessed April 20, 2011).

Paterson, K. and Hughes, B. (1999). Disability Studies and Phenomenology: The Carnal Politics of Everyday Life. *Disability & Society*, 14(5), 597–610.

Singer, P. (2001). *Writings on an Ethical Life.* New York: Harper Collins.

Singer, P. (2008, December 28). Happy Nevertheless: Harriet McBryde Johnson, b. 1957. *New York Times*, MM34.

Titchkosky, T. (2003). Betwixt and Between: Disability is No-Thing. In T. Titchkosky (Ed.), *Disability, Self and Society* (pp. 209–239). Toronto: University of Toronto Press.

Titchkosky, T. (2011). *The Question of Access: Disability, Space, Meaning.* Toronto: University of Toronto Press.

Walcott, R. (2011, October 27). Black Queer and Black Trans—Imagine Imagination Imaginary Futures. *FedCan Equity Matters.* http://blog.fedcan.ca/2011/10/27/black-queer-and-black-trans-%e2%80%93-imagine-imagination-imaginary-futures/ (accessed November 21, 2011).

Weber, M. (1947). *The Theory of Social and Economic Organization.* New York: Oxford University Press.

Weiss, G. (2008). *Refiguring the Ordinary.* Bloomington: Indiana University Press.

World Health Organization. (2011). *World Report on Disability.* Geneva, Switzerland: Author. http://www.who.int/disabilities/world_report/2011/report/en/index.html.

Why Do Dolls Die? The Power of Passivity and the Embodied Interplay Between Disability and Sex Dolls[1]

Eunjung Kim

Philosophers engaging in bioethical questions about what constitutes life worth living often imagine a subject whose cognitive and physical disabilities are so "severe" that she is not able to communicate, move, or show signs of consciousness. This imagined subject is a being who needs to be fed, cleaned, kept warm, moved, and cared for, but lacks any other sign of "humanity," such as self-consciousness, autonomy, rationality, or even sentience. One wonders, is this a human life? The utilitarian philosopher Peter Singer posed this question to Harriet McBryde Johnson in their debate about the worthwhile life: "Let's assume we can prove, absolutely, that the individual is totally unconscious and that we can know, absolutely, that the individual will never regain consciousness. Assuming all that, don't you think continuing to take care of that individual would be a bit—weird?" (quoted in Johnson 2003, 55). Disability studies scholars have defended the unqualified category of "human being" and argue on the side of caution, urging the inclusion of every human born, so that past catastrophes might be avoided, and condemning genocide committed in the name of the "subhuman" status of certain groups of people (Bérubé 2008). Given that the expansion of rights to sentient nonhuman animals in Singer's argument has not necessarily ensured the recognition of some individuals with disabilities as human beings, disability studies scholars have been understandably reluctant to step outside of the boundary of human beings. As Michael Bérubé (2009) argues in response to Singer: "Better, I think, to add some animals to the category of rights-bearing entities without kicking any humans out. It needn't be a zero-sum affair" (363).

Instead of defending the fraught definition of "human" as the basis of a "moral" and caring world in order to valorize disabled existence, I suggest recognizing the intercorporeal ontology of objects, with the aim not of conferring inherent rights on them but, rather, of undermining efforts to deny a being humanness on the basis of object-like status. As the absoluteness presumed by Singer is medically impossible, one has to start by imagining an object and thus must completely leave the category of human. In the filmic representations of this imagining that I consider here, when the characters take care of life-size dolls that absolutely cannot move, communicate, feel pain, or express consciousness, the "weirdness" to which Singer gestures transforms into something else. *Lars and the Real Girl* (Gillespie 2007) is premised on the audience's acceptance of the protagonist's attachment to an object that is no longer an object. And weirdness alone does not explain how an audience can become attached to a doll played by a living woman, as in the film *Air Doll* (Koreeda 2009). I do not suggest that life-size dolls in films have inherent value or automatically generate affective depth; rather, I believe that theoretical insights into passivity as agency might be gleaned by seriously considering the figure of the doll in these films as an embodiment of disability. Such representations of the interactions between female-gendered dolls and human beings frame the social recognitions for both objects and human beings that constitute life, care, and death.

What meanings and affects do objects generate in a neoliberal world increasingly dependent on the expendability and substitutability of objects and on the individuality of persons? I want to confront the "weirdness" introduced by Singer and its implications: namely, that it is purposeless, worthless, or pointless to care for an unresponsive human being under the condition of the "absolute impossibility" of improvement, as if the potential to improve were the only justification for care. The possibility that an object can be valorized through a network of recognition and the way that it is—and needs to be—cared for requires that we discard as irrelevant any definitions of *human being* that are based on prerequisites of mental and bodily functioning and progress. By examining human-objects in various representations and analyzing two films, *Lars and the Real Girl* and *Air Doll*, I explore how doll bodies make visible and enact passivity in its extreme form, thereby creating a condition for accommodation. The ethics of passivity is to recognize the unmodifiable aspect of *object being* that enables a subject to become an object to be acted upon, and to actualize the other within the self.

MAGICAL THINKING IN THE UNCANNY VALLEY

The roboticist Masahiro Mori (1970 [2005]) introduced the notion of the "uncanny valley," which describes the dramatic drop of acceptance of and familiarity with both moving and still objects as their likeness to human beings increases. According to Mori, as objects become more humanlike in appearance, we perceive them to be more familiar. However, at a certain point, there is an interruption—a sudden drop—in this positive correlation between familiarity and human resemblance. Mori places the toy robot at the top of the first peak and healthy human beings at the higher second peak, with a deep valley between them. When a prosthetic arm has achieved a degree of human verisimilitude, Mori says, it becomes "too real and when we notice it is prosthetic, we have a sense of strangeness. So if we shake the hand, we are surprised by the lack of soft tissue and cold temperature. In this case, there is no longer a sense of familiarity. It is uncanny. . . . [T]he appearance is quite human-like, but the familiarity is negative. This is the uncanny valley" (n.p.). There are a couple of logical problems with Mori's explanation. It is premised on a violated sensory expectation at the moment of contact instead of an emotional reaction to the appearance of the object itself. It also assumes a universal human response to universalized objects, including prosthetic hands and robots that resemble uniform human counterparts, without considering the individual degree of familiarity based on exposure and experience, let alone the diversity of human bodies.

Mori asks, "Why do we humans have such a feeling of strangeness? Is this necessary? I have not yet considered it deeply, but it may be important to our self-preservation." Some commentators have translated Mori's speculations that uncanny feelings stem from "self-preservation" into an argument about "natural" reactions to living bodies that carry diseases. A 2007 article in *New Scientist* describes Karl MacDorman's research on human–robot interaction as follows: "The result shows that those which prompt feelings of uncanniness also tend to provoke fear, shock, disgust and nervousness. Since these emotions are typical responses to diseased bodies, MacDorman suggests that the uncanny valley phenomenon may stem from a 'fear of one's own mortality' and an 'evolved mechanism for avoiding pathogens'" (Giles 2007). The article emphasizes MacDorman's conjecture, which expands the uncanny valley of humanlike objects to certain human bodies by placing Othered bodies outside the human. In addition, it represents the so-called intrinsic emotional and bodily reaction to "unhealthy" bodies and bodies with prostheses as a fear of contagion without acknowledging how historical and social processes of marking and excluding certain bodies are embedded in those emotional responses.

Virtual sex toys, blow-up dolls, or life-size silicone dolls, collectively known as sex dolls or love dolls, are representations of the female body crafted for sexual use.[2] As they become more lifelike, constructed with silicone flesh and realistic skin texture, they are often associated with "uncanny" or "creepy" feelings. Men who use sex dolls are also judged for their sexual "perversion." Because sex dolls, in their similarity of size and "anatomical correctness," are woman-objects designed to be fused physically with male bodies in accord with a version of heterosexual male desire, these dolls evoke a great deal of nervousness among feminists. Moreover, the nervousness about sex dolls manufactured for adult men may also derive from the sexualization of childhood innocence represented by the dolls, from erotophobia, and from the belief that sex dolls are a manifestation of the objectification of women, and therefore a form of misogyny. Feminist theories have neither fully articulated the ways in which objectification and negated humanity lead to violence and oppression (and vice versa), nor taken into account the diverse contexts in which certain objects are treated. In Catharine MacKinnon's (2006) logic, there is a direct relationship between images of women and real women: consequently, what some men do to or with the images is a violation of the women that those images represent. Arguing that pornography is a form of trafficking in women, MacKinnon writes, "From the standpoint of the person used to make the materials, the image of the person is still that person. And the sexual use of the person in the materials by the consumer is a real, actual, sexual act for the user" (248). Yet, pornography and sex dolls modeled on an image of a woman are copies without an original—though molded with the age, racial, bodily, sexual, and cultural characteristics of living bodies. They thus resist such simple equation of images and reality and, as re-representations of images, produce different meanings.

Although the sexual uses of female dolls without consent (which dolls cannot and do not give), their mutilation, and their abuse may demonstrate the prevalence of violence against women, it is questionable whether women are automatically implicated as victims when dolls are used as sexual devices. How are women imagined when the dolls become objects of care, a move that may expand their belonging and vitality? What interests me here is that sex dolls in fact become characters in film and other visual media, thereby constituting multiple layers of virtuality beyond the representation of real women. What do doll films say about agency, passivity, and the human condition? And, if dolls are not recognized as having agency or sentience but are viewed merely as prostheses, with whose agency, desire, and volition are these films concerned? In *What Do Pictures Want?*, W. J. T. Mitchell (2005) addresses some of these questions by examining instances of people who damage images when they are offended by them. In his view, two beliefs are operating on such occasions: "the image is transparently and immediately linked to what it represents" and "the image possesses a kind of vital, living character that makes it capable of feeling what is done to it" (127). Mitchell further explains that the image

> is not merely a transparent medium for communicating a message but something like an animated, living thing, an object with feelings, intentions, desires, and agency. Indeed images are sometimes treated as pseudopersons—not merely as sentient creatures that can feel pain and pleasure but as responsible and responsive social beings. Images of this sort seem to look back at us, to speak to us, even to be capable of suffering harm or of magically transmitting harm when violence is done to them. (127)

Mitchell argues against the tendency to think that such beliefs about images no longer exist, or to dismiss them as the superstitions abandoned by modern and urbanized societies: "While there are important historical and cultural differences in the power attributed to images, the tendency to endow them with life and immediacy (and then to disavow that endowment or project it on someone else) is fundamental to the ontology of images as such, or to a form of life we might call 'being with images'" (128). He further points out that "images are one of the last bastions of magical thinking" (128). This "magical thinking" approaches the uncanny by projecting threat and power onto the images and objects whose ontologies may spill over the coherently drawn, yet imagined, lines between real and unreal.

These overflowing ontologies do not simply evoke the surreal. In his theorization of disability aesthetics, in which damaged art represents a "category shift" that does not allow any possibility of restoration (Barkan 1999 quoted in Siebers 2008), Tobin Siebers argues that disability has been "deliberately and explicitly represented as disability not in the name of surrealism but in the name of a different aesthetic value—disability itself" (n.p.). In the case of female dolls in films, anchoring evasive surrealism in the ontology of disability and "being with images" produce a different reading of doll bodies as disabled bodies. The category shift from surreal to corporeal reality concerns the intelligibility of vitality, because humanlike dolls fall outside of "the categories and concepts by which we can be understood and made intelligible to others" (Kittay 2006, 106).

ON IMPASSIVITY

In *I Can't Feel It Anyway* (O'Brien 2010a), a short video released online, the transgender-identified video artist Kean O'Brien hugs and kisses a blow-up doll on a bed. O'Brien appears to hear something from the doll and replies, "Do you wanna fuck? Do you wanna fuck? Okay. I need to put it on." He takes off his pants, his vulva facing the camera, before putting on a strap-on dildo. His action manifests as a response to the doll's initiation of sex for the doll's pleasure, not just as an attempt to satisfy his own desire. The doll and O'Brien exchange penetrative and oral sex as he puts the doll in various positions. The title, *I Can't Feel It Anyway*, can be variously interpreted, since neither the *I* nor the *It* is clearly identified. The *I* might be the doll, who can't feel it, whether "it" be desire, arousal, sexual pleasure, orgasm, or anything at all. Or the *I* might be O'Brien, who can't feel the virtual penis or other things. Or the *I* might be a viewer who is watching the film. Used to intensify the ambiguity, "anyway" also suggests the passivity of the subjects involved and the insignificance of the activity presented in the film. Their bodies are impassive entities and impassive results of actions and passions. As Gilles Deleuze (1990) puts it, they act and are acted upon, living in the present moment in bodies, but at the same time they become entities "infinitely divisible into past and future, and into the incorporeal effects which result from bodies, their actions and their passions" (5).

The scenes could be perceived as simply recording O'Brien's performance of autosexual activity as he uses an object as a surrogate partner and sexual prosthesis. Yet, there seems to be much more happening in this short film. O'Brien's intersex/trans-embodiment having sex with a virtual doll emphasizes the performance of sex as occurring between two subjects fused through the contact of two object-organs. The film frames sexualities as simulacra and "event-effects," not only through the presence of the camera but also through the multiple layers of virtuality of the two bodies. "All bodies are causes in relation to each other, and causes for each other—but causes of what?" Deleuze asks. "They are causes of certain things of an entirely different nature. These effects are not bodies, but, properly speaking, 'incorporeal' entities. They are not physical qualities and properties, but rather logical or dialectical attributes. They are not things or facts, but events" (1990, 4–5). Nonetheless, O'Brien and the doll create the opposite of an incorporeal entity, forging an event that is based on the temporal corporealities of both bodies and that generates an effect beyond logic and a dialectics of humanness and objecthood.

"Through video," O'Brien writes, "I explore my personal tension between desire and impairment, the loss of connection. I seek to enable a place for that contact to be found" (2010b, n.p.). What is lost and found in the virtual relationship between dolls and human beings is the connection through simulacra and the fusion of object and subject, of active and passive. Baudrillard (1994) perceives the moment when simulation begins as an indifferentiation of the active and the passive (31). Creating an event together, O'Brien and the inflated doll erase the distinction between the actor and the acted upon. The doll, like television in Baudrillard's formulation, "is watching us, alienates us, manipulates us, and informs us" (30). What kind of rhetorical and visual power is generated when individuals actualize themselves by imagining the virtual intentions and actions of dolls imposed on them? Given that a relationship with a doll requires a great deal of imagination of the doll's agency and activeness, how can the power of passivity be understood through the dolls' bodies of inaction?

DOLLNESS AND DISABILITY

Aside from any connection to the uncanny valley, sex dolls have had a close relationship, both historically and conceptually, with disability. First, in 1980, a British rehabilitation professional, working under the assumption that disabled men and women have difficulty finding human sexual partners, suggested that they use female and male dolls for their sexual encounters (Goodman 1980). Disabled men are invoked most often to justify such technologies on the "charitable" grounds that they need a surrogate. Second, the marginality of doll-loving men shown in the media, such as in the British documentary film, *Guys and Dolls* (Holt 2007), is closely connected with a pathology, understood as sexual "perversity" or mental disability. Meghan Laslocky (2005) speculates that doll love might be an indication of schizoid personality disorder, Asperger syndrome, or autism, rendering it difficult for doll-loving men to relate to any other human beings. Although Laslocky emphasizes their diversity and represents their doll love as a form of sexual preference, she attempts to diagnose the men she interviewed with the help of a psychiatrist, not because they claimed to have disabilities but because their behaviors might fit into a diagnostic profile.

Third, because of their immobility, female dolls are often portrayed as having multiple disabilities. An online cartoon presents two stick figures looking over a body with blonde hair, its lower part drawn as a triangle, lying on a couch (Dave 2008). Figure 1 says, "Heh, nice sex doll." Figure 2 replies, "Actually, that's my disabled sister." Figure 1 responds, while dropping his pants, "Disabled? Looks like she's in perfect working order to me!" The cartoon displays the virtual and functional indistinguishability, for sexual purposes, of the two bodies. A disabled sister and an object are both bodies reduced to an organ, a receptacle, presumed to be in working order merely because they possess orifices. Figure 1 resists labeling the prone body as disabled, since she is functioning in the way he desires. On seeing the word "actually," it is quite possible that most readers perceive Figure 2's ascription as her real identity. Readers may believe it is more likely for a woman to be objectified than an object personified. If, instead, they see Figure 1's initial assessment as her identity, then Figure 2 is anthropomorphizing a sex doll as his disabled sister. Figure 1 designates the doll on the basis of his primary desire, and Figure 2 defies that naming in his belief that the doll is a live human being. That the sex doll/disabled sister is silent and unresponsive in this debate leaves her status unresolved.

In highlighting the fusion between the disabled body and the doll body, the virtual depiction of the virtual can be read not just as signifying the reduction of women to sexual organs without bodies or as revealing icons of a degrading objectification of women who should not be objectified. In their filmic representations, dolls can be read as a species coded with disability, race, a/sexuality, and femininity. In urging us to understand inaction and unresponsiveness as exertions of power and agency, representations of sex dolls become potential sources for reconceptualizing human qualities and capabilities in ways that confront the ableist prerequisites for a human being to qualify as a human being. The unmodifiable and radical passivity of doll agency leads the community around dolls either to discard them entirely or to surrender to them so fully that some human beings become prostheses to the doll in the process of its becoming real and alive. As individuals interacting with dolls also make the dolls issue commands, this mode of communication projects a context in which the dolls initiate actions, while also setting the parameters of individuals' possible responses. Tellingly, their immobility, inaction, incommunicativeness, stupor, and catatonia pose such a dangerous challenge to the able-bodied, normative ontology that the dolls in films must die. This death, usually portrayed at the end of the film, is disturbingly similar to the deaths, the suicides of disabled characters, or the elimination of disability through cure that films frequently depict.

THE DEATHS OF DOLLS

A North American film, *Lars and the Real Girl* (2007), and a Japanese film, *Air Doll* (2009), both employ sex dolls, to different degrees, as central characters rather than as props. *Lars and the Real Girl* depicts a silicone doll, named Bianca, whom Lars (Ryan Gosling) brings into his small, homogeneous, rural town in the Midwest. Presented as a young man who is not social and finds it painful to be touched, Lars is what Nicole Markotić (1999) calls a "problem body" beyond the scope of expected normality, "its figural overdeterminations" based on his avoidance of social contacts and occasions (6). The extent of the problem is dramatized in the scene in which his sister-in-law, Karin (Emily Mortimer), insists on having him over for a meal and physically holds him down on the ground to prevent him from avoiding her. The problem body addresses "the variable determining factors defining the problematic relationship between 'normal' and 'abnormal' bodies" and "denotes a complicated approach to bodies deemed physically problematic due to multiple forms of difference, including racialization, gender, age, queerness, and disability" (Markotić 1999, 6; 2008, 9). Lars' aloneness and disinterest in romance invite several interventions from his social and familial circles. After asking if he is gay in an attempt to understand his aheterosexual life as a guise of homosexuality, his church friend, Mrs. Gruner, suggests that he initiate romantic gestures toward any woman; Karin and his brother, Gus (Paul Schnieder), invite him for meals; a new co-worker, Margo (Kelli Garner), shows interest in becoming friends with him; and a receptionist suggests that he date Margo. One day, Lars brings his half-Brazilian, half-Danish girlfriend Bianca to Karin and Gus' house, rendering them speechless at the sight of a life-size doll. As "Real Doll" becomes a real girl, Lars reconfigures her dollness as foreignness and disability. Bianca, trained as a nurse, has worked as a missionary, does not speak much English, and uses a wheelchair.

In a poetic and image-driven style with minimal dialogue, *Air Doll* employs an inflatable sex doll named Nozomi as a central character. She is initially owned by Hideo (Itsuji Itao), a middle-aged man who lives alone and works as an inefficient waiter, disliked and harassed by his boss. When left alone, Nozomi becomes animated as a doll-woman (performed by Bae Doo Na).[3] Yet, Nozomi's moving body remains a doll body: filled with air, with a valve in her belly, and seams throughout her light-penetrating skin. After becoming animated for the first time, Nozomi starts to explore the outside world, finding a job at a local video store while her owner Hideo is at work. When Hideo comes home, she has to once again become an inanimate object; in a reverse simulation, the role is still performed by Bae. Hideo does not question Nozomi's dollness and moves her in a wheelchair. Conversely, the other characters she runs into do not question her humanness: her doll-like embodiment does not register as strange in the modern and urban space characterized by atomized indifference, hollowness, and loss. Nozomi starts to feel an affinity toward hollow objects, such as empty bottles in the trash, and starts to collect them.

Given a voice in the film, Nozomi repeats her identity several times: "I am an air doll, a substitute, for sexual desire." By observing a person who divides trash into two piles as he loads garbage into a truck, she learns that everything is sorted into the "burnable" and "nonburnable." This distinction becomes important in setting her apart from other humans when her creator at the factory informs her that all dolls are "nonburnable." She is saddened because of the replaceable nature of her existence. According to this film, having a birthday celebration and being able to age, die, and burn are the characteristics fundamental to being human.[4] Nozomi meets an old man sitting in the park who says that he is empty inside, just like mayflies with their vestigial digestive system filled with air who die after emptying their insides by laying eggs. Their common emptiness erases species distinctions between humans, insects, and dolls. Nozomi exists as a living being and a replaceable object at the same time, tolerating her unique vulnerability—a cut on her skin can deflate her—and her phantasmic and surreal presence in the world.

In contrast, Bianca never comes to life in the film by functioning in any way as a living, able-bodied woman would. Instead, she becomes a living person by being made intelligible to others as a living woman through Lars' belief. When Lars' doctor, Dagmar (Patricia Clarkson), tells his family to go along with his "delusion" and treat Bianca as if she were a real person, his brother Gus, who initially wants to hospitalize Lars, resists strenuously: "Oh, my. No, no, no, no. No. No, I mean, pretend that she's real? I'm not gonna do that. I mean, I can't. I'm just not gonna do it." Dagmar replies, "She *is* real. I mean, she is right out there," pointing to the bodily existence that occupies space and makes it impossible to deny its realness. Lacking other options, Gus and Karin invite church members to participate in Lars' belief as well, and several members resist. One even suggests that the doll is "a golden calf," a religious interpretation that casts belief in the doll's vitality as sinful idolatry. The recognition of a doll as a person elevates the doll to being a god or a symbol of godly power and of the human fallibility that such worship represents. To change the dominant way of weirding[5] Bianca, Mrs. Gruner points out that attachments to objects and nonhuman animals, as well as object-seeking conditions, are common and therefore unweird: "Oh, for heaven's sake, what's the big deal? Sally, your cousin puts dresses on his cats. Hazel, your nephew gave all his money to a UFO club. Arnie, everybody knows your first wife was a klepto." This succinct list persuades people as it does not promote abjection of the subject but, instead, achieves the opposite: embracing the strangeness and idiosyncrasy that exists in most families.

Rather than interpreting Bianca as a prosthesis for Lars that enables him to become more social, Markotić (2008) argues that,

> as a disabled 'person,' Bianca serves as a prosthetic for the *town*, an enabling device for the community to recognize that Lars is not lonely or emotionally needy, nor does he require the town's help to be romantically 'fixed-up.' . . . It is almost as if *he* is taking care of *them* by getting this mail-order doll and treating it as his girlfriend. (3, emphasis in original)

Markotić focuses on the town's need to cope with Lars' difference, a problem that Lars solves by introducing Bianca as a surrogate locus of their attention and care. Furthermore, if one looks at Bianca—not Lars' difference or the town's fixation on heterosexual coupling—as the film's main subject, then Lars and the townspeople serve as the critical device in Bianca's becoming human. They recognize her as a living person and inform each other of the organizing principle of her presence, participating in her becoming a human character and creating intersubjectivity. In an environment inaccessible to wheelchair users, Bianca is bathed, dressed, and carried from wheelchair to bed and from house to car, requiring the labor of physical care. During production, too, the film crew and cast treated Bianca just as they would a lead actress. This behavior indicates that personhood, once created, spills beyond the filmic frame. Gosling emphasizes the power of her passivity during filming: "Even when she's not saying anything she's communicating everything. It was amazing to watch. And it's a really rare, rare quality. It's intimidating, to be honest, because she has no agenda for a scene" (Production Notes n.d., 12).

Lars suggests that Karin's pregnancy has recalled the tragic death of Lars' mother during his birth as well as his isolated childhood with a grieving father, and that his emotions explain why Bianca came to exist. As he continues working through these issues in therapy, the camera captures his gaze toward Margo, implying that he is developing some interest in her. This is followed by Bianca's loss of consciousness, which signals that the context of her life is changing. Dagmar reminds Karin and Gus, who are panicking over Bianca's ill health: "It's always been Lars. He is making the decisions. He is the one who found her unconscious. He is the one who said she is dying." When Lars and Bianca go out to the lake, Bianca drowns. Her death is presented as an accident, not a murder, as Lars is shown attempting to rescue Bianca from the water, or a suicide. The lake acts as the force of nature to which Lars and Bianca need to surrender.

This event is followed by the funeral for and burial of Bianca's body, which conclude the process of framing her death.

In *Air Doll*, Nozomi has a dream of being drowned. Air bubbles come out of her body, indicating that the ability to drown is another human characteristic to which she aspires. Indeed, Nozomi dies not by taking in water but by releasing air. Toward the end of the film, when she tells Junichi (Arata), with whom she has begun to develop intimacy, that she will do anything for him—thereby turning her passivity into her ability to fulfill his wish—he asks her to let him deflate her body and refill her with his breath. In his bedroom, he deflates and reinflates her body several times. Believing that he is one of her kind, she tries to do the same thing to him and cuts his skin while he is asleep. Instead of air, it is his blood that gushes out, but she fails to recognize bleeding as a characteristic of a living human being. While she tries without success to seal the cut with tape and to inflate his body through his mouth, she laments in voice-over, "My breath cannot fill Junichi." Nozomi views her failure as a sign of her inability and sterility, not of his species difference. She leaves his dead body in a garbage bag outside and aimlessly walks around the empty streets. She sits down on a bench and takes off the tape that Junichi put on her wrist after she was cut. She lets the air out of her body and inhales, as if feeling his breath once again. In the next scene, facing the death that she herself has brought on, she places her body next to the garbage bags outside the houses, surrounding herself with her collection of empty objects. As Nozomi collapses, a baby doll left in her arm by a girl makes a sound, "Mommy." A bulimic woman waking up in the middle of her object-filled room bears witness to the death of Nozomi, as the doll undergoes a category shift from a live being to trash. Looking down the street through the window, she sees Nozomi's dead body and the assemblages of objects and says, "Beautiful."

The aesthetics of her doll body and the assemblages in the garbage site, observed by the woman who surrounds herself with objects but feels empty inside, break the boundary between nonhuman objects and human existence. In fact, "beautiful" is the first word uttered by Nozomi when she comes to life and feels the touch of a water drop on her plastic skin. Jane Bennett (2004) calls the ability of trash to generate the awareness of energy and the claim to autonomy of matter placed in a mise-en-scène the "thing-power" of stuff, which "commands attention as vital and alive in its own right, as an existant in excess of its reference to human flaws or projects": It "exudes a kind of dignity, provokes poetry, or inspires fear" (350). The scenes of Nozomi's body with other objects make visible this poetry and the effect of her transformation transmitted to others. As she exhales her last breath, the seeds of a dandelion drift by, and the camera revisits the characters presented earlier in the film, now shown at later times and in various spaces. Life is constituted when the body, though it seems empty, is filled with air exhaled by other life. Conversely, death is the condition of losing sociability, when the inside and outside of the skin become indistinguishable.

Although the two films present the vitality of dolls differently—through social recognition and bodily constitution—*Lars and the Real Girl* and *Air Doll* come to the same conclusion: the deaths of dolls. Do the dolls die because they fail as nonhuman beings to live together with human beings after fulfilling their purpose in meeting human needs? Does the age of neoliberal consumption make death and the mode of disposal the most important factors in classifying bodies, as if their permanence might violate environmental sustainability? Bianca and Nozomi died because they lived. Their transition from objects to vital subjects is only partially successful or context-bound, as *Lars and the Real Girl* and *Air Doll* conclude that the vitality of dolls cannot continue, for life and death become meaningless in their existence: rather than moving from one category to the other, they put into question "the distinction between cause and effect, between active and passive, between subject and object, between the end and the means" (Baudrillard 1994, 30). For these two films, a person's desire and the objecthood of dolls fulfilling that desire are put into question by the radical passivity of dolls and the performative passivity of humans. There is no single agent who possesses autonomous agency and escapes passivity as a force controlling his or her own circumstances. Nozomi's death and Bianca's death are the same in that both are replaced by other bodies that take their roles in relation to the other characters. To spare humans from having to face the dolls' immortal bodies, one is buried in the ground and the other is thrown away in the trash.

In their respective theorizations of transnational organ trafficking and pornography, Michael Davidson (2008) and Slavoj Žižek (2004) both reversed the "Body without Organs" described by Gilles Deleuze and Félix Guattari (2004) into "Organs without Bodies." Žižek claims that "the entire human body, inclusive of the head, is nothing but a combination of such partial organs—the head itself is reduced to just another partial organ of *jouissance*" (172). In the two films, sex dolls are the very presence of object-being made intelligible to others rather than organs or bodies. But both their unmodifiable and permanent nature and their radical passivity in animated and unanimated forms are rejected by the able-bodied society. If the "loss of connection" is, as O'Brien (2010b) frames it, an impairment, then sex dolls function mainly as a prosthetic device. If the lack of connection is an ontological condition, then dolls, as disabled bodies, enable viewers to redefine humanness so that it is based on the effort to fuse with objects, not on autonomous capabilities and sociability.

THE ETHICS OF PASSIVITY AND DISABILITY: DEFYING INTELLIGIBILITY

In the end, what Singer thinks "a bit weird" is "*continuing* to take care of" a totally unconscious individual (emphasis added), which brings up the temporal dimension of care. If one is to take care of objects and persons, for how long can it last before it becomes weird? The film *The Safety of Objects* (Troche 2001) connects the attachment to an object with caring for an unresponsive person. The film traverses familiar territory by weirding the mother, Esther, who cares for her unresponsive, seemingly unconscious son, Paul, at home. Complying with the wish of her able-bodied daughter, Esther enters into the "hand-on-the-car" contest: If she can keep one hand in contact with the car longer than anyone else, she will win it. She endures more than 70 hours, until only one other contender remains—but then she suddenly lets go, overwhelmed by a flashback of Paul's accident.

She returns home in tears, says a tender good bye to him, and puts a plastic bag over his head. The scene is followed by the reconciliation of Esther and her neglected daughter. The film tries to persuade the audience to understand the loving mother's choice to kill her unresponsive son, suggesting an analogy that we all eventually have to let go of objects we feel attached to, although objects and disabled persons care for others around them.

As human beings are circumscribed by humanlike objects that would not, by themselves, accommodate humanness, the objects demand that a system be created that recognizes them. Certain bodies are oppressed not by "thingification" (Chakrabarty 2002, 142), but by the specific mode of intelligibility with which the thing and other things are treated. When it becomes possible to refuse to feel that humanlike objects are uncanny, the imagined uncanny valley of disabled, diseased, and prostheticized bodies fused with objects reveals a space of aesthetic and ethical differences. I end with Harriet McBryde Johnson's (2003) reply to Peter Singer's question about the weirdness of continuing to take care of an unconscious individual: "No. Done right, it could be profoundly beautiful" (55). Refeeling and rethinking how the weird, uncanny, abject, and beautiful are involved in object beings make us aware of overflowing, intersubjective ontologies beyond those of qualified personhood and degraded objecthood.

NOTES

1. I am deeply grateful to Nicole Markotić, Tobin Siebers, Cynthia Wu, Jenell Johnson, Janice Hladki, Sarah Brophy, Michael Gill, and the anonymous reviewers for their helpful suggestions, insights, and support.
2. There are sex dolls in male form marketed for male and female customers. However, male dolls are rarely represented as characters in American, British, and Japanese television programs and films.
3. In 2010, Bae Doo Na received the Best Actress award both from the Tokyo Sports Film Awards and from the Takasaki Film Festival; thus, a nondisabled actor performing the role of a doll was commended for skillfully performing different embodiment, much as nondisabled actors often receive recognition for acting as disabled characters.
4. This is in a clear contrast to the recent remake of *The Stepford Wives* (Oz 2004), a film in which Joanna persuades her husband not to make her into a robot by emphasizing that a robot saying "I love you" cannot mean it. Thus, the quality of being human in *The Stepford Wives* presents humanness as having the emotional ability to feel and the autonomy to express genuine love, rather than the corporeal capacity of aging and of being reducible to ashes. This focus on abilities as criteria for human status is in line with Singer's "weirding" of the care given to unexpressive being without such capacities.
5. The use of *weird* as a verb is adopted from Mel Chen's (2011) theorization of "weirding families" as "the placing of idealized family under a weird lens, one that is racially quirky or posthuman" (Chen 2011, n.p.).

REFERENCES

Barkan, L. (1999). *Unearthing the Past*. New Haven, CT: Yale University Press.

Baudrillard, J. (1994). *Simulacra and Simulation*. Ann Arbor: University of Michigan Press.

Bérubé, M. (2008). Wandering Back In. http://www.michaelberube.com/index.php/weblog/wandering_back_in (accessed January 6, 2012).

Bérubé, M. (2009). Equality, Freedom, and/or Justice for All: A Response to Martha Nussbaum. *Metaphilosophy*, *40*(3–4), 352–364.

Bennett, J. (2004). The Force of Things: Steps toward an Ecology of Matter. *Political Theory, 32*(3), 347–372.

Chen, M. (2011, November 13). Chinese Toys and Weirding Families. National Women's Studies Association Conference, Atlanta, GA.

Chakrabarty, D. (2002). *Habitations of Modernity: Essays in the Wake of Subaltern Studies*. Chicago: University of Chicago Press.

Dave [pseudonym]. (2008, March 24.). Cyanide and Happiness. *Explosm.net*. http://www.explosm.net/comics/1215/ (accessed April 22, 2011).

Davidson, M. (2008). *The Concerto for Left Hand: Disability and the Defamiliar Body*. Ann Arbor: University of Michigan Press.

Deleuze, G. (1990). *The Logic of Sense*. Translated by Mark Lester. New York: Columbia University Press.

Deleuze, G. and Guattari, F. (2004). *A Thousand Plateaus: Capitalism and Schizophrenia*. Minneapolis: University of Minnesota Press.

Giles, J. (2007, October 27). What Puts the Creepy into Robot Crawlies? *New Scientist*, http://www.newscientist.com/article/mg19626276.500-what-puts-the-creepy-into-robot-crawlies.html (accessed March 8, 2012).

Gillespie, C. (Dir.) (2007). *Lars and the Real Girl* [DVD]. USA: MGM.

Goodman, R. E. (1980). Sex Aid and the Disabled. *Sexuality and Disability, 3*(3), 232–235.

Holt, N. (Dir.) (2007, January 17). *Guys and Dolls*. London: BBC.

Johnson, H. M. (2003, February 16). Unspeakable Conversations: Or How I Spent One Day as a Token Cripple at Princeton University. *The New York Times Magazine, 50–55*(74), 78–79.

Kittay, E. (2006). Thoughts on the Desire for Normality. In E. Parens (Ed.), *Surgically Shaping Children: Technology, Ethics, and the Pursuit of Normality* (pp. 90–110). Baltimore: Johns Hopkins University Press.

Koreeda, H. (Dir.) (2009). *Air Doll (Kûki ningyô)* [DVD]. Hong Kong: EDKO Film.

Laslocky, M. (2005, October 17). *Real Dolls: Love in the Age of Silicone*. http://www.saltmag.net/display.php?article_id=240&author_id=94 (accessed April 22, 2011).

MacKinnon, C. (2006). Pornography as Trafficking. In C. MacKinnon (Ed.), *Are Women Human? And Other International Dialogues* (pp. 247–258). Cambridge, MA: Harvard University Press.

Markotić, N. (1999). Introduction "Coincidence of the Page. " *Tessera, 27*, 6–15.

Markotić, N. (2008). Punching Up the Story: Disability and Film. *Journal of Canadian Film Studies, 17*(1), 2–10.

Mitchell, W. J. T. (2005). *What Do Pictures Want?* Chicago: University of Chicago Press.

Mori, M. (1970 [2005]). Bukimi no tani [the uncanny valley]. Translated by Karl MacDorman and Takashi Minato. In K. MacDorman (Ed.), "Androids As An Experimental Apparatus: Why Is There An Uncanny Valley And Can We Exploit It?" *CogSci Workshop Toward Social Mechanisms of Android Science Proceedings* (pp. 106–118). http://www.androidscience.com/ (accessed April 22, 2011).

O'Brien, K. (2010a). *I Can't Feel It Anyway*. Vimeo.com. http://vimeo.com/16479526 (accessed January 31, 2011; video removed on March 5, 2011).

O'Brien, K. (2010b, March 17). *Kean O'Brien*. http://alum.calarts.edu/~studio/672/kean-obrien/ (accessed January 6, 2012).

Oz, F. (Dir.) (2004). *The Stepford Wives* [DVD]. USA: Paramount.

Production Notes. (n.d.). Lars and the Real Girl. http://www.vervepics.com/docs/larsnotes.pdf (accessed January 7, 2012).

Siebers, T. (2008, August 31). Disability in the Mirror of Art. *Literature, Art, and Medicine Blog*. http://medhum.med.nyu.edu/blog/?p=130 (accessed April 30, 2011).

Troche, R. (Dir.) 2001. *The Safety of Objects* [DVD]. USA: MGM.

Augmented Spirit/Extreme Embodiment: A Mapped Landscape of Vent Life[1]

Katerie Gladdys and Deshae E. Lott

What are the consequences of fixating our gaze upon the machine? Are we like Ovid's Pygmalion, who so romanticized his statue that he replaced extant human relations with a supernatural one? Alternatively, do we subscribe to fictions like those exemplified by Doc Ock in *Spider-Man 2* (Raimi 2004), the Borg in *Star Trek: First Contact* (Frakes 1996), or even Maggie Fitzgerald in *Million Dollar Baby* (Eastwood 2004), through which we project such irresistible, unmitigated power upon the apparatus that we doubt its constructive contributions to our lifestyle and fear its role in our communities? Our cultural narratives suggest that we often forge dangerous connections with creations that, in our imaginations, border between two realities: the objectified subject and the fantastic. We begin responding to machines that bridge those realms in ways that compromise or obscure our sense of humanity. Certainly, as Donna J. Haraway (1991) asserts, "human beings, like any other component or subsystem, must be localized in a system architecture . . . Communications technologies and biotechnologies are the crucial tools recrafting our bodies" (163–164). Yet, when the unfamiliarity with or data-production generated by a machine dominates relationships with the human body, interpersonal relationships can become pre-scripted by the interface in ways that discount the human mind's positive creative powers—something we accept more readily when machines (e.g., cell phones, computers, and touch pads) appear outside of medical contexts or accessorize rather than meld with the human form. In the collaborative artwork *Augmented Spirit: Extreme Embodiment*, we highlight fragments from Deshae's life text in an effort to achieve our artistic missions. Debunking human–machine melds as fantastical or impersonal, this investigation uses an interactive sonic art installation to poeticize both the uncomfortable and aesthetic aspects integral to the life of a mechanical ventilator-dependent individual. The sustained life becomes a locus for recognizing that our fascination with the supernatural capabilities of the machine in fact translate into something very basic: a high-maintenance form of survival that presents acute vulnerabilities and impositions as well as ordinary celebrations of life. This collaborative artwork seeks to activate the observer, the observed, and the social infrastructure toward co-constructing a polyphony that, if not harmonious, goes beyond any cacophonic, fantastic, and horrific stereotypes that characterize dominant cultural narratives on disability and its accompanying apparatuses.

Trach cuff deflated; Remote to "noise maker" stored[2]

According to John J. McDermott (2006), "medical technology, despite its brilliant, startling successes, cloaks a pervasive sense of interpersonal distance, loss of personal control, and often subjects us to an impersonal paternalism" (255). Our sonically interactive, textile-based art installation specifically challenges assumptions about what constitutes positive human–machine melds by uncovering traces of the life embodied alongside the machines. As relational art, *Augmented Spirit/Extreme Embodiment* translates a particular set of social relations that exist in the world (in this case Deshae's world as a ventilator user) into an art piece that asks the audience physically to participate in or locate themselves in or enter into an intersubjective relationship with the ideas presented and their relationship to the larger ideas that the art intimates (cf. Bourriaud 2002). In our case, the relational art piece challenges and stimulates perceptions about how one turns disability into a creative act not just as a piece but as a life lived.

Rotating mattress overlay & oxygen concentrator turned off

For all of the disconnections persons can attribute to technology, technology continues to create new, accessible interpersonal and global connections among many of us, whether for work or recreation, protest or service. Haraway's "A Cyborg Manifesto" (1991) is prophetic about such possibilities:

> Writing is pre-eminently the technology of cyborgs . . . Cyborg politics is the struggle for language and the struggle against perfect communication, against the one code that translates all meaning perfectly, the central dogma of phallogocentrism. That is why cyborg politics insist on noise and advocate pollution, rejoicing in the illegitimate fusions of animal and machine. These are the couplings which make Man and Woman so problematic, subverting the structure of desire, the force imagined to generate language and gender, and so subverting the structure and modes of reproduction of "Western" identity, of nature and culture, of mirror and eye, slave and master, body and mind. (176)

The cyborg—both as a myth and as an actual hybrid of human and machine—restructures misrecognitions into re-cognitions by disassembling and splicing dominant discourses with alternatives that reconstitute how we perceive and articulate embodied reality. However unnatural the fusion of woman and machine, lives now transgress such boundaries.

In bed, physical therapy/passive range of motion, round 1 of 3

Health machinery born of advancing medical technology inspires new understandings of cyborg existences. Vent-user Deshae Lott's life demonstrates the complications and triumphs that emerge in using technology to sustain life and invites others to locate embodiment and commonality amidst the biomechanical and unusual. The machines necessary to sustain her life—ventilator, suction canister, oxygen concentrator, wheelchair, chest vest, in-exsufflator, nebulizer—(Lott 2011) whoosh, whirl, alarm, drone, buzz, vibrate, chime, and tone around her, creating interfaces of intrusive, cumbersome, and cacophonous tubes and devices that seem antithetical to personal freedom. The frail body and the engineering feats that sustain it demand unrelenting attention, yet, in this case, the very presence of an individual life connected to the interfaces fosters a creative process whereby the patient and caregivers cooperate with the interfaces without being dictated to or dominated by them. Interdependencies with machines, people, and systems add texture to the song while Deshae's voice carries the melody and, faint though it is, vibrantly arises amidst and because of the interfaces. Through the use of interactive textiles, we present a multilayered sculptural installation mapping how the human consciousness, sustained by medical interfaces, emerges to create meaningful connections with others and the surrounding environment. Viewers of the piece will be led, as persons are in Deshae's presence, to see the life itself in the foreground, rather than the unfamiliar and imposing infrastructure sustaining that life.

Detachment from bed-side vent; transfer body, bed to chair

IMPETUS FOR THE COLLABORATION

Our academic fields intersect in the study of how individuals shape and respond to processes that become part of a community's landscape.

Attachment to wheelchair vent; bed-side vent moved by toilet

Deshae Lott, a person with one of the two most severe forms of Limb Girdle Muscular Dystrophy, uses her own life as a malleable medium. In her published articles and public speaking engagements, she creates a lexicon inspired by her physical condition in order to invite others to enter her landscape. Deshae finds ways to allow difference to strengthen both the individual and the community. Then, through spoken, written, or typed words and other physical expressions, she proposes approaches for understanding and constructively responding to such differences. An activist practice emerges from the text of her life. Although one experience, such as hers as a vent user, can never represent the full range of human experiences because each life has unique elements, the whole can be better understood by explorations of its disparate parts. Even if her story serves as but one model—and one that cannot speak for every person living with a disability—Deshae combats misunderstandings about disability that lead to exclusion. She disassembles and creatively reassembles factual evidence (images and sounds and patterns) from her environment and life, arguing that even when disability disrupts familiar patterns and rhythms, the fostering of inclusion benefits both individuals and communities.

Wheelchair & vent batteries unplugged from their chargers

Exploration and the literal path-less-traveled inform Katerie Gladdys' art practice. Her work transforms mapped landscapes and familiar interactions into alternative geographies that transform how we experience a place, space, and dynamic. As she transmits her own sense of wonder, she seeks to encourage others to look more closely at what constitutes their everyday existence. Listening to the stories of others allows her to engage the audience in a familiar modality as an entrance into unfamiliar terrain. Cultivating alternative modes of categorizing information opens a discourse that produces new opportunities for problem recognition and solving that have the potential to influence other fields. Katerie endeavors to make art that awakens curiosity about the quotidian in her viewers, transforming spectators into participants yearning to explore their surrounding environments, and perhaps developing their own unique strategies to connect with the world around them.

Bathing & dressing; Tracheostomy stoma cleaned

PROCESS

Augmented Spirit: Extreme Embodiment responds to Jacqueline Ann K. Kegley's (2006) call that we "pay attention to the conditions necessary for creative living even when terminal or ill" (75). In part, we believe such attention can emerge only when our culture understands more about what it means to live with an illness and about the possibilities and resources necessary for creatively inhabiting a body sustained by biomedical interfaces. Kegley attests that medicine "ignores the person's story and its relevance to the healing process":

> Josiah Royce and others have argued that the person is his or her story, his or her life-project, and to ignore this is to degrade the person and to trespass on individual autonomy . . . Medicine and medical education have tended to devalue the voice of the patient - . . . the patient becomes objectified and rationalized, and the person's lived experience and personal meaning of the illness are ignored. (75–76)

One way of acknowledging the story is by examining the landscape of an individual body and using it as material for art-making, including the art of introducing alternative rhetorics of what it means to inhabit the human body. In this iteration we choose to sonically map some of the social networks and mechanical interfaces Deshae encounters daily.

Oral medications; Respiratory treatment 1 of 4

What becomes vital to responding to Kegley's call is not the structures and machines that sustain life but, rather, how Deshae goes about creating conditions that afford her creative spaces within that essential infrastructure. John J. McDermott distinguishes between our landscape, as that which we inherit, and our personscape, or how we manipulate our landscape with our hands, tools, and modern technology (Hart 2006, 157). Our installation reflects how the inherited landscape and the unique personscape merge and, then, how various personscapes interact with Deshae's disability and personality in ways that develop new awarenesses and beauties in a difficult landscape. Even though the disability limits the landscapes through which interpersonal relationships emerge, it also expands the community of people with whom Deshae engages. For example, as an Americanist concentrating in religious studies and disability studies, Deshae, with a healthier body, might never have navigated a maze of healthcare exchanges or done so in contexts in which she cultivated more than surface-level interactions with doctors, nurses, hospital advocates, insurance case managers, home health agencies and employees, attorneys, and medical equipment suppliers.

Nebulization, Chest Vest, Cough Assist, Lungs suctioned

Our piece conveys both the fluidity and disruption inherent in a vent user's existence while also capturing, to use Haraway's (1991) phrase, "frozen moments":

> Technologies and scientific discourses can be partially understood as formalizations, i.e., as frozen moments, of the fluid social interactions constituting them, but they should also be viewed as instruments for enforcing meanings. The boundary is permeable between tool and myth, instrument and concept, historical systems of social relations and historical anatomies of possible bodies, including objects of knowledge. Indeed, myth and tool mutually constitute each other. (164)

While we present realities of the disease process such as bureaucracies, invasive technologies, and social mores, the project combats dis-ease by inviting the participant to engage the installation in a playful manner. In that play we hope the audience might ask "What is this?" "What does it mean?" and "What does it mean to me?" in such a way that the analysis is neither sterile nor voyeuristic but, instead, an intriguing opportunity to explore potentially unmapped terrain. Just as Kegley calls medical practitioners to listen to their patients' stories, we encourage audiences to listen to and engage with one patient's story through their curiosity about and interaction with the art piece's interfaces. While Katerie works elements of "playfulness" into her various digital installations, in *Augmented Spirit/Extreme Embodiment* such play perfectly relates to and reflects the creative, joyful method by which Deshae approaches her life and disrupts conventional notions of dis-ability.

Leg & arm braces worn to stretch tendons

DAY IN THE LIFE OF DESHAE

With her vent dependency in November 2002, a new series of regular rhythms and movements emerged in Deshae's life. Deshae's survival strategies now dominate her daily schedule, disrupting and restricting its non-health-related activities in unrelenting intervals just as do the lines of text appearing beneath each paragraph in this article, where each such line details aspects of Deshae's survival routine. This schedule for living—with constricted vistas for productivity beyond survival and maintenance periods—promotes peace, order, and stability in the midst of chaos and dissolution. Deshae's artistry has a two-fold effect: Deshae is able to maximize her situation, orchestrating quality-of-life moments within the limitations imposed by her body and other resources (time, money, energy); and her companions cultivate such a sense of comfort in the spaces where the cacophony of her machines and the dissolution of her body pervade the landscape that, sometimes, they feel greater comfort in Deshae's spaces than in their alternative environments. Her careful management of her lifestyle models the human potential to navigate one's terrain with receptivity rather than resentment. In a pronounced way, the personscape informs and manipulates the landscape.

In chair, physical therapy/passive range of motion, round 2 of 3

MAPPING UNRECOGNIZED SPACE

Much of Katerie's work uncovers and re-presents experiences of marginalized landscapes in the natural world—landscapes that are both very present and accessible but also forgotten or even unrecognized. The mythology of a utopian future inhabited by cyborgs recurs as a theme in contemporary culture and in the content of digital media art. The cyborg exists as part of a future almost here but just beyond our grasp. As both colleagues and friends, Deshae and Katerie have had engaged discussions about disability and creative work. After Deshae became vent dependent in 2002, Katerie became aware of the ever-present apparatuses sustaining Deshae's physical life and how their physical forms recall popular notions of what constitutes a cyborg, or an augmented body. Katerie noticed, too, that the context and purpose the apparatuses serve differ greatly from their fictive representations.

Food and drink; teeth flossed & brushed

AURAL AND VISUAL SPACE OF DESHAE'S HOUSE

Deshae lives in a suburban development where little is unique to the exteriors of the neighborhood houses. In contrast, as one would expect, the interior feels more personalized by furniture, bric-a-brac, and books but still rests within the range of middle-class American expectations. The generic neighborhood belies what happens inside the domestic space Deshae calls home. At the same time, despite the abundant medical interfaces prominent in every room of Deshae's home, the experiences of the visitor prove markedly different from when the same visitor enters into institutionalized home settings such as a group home, a convalescent home, an assisted-living complex, a rehabilitation facility, or even an intensive care room—which Deshae actually now refers to as her "home away from home."

Deshae assisted in restroom—transfers, ventilation, wiping

Due to Deshae's medical condition and its requisite survival apparatuses, Deshae's home and body do present any novice visitor with an unrecognizable landscape. In terms of her body itself, unfamiliar gestures can signal something quite familiar. Deshae cannot lift her arms for hugs, or her hand to shake that of another. A guest must decipher, learn, and re-code that, with Deshae, her palm extended on her wheelchair's armrest is a welcoming gesture. In actuality, a great deal of Deshae's lifestyle corresponds to landscapes that very much pervade the typical person's lifestyle: the neighbor who does not get out much because of health reasons, and so who is only occasionally seen yet still seems as present and real as she is mysterious and unknown; or, more basically, the fellow human being who breathes, eats, drinks, and dwells—sleeping or awake—within a framed housing structure. In fact, Deshae's life is akin to so many of the lives most of us acknowledge on some level. It is to the typical passerby simply the life of another stranger whose unique and challenging story that passerby might never witness up close, as it actually transpires behind the walls and on the walls and beyond any walls at all. Our work invites an audience to engage with a slice-of-life perhaps not previously seen and, thus, to cultivate a deeper sensibility about what being human can entail.

Respiratory treatment 2 of 4

In a domestic setting, Deshae's disability becomes tangible in a two ways that the installation reflects: the traces of literal paths on the carpet that Deshae's powerchair travels from room to room; and the constant sounds of the machines that sustain her life and that contrast with the sounds of everyday living. In Deshae's home, all movement occurs within a restricted space. Restrictions emerge both in terms of the boundaries of the walls of the house and its plot of land, further, in terms of which area of which room contains the specific life-sustaining machines needed at set times of the day. Accordingly, the aural-visual, interactive digital installation poetically represents such an alternative universe and its complexity so that others both learn about restriction and, concurrently, glimpse the creativity that it takes to lead a rich life within limited space. *Augmented Spirit/Extreme Embodiment* thereby captures one potential narrative of the daily life of a vent user.

Mechanical Compression arm sleeve worn for lymphedema

The first evidence of deviance in Deshae's house, which is thus reflected in the installation *Augmented Spirit/Extreme Embodiment*, is the neutral-toned carpet and the traces left on it by her wheelchair. The smudged imprints and compressed carpet fiber reveal Deshae's well-worn path from her bedroom to the kitchen to the living room and, finally, to her study. This path is wider than a foot-path dotted with tufts of upstanding carpet. The path winding through the house forms a kind of map, inspiring artistic play with the evidence of Deshae's movements throughout the house—evidence unique to Deshae's mode and path of locomotion. Traced, this evidence formed a map demonstrating proof of the life lived.

Fresh ballard & heat-moisture-exchange replace day-old set

When some people return to their own homes after spending time at Deshae's, they—like Katerie—may feel struck by the relative quiet as well as the ability to listen to ambient sounds from the outside. At Deshae's house there is constant mechanized sound at any given time: the ventilator itself, its alarm, the periodic suctioning of fluid from her lungs. The din is punctuated by laughter, teaching, conversation, and poetry, as well as the household sounds that we take for granted, such as the buzzing of an alarm clock, the running of water, the flushing of toilets, the churning of the dishwasher, the toning of doorbells, and the ringing of phones. Human beings have designed a host of machines, the working sounds of which deliberately interrupt our lives in order to increase convenience or efficiency. Such sounds arise in Deshae's home alongside an equally large host of sounds from devices required not simply for convenience or efficiency, but to sustain life. Listening to these life-sustaining mechanical sounds as an observer, a pattern or rhythm emerges. The house/space becomes simultaneously a map and an instrument reflective of the creativity with which Deshae approaches her life.

In chair, physical therapy/passive range of motion, round 3 of 3

THE ROLE OF COLLABORATION

Deshae's survival depends on a complicated dance of support people. Her existence is a carefully orchestrated collaboration in which Katerie now takes part. Katerie grapples with the idea of representing Deshae's living space in terms of sound and imagery because the mapping itself is a subjective and limiting activity. Although we discuss the nature and product of the collaboration, the process of distillation and creation requires Katerie, as an artist, to make choices about which situations to represent—and how to represent these situations that are not her own. In a sense, the collaboration doubly functions as a relational artwork, where the artist of the life portrayed reflects on her creativity and her creative process and, at the same time, the installation itself captures glimpses of both the process and the artists' reflections. All the while, we invite the audience to observe this process of negotiations and explorations in hopes that the audience, in turn, meaningfully will negotiate and explore the installation and the ideas it represents, challenges, and celebrates.

Respiratory treatment 3 of 4

The process of collaboration highly informs the nature of the audience's interaction with the piece. The installation ideally provides a place where people have opportunities to learn about the landscape of disability and simultaneously are able to/have to/are compelled to co-create this environment with others. This co-creation allows participants to physically "feel," to some small but measurable degree, the bodily inconvenience and mental irritation of disability during their processes of creating a soundscape unique to their movements even as they encounter the sonic textures added by other persons also moving through the piece. The experience has the potential to become a rich tapestry of sound and, at the same time, has the possibility to sink into cacophony when two or more people participate and "play" in the space. This reflects the life Deshae leads, where the constant presence of others (machines and human beings) necessary for her survival sometimes feels quite unpleasant, and, at other times, offers such a beautiful scene that the laborious and disharmonious dimensions of the lifestyle slip from the foreground of each co-participant's consciousness. The installation thus aims to capture the poetic triumphs as well as the chaos and rigorous methods of the vent user's lifestyle. In both the art piece and the life it represents, this tension between coexistent realities of the vent user's situation dominates the visual, aural, and interpersonal landscapes.

Food and drink; teeth flossed & brushed; oral medications

DESCRIPTION OF THE PIECE

The physical work consists of a piece of carpet cut in the shape of the floor plan of Deshae's house. Stitched or embroidered into the carpet using conductive thread are two parallel paths or tracks representing the imprints of wheelchair wheels. On two small-sized versions of the piece, Katerie's embroidering of the path gestures, additionally, to the domesticity of the environment. The medical apparatus is in full view of the audience, and the juxtaposition of the represented machines against the very domesticity of the installation materials—the carpet and the furniture-like stand with the apparatus—imparts a tension that is inherent in Deshae's home environment as well as in the environments of other people in her situation who live at home.

Respiratory treatment 4 of 4

Contingent on the space allotted to the installation, the audience's bodies—fingers, hands, feet, wheels of other wheelchair users' chairs—come into contact with either or both tracks on the carpet, thereby triggering sets of sounds typical of Deshae's aural experience in a particular room in her house. The participants navigate the space by simultaneously tracing with fingers or walking/shuffling their feet on the two paths, applying pressure (see Figure 1). Different points on the path elicit different sounds or layerings of sound. Sets of wall speakers that broadcast the various mechanical and human sounds surround the carpet. (The latter sounds may be familiar ones, such as conversations, or unfamiliar ones, such as Deshae's physical reactions to various machines interacting with her body.) In one version of the piece, portable DVD players boxed to resemble decorative pictures typically hung in domestic interior spaces play video that, on first glance, appears to be an abstracted landscape but that, on closer examination, is the landscape of Deshae's body undergoing some of her daily therapies. Specifically, the images capture aspects of Deshae undergoing her physical therapy or passive range of motion with the help of her husband (see Figure 2).

Vent moved from beside toilet to bed-side

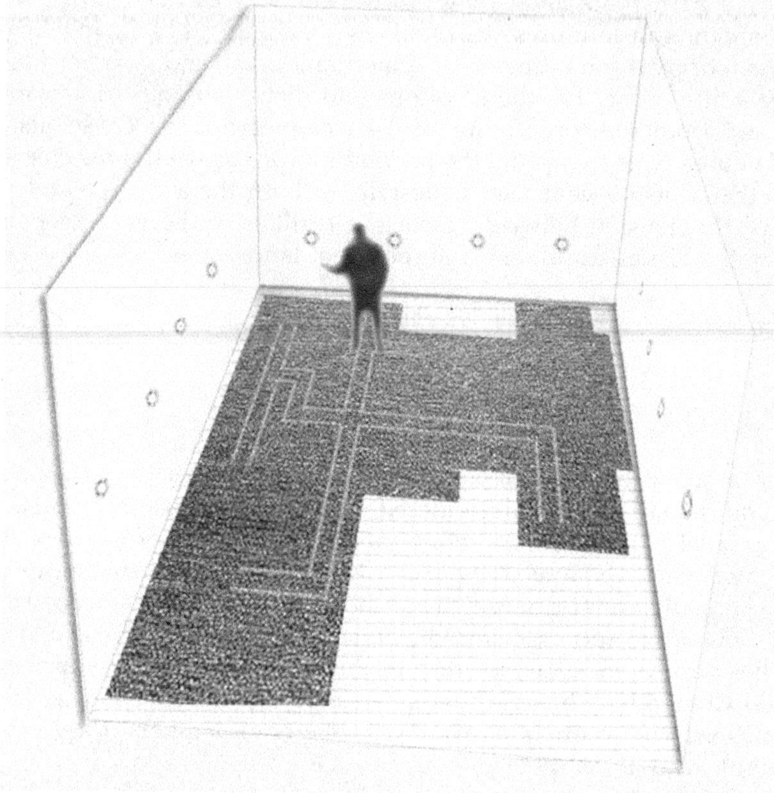

Figure 1. Diagram 1: Participant on mapped path.

Our multilayered sculptural installation represents Deshae's experiences through the use of images hung on museum room walls and sounds emerging from the audience's tactile interaction with textiles centered in that same room; observers become participants (Gladdys 2010). The installation connects something common to many persons' lives (carpet) with a fairly uncommon lifestyle (vent dependency). The impressionist piece ideally invites the listener/viewer/sound-activator to approach alternative realities with curiosity and personal involvement.

Rotating mattress overlay & oxygen concentrator turned on

SIZE AND SCOPE

As it appears in museums and similar fora, this piece is an installation where people walk or "wheel" the paths. This installation is site-specific, so its size and scope typically depend on the location specifics wherever the piece appears

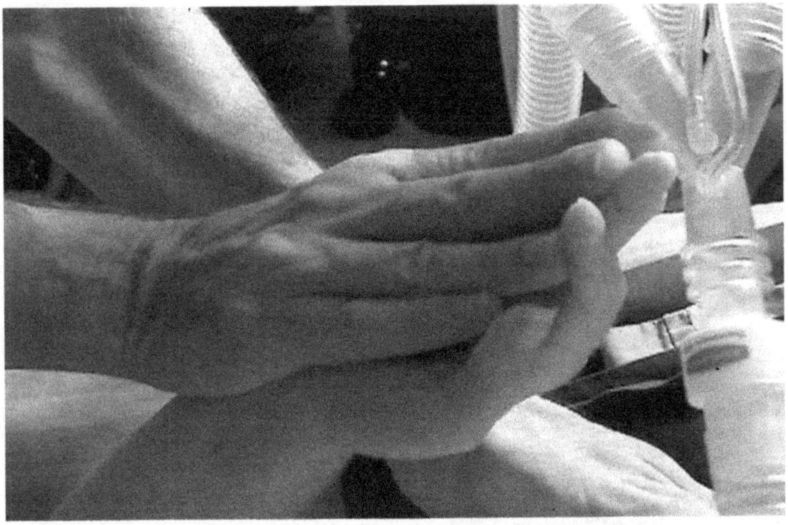

Figure 2. Abstracted landscape video of Deshae's body undergoing physical therapy.

for public display/co-performance. Ideally, there would be a large floor space to lay the carpet and walls for the speakers (see Figure 3). The area would allow for both foot traffic and spaces for participating in the installation itself. Currently constructed pieces are sonic sculptures that use the hands or fingers to follow the path and trigger the audio.

Detachment from chair vent; transfer body, chair to bed

MOVEMENT IN THE PIECE

In *Augmented Spirit/Extreme Embodiment*, participants navigate the space by simultaneously placing their feet or fingers on two parallel tracks—representative of wheelchair paths through Deshae's home—and walking or shuffling or tracing atop those paths, following the trail as they desire.

Attachment to bedside vent; Deshae voids via a urinal

The motion of the participant triggers sounds, voices, and noises specific to the sonic environment either of Deshae's home or, sometimes, of homes in general. The restrictions on movement placed both on the space itself (the plane of the carpet) and on the mode of locomotion (having to walk wide-legged or to trace with fingers in order to touch the two tracks and activate more sounds) convey, gently and in a small way, the inconvenience of disability. At the same time, these restrictions evoke the play of a game like Twister, where successful players place their bodies in "unnatural" or awkward positions. The human-body-scaled installation allows the participant to perform/experience disability. And, with both the smaller and larger installations, those who interact with the carpet become part of an electronic instrument where movement encourages the

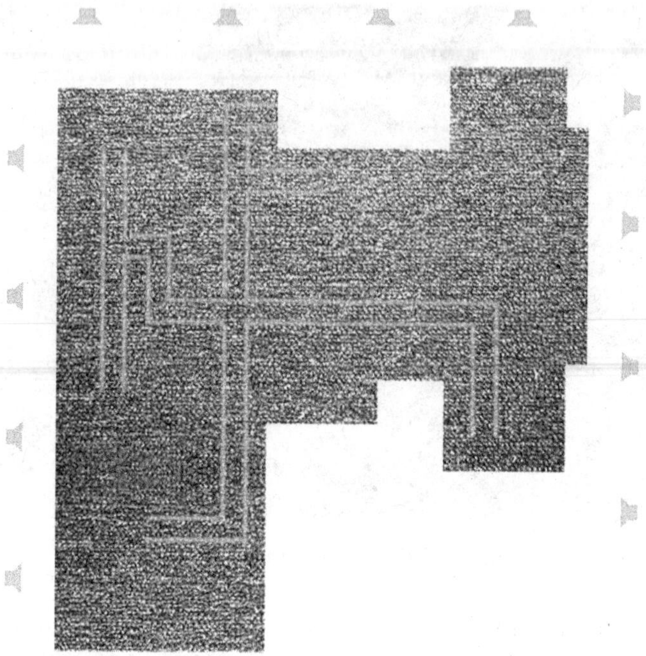

Figure 3. Diagram 2: View from above.

audience to experiment with sound and, potentially, to realize an alternative perspective on disability. Additionally, a video playing on a portable DVD player illustrates the minutia of Deshae's various therapies and makes them into their own landscapes.

Wheelchair & vent batteries plugged into their chargers

TECHNOLOGY AND MATERIALS

The parallel wheelchair tracks are stitched into the carpet with conductive thread. The stitches appear to be different-colored loops in the carpet and variably blend into the weave of the carpet. (Conductive thread does not carry a current that is strong enough to cause injury to human beings; the charge of static electricity potentially created by rubbing carpet in a dry environment is stronger than the current of the conductive thread.) The ends of the conductive thread are connected to very thin wires that lead to a circuit board containing touch sensors. The touch sensors have their own wires, which lead to an Arduino device that is connected to a USB port of a computer running the program Max MSP. Touching the carpet sends a message to the computer to play a particular sound or sets of sounds, which the computer then sends to the speakers via a multi-channel audio interface that sends a discrete sound to a particular speaker.

Deshae given remote that activates her "noise maker"

ART PROJECT DOCUMENTATION

See Figures 4 and 5 for art project documentation.

Figure 4. Hand touching stitches. Augmented Spirit/Extreme Embodiment: Sonic sculpture mapping the interior space of a vent user.

Figure 5. Two participants playing with sculpture. Augmented Spirit/Extreme Embodiment: Sonic sculpture mapping the interior space of a vent user.

CONCLUSION

The art project *Augmented Spirit/Extreme Embodiment* tries to connect something common to many persons' lives (carpet) with a fairly uncommon lifestyle (vent dependency); the tangible aspect of the carpet where sounds activate at the touch of a viewer-participant links, in a real way, the more typical human's experience with the ventilator user's more atypical experiences. The carpet, however, serves as only one co-structure shared between the vent user and non-vent user, the artist and the audience. Other co-structures emerge when the audience, through the pressure of touch, triggers familiar sounds of domestic life or the voice of Deshae alongside the unfamiliar sounds. In effect, the audience's own unique physical motions through the installation set off unique sequences of aural sensation.

Trach cuff inflated; lungs suctioned

Like other museum installations, an audience can engage with this piece by reading the tag with its brief description, artists' names, and the related artists' websites addresses. Yet, given the sonic sculptures in the piece, a varied audience is invited to engage with *Augmented Spirit/Extreme Embodiment* by activating sound sensors. In particular, sounds typical to a person's day (e.g., discussions on choices of salad dressing or family member frustrations, silverware hitting a plate, clocks chiming, a toothbrush rubbing against one's teeth) contrast with the roar of the suction canister, the whir of a rotating bed mat, and discussions about medical equipment. Excerpts from Deshae's autobiographical poems and her teaching seminars also correspond with locations on the map of the house in which such kinds of living occur.

By twenty-one she had acquired
A decade of practice
Waiting like this,
Waiting
For someone else
To button her shirt
Zip her pants
Tie her shoes
Lift her frame
From a chair, a bed, a toilet, a seat in the van...
At thirty-one she stopped breathing
Without electricity and a machine with tubes and alarms.
Inhalation and exhalation mechanized,
Her nose and mouth and diaphragm became
Mere accessories.
She could not be left alone ever:
A tube might pop loose;
The trach might plug up;
The electricity might go out.[3]

Through such interaction with the project, then, we hope to compel participants in a small way to approach realties different from their own with greater curiosity and personal involvement. Despite any discordant differences that inform and dominate the individual's first impressions, curiosity and personal involvement might help audience members at least to recognize and perhaps even to develop resonance with the very human aspects present in these, to them, unfamiliar situations. One of our hopes is that, by participating in the installation, the audience will experience something akin to the experiences of those who enter Deshae's home. The discordant sounds and unfamiliar machines, dialog, and interfaces slip into the background when a shared humanness emerges and becomes the communal focus. The interfaces gradually lessen their seductive grasp on a visitor's attention; instead, by stimulating the installation and, in turn, being stimulated themselves on a variety of levels (including the very direct sensation of feeling sound reverberations or creating static electricity), the vibrancy of the co-creative human exchange compels all participants' attention. In a way, we use machines to promote and deepen understanding about and empathy for health machinery. Unlike an advertisement, however, we do not promote or endorse a product. Our work seeks to promote personscapes and to suggest that positive outcomes can surface through convergences of dramatically different personscapes. Like much art, the installation proves impressionistic in character, thereby inviting the listener/viewer/carpet-trodder/sound-activator to form unique relations with, and perchance because of, *Augmented Spirit/Extreme Embodiment*.

Unpredictably, and briefly,
Freedom would return to her.
She could ride in the van to attend
Her nephew's track meet,
Her niece's dance recital,
Her physical therapist's rock concert,
A meal out with friends.
Each time freedom came,
She wept,
Grateful to practice ordinary life again,
Grateful to be present and glad at heart.[4]

NOTES

1. Acknowledgements of financial support: For conference travel, the University of Florida School of Art and Art History Travel Grant, 2009–2010. And, for material and equipment, the University of Florida College of Fine Arts Scholarship Enhancement Fund, 2008–2009.
2. For more information about Deshae's health care routine, see http://www.deshae.info/health_-care/use.htm.
3. Lines excerpted from "The Sick Wife," an unpublished poem by Deshae E. Lott.
4. Lines excerpted from "The Sick Wife," an unpublished poem by Deshae E. Lott.

REFERENCES

Bourriaud, N. (2002). *Nicolas Bourriaud: Relational Aesthetics*. Paris: Les Presses du réel.
Eastwood, C. (Dir.) (2004). *Million Dollar Baby* [DVD]. USA: Warner.
Frakes, J. (Dir.) (1996). *Star Trek: First Contact* [DVD]. USA: Paramount.

Gladdys, K. (2010). Getting a Lay of the Land. http://layoftheland.net/augmentedGladdysLott/ (accessed April 4, 2011).

Haraway, D. J. (1991). *Simians, Cyborgs, and Women: The Reinvention of Nature.* New York: Routledge.

Hart, R. E. (2006). Landsccape and Personscape in Urban Aesthetics In J. Campbell & R. E. Hart (Eds.), *Experience as Philosophy: On the Work of John J. McDermott* (pp. 140–161). Bronx, NY: Fordham University Press.

Kegley, J. A. K. (2006). Living Creatively, While Terminal. In J. Campbell & R. E. Hart (Eds.), *Experience as Philosophy: On the Work of John J. McDermott* (pp. 58–83). Bronx, NY: Fordham University Press.

Lott, D. E. (2011). *Description of Deshae's Equipment Use.* http://www.deshae.info/health_care/use.htm (accessed April 7, 2011).

McDermott, J. J. (2006). Afterword: You Are Really Able In J. Campbell & R. E. Hart (Eds.), *Experience as Philosophy: On the Work of John J. McDermott* (pp. 237–272). Bronx, NY: Fordham University Press.

Raimi, S. (Dir.) (2004). *Spider-Man 2* [DVD]. USA: Sony.

The Reworking of Spatial Attribution: People with Intellectual Disabilities and the Micropolitics of Dissensus

Ann Fudge Schormans and Adrienne Chambon

Space, as conceptualized by Pierre Bourdieu (1989), is always relational and always an indication of social positioning. Symbolic of the often entrenched and violent social divisions that exist in a given society, space explicates the symbolic status or capital with which one is or is not attributed. Considering social space and subjectivity for people with intellectual disabilities, Rob Kitchin (1998) writes of the restrictions imposed on the spaces open to people labeled intellectually disabled; such restricted spaces and positionings keep labeled persons "in their place" and "out of place." Here, we take up these ideas in order to build on earlier work, in which we reported on a research project involving a group of people with intellectual disabilities who critiqued, re-imaged, and re-imagined public photographs of people with intellectual disabilities (Fudge Schormans and Chambon 2010, in press). Approaching the project from the perspective of its value as or to autobiography, we dealt with notions of space and place in limited terms. Prompted by the musings of audience members and panel presenters, in this article we actively take up questions of space and place in our (re)consideration of the work done by this group of people with intellectual disabilities with visual imagery of people so labeled. We look, in particular, at the ways in which the group's work with photographic imagery can be recognized as a political act of dissensus that begins to disrupt the ableist consensus about what are/are not acceptable spaces and subjectivities for people with intellectual disabilities.

VISUAL REPRESENTATIONS AS PUTTING AND KEEPING PEOPLE WITH INTELLECTUAL DISABILITIES "IN THEIR PLACE"

"Space" can be understood to refer to the structural qualities of a physical environment, whereas "place" is the notion that includes the dimensions of lived experience, interaction, and use of space by its inhabitants (Hornecker 2008). But space is not only a physical dimension; it also holds social, emotional, and symbolic meaning. People's lives are grounded in different spatial arrangements and in the meanings that particular places have for different social groups. For Bourdieu (1989), spaces are not neutral: They are specialized and ordered in ways that manifest and reflect social hierarchies among citizens. Specific settings and activities organize lived experiences and *produce* social practices, and, in this way, space works to construct a "sense of one's place" (Bourdieu 1989, 17). As political scientist Chantal Mouffe (2006) has remarked, "every form of space is always some configuration of power relations" (n.p.). Controlled exclusively by non-disabled outsiders (Hevey 1997), the space of visual representation of people with intellectual disabilities is not merely one in which social position and interaction are represented; it also works to structure such positions and interactions (Freund 2001). Such representations are spaces of division that emphasize difference and effect particular relations of power.

People with intellectual disabilities rarely have any choice over the spaces they are placed in and the resultant identities imposed on them in and by these spaces (Power 2010). Afforded access—in visual representations as in real life—to only a very limited range of spaces in the world, they are thus excluded from those physical and social spaces that non-disabled others take for granted and take up freely (Kitchin 1998). Usually stereotypic and dysfunctional, visual representations—in particular, public photographic imagery—depict labeled people primarily in terms of the biological-biomedical perceptions of their lives: as in need of medicalization and therefore dependent and vulnerable; or within institutional spaces, agentless and singularly and dys-functionally "other" (Garland-Thomson 2001; Hevey 1997). Yet, the lived reality for many people with intellectual disabilities may include (often involuntary) institutional living—for example, large institutional-style group home living, incarceration in the corrections system, hospitalization in mental health or long-term care settings—and, in this sense, these representations may closely approximate their lives. Deinstitutionalization and community living, however, have meant that this is less often the case and, as a result, these stereotypical images fail to reflect alternative experiences. Constructed as incommensurable subjects in both representational and public space, people with intellectual disabilities are spatially and socially located outside of the everyday world. They are kept "in their place," or else, as Kitchin (1998) forcefully argues, when they are located in "ordinary" spaces, they are understood as being "out of place": always on the outside, never quite belonging (345). In this way "disabled people are taught to 'know their place'" (whether they accept this or not)—taught to know the spaces to which they do and don't belong and their position on the social ladder (346). Noting that these are often unconscious strategies, Bourdieu (1989), like Kitchin, argues that their result is that social place and social distances are inscribed in bodies, into relations to the body, and into language and time. For Bourdieu, social classifications, notably those that work through dualist oppositions such as abled/disabled, work to organize our perception of the social world and, under certain conditions, move beyond perception to organize the world itself. Thus, the spatialities of disability powerfully shape well-being, identity, and experiences of space (Kitchin 1998; Power 2010).

Another important aspect of visual representation for people with intellectual disabilities is their exclusion from the role of viewer or commentator. This appears rooted in hegemonic, long-standing (if false) assumptions about "ability" and "intellectual disability": labeled people are believed incapable of understanding, having an opinion, commenting upon, or responding (individually, collectively, socially, or politically) to public images of people with intellectual disabilities. Regarded simply as objects—and not subjects—of our non-dis-abled gaze, we believe they are neither able (nor desiring) to return our gaze nor to gaze themselves. They have thus been silenced, afforded neither the right nor the opportunity to speak to or against these visual representations and spatial attributions. Created from the hegemonic (non-disabled) perspective, and excluding potentially dissenting (disabled) understandings, these public imagings and imaginings of intellectual disability foster the illusion of consensus—the notion that all viewers will see intellectual disability and people labeled intellectually disabled in the same way (Sontag 2003). As Mouffe (2000) writes, "we have to accept that every consensus exists as a temporary result of a provisional hegemony, as a stabilization of power, and that it always entails some form of exclusion" (17). This "culture of consensus" is exclusive. Restricting not only what can/cannot be seen and whose voices are/are not included, it means, too, that it is not considered possible—or necessary—to envisage that things could be different from how they are now (Mouffe 2006).

We turn our attention now to the research project under discussion here. Named the "What's Wrong with this Picture?" project by one of the research participants, it was an inclusive, arts-informed interpretive inquiry into the ways public photographic images serve to (dysfunctionally) represent people with intellectual disabilities, influencing how and what we come to know about them. It was concerned with how labeled people would, themselves, see and respond to these cultural representations and means of knowing and with how they might use photography to problematize these (dis)abling re-presentations, to trouble non-disabled knowing, and for self-representation.[1]

A group of four people labeled intellectually disabled accepted the invitation to participate in the project. Working with a selection of public photographic images of people with intellectual disabilities, the research project members first critique the images, addressing what they like/do not like about them, the stories they believe the images tell/do not tell, how non-disabled others might interpret them, and the potential consequences of such to their own lives. But they do more than express dissatisfaction with these representations. Using the computer software program *Photoshop* and/or by taking new photographs, they transform these images and, in doing so, they intervene: "commandeering space and commenting on the kinds of power expressed in certain spatial layouts," they rewrite the original images as political sites (Tonkiss 2005, 141). Their counter-images modify the (un)livable spaces to which labeled people are assigned and liberate the figures thus represented from these bonds, from the vividness of otherness, thereby rendering them more mobile, more in relation; living and livable. Through these visual manipulations, they make these exclusionary spaces their own, inviting others into a heterological space (Foucault 1986) of their design and creation. Going further, the transformed images—strategically paired with the originals—are exhibited (in an art gallery styling designed by the group members) to different audiences. This pairing of the original visual representations produced by non-disabled outsiders with the group members' counter-images serves as a spatial tactic that works to unsettle and transform accepted organizations of social and physical space for disabled persons. It is about the political work of dissensus (Mouffe 2006): an intervention into the modes of public representation that, in challenging dysfunctional spatial attributions effected in and through visual representation, reflects a taking of power, a (re)positioning of the disabled self as citizen, and an occupying of the space of debate.

WHAT'S WRONG WITH THIS PICTURE?

The research group members—Bob, Robin, Sam, and Donna—chose eleven images in total to work with over the course of the project. At this juncture, we wish to introduce three of these, for it is their work with these particular images that we will talk about in this article.

One image in particular proved to have a powerful effect on the group members. It is an image of a young man with intellectual and physical disabilities. Alternately averting their eyes and pushing the image away, or else drawing the image close in a protective, caring, and care-full caress, the group members had mixed feelings about working with this image. Wanting, in many ways, to simply make it go away, they were drawn, too, to its representativeness of all that they found troubling about intellectual disability imagery. They identified its power over non-disabled viewers' understandings of intellectual disability and over their own lives. Drawn from a national newspaper, it was accompanied by two other images and a lengthy text. The image is sparse, bare, and barren—little has been included and what has is bleak. In accordance with this staging, the man has been photographed wearing only a diaper. To the group's dismay (most are brought to tears), his near naked body is exposed to the camera, to the viewer. He lies, alone, on a thin quilted blanket partially covering a plastic-protected mattress lying on a carpeted floor,[2] his head resting on the carpeted edge of a raised floor or step. Photographed in black and white, the image is dark: the dark walls of the carpeted floor that surround the man press the bits of light contained within the image toward its center, toward the mattress, the body, and the diaper. The man is very thin, seemingly barely alive. Attending to this, the group members hold the image gently, as if he will break. His knees are tightly held together. His arms are drawn close to his body, framing his chest, and one hand rests against his chin. His face is turned away from the camera.

The second image is a color photograph that was the lead-in to a feature article in a national newspaper. The right side of the image is filled with the body of a teenage girl with visible physical disabilities, photographed sprawled across the lap of a diminutive woman sitting on a chair. The girl's limbs flay out and away from her body and her back arches at a distressing angle. Her head seems to be falling backwards, at risk of banging into a small table with a lit lamp behind her; the lamplight shines upon her face. Her eyes are closed and her face is turned towards the ceiling, prompting Robin to quietly state that she looks as if she had committed suicide, and Bob to sadly suggest that she is in great pain. The other woman smiles at the girl as she tightly grips her around the waist. Gripping the image tightly in his own large hands, Sam worries that the woman will drop her. The colorful clothing of the woman and girl is in contrast to the subdued, dark shades on the left-hand side of the image; this half over-encumbered by a wheelchair. The wheelchair's size is exaggerated by the way it is not fully contained within the frame of the image, and, as large as the girl's body appears in the staging, it, too, is diminished by the wheelchair. Behind the women, a hospital-style bed laden with medical/therapeutic equipment is barely visible. The unadorned walls and floor of what appears to be a very small room are a pale grey in color. The group members identify this to be a hospital room.

Waving the image in the air, smiling and talking excitedly, the group members were initially happy to be working with the third image, a movie poster for the Hallmark Hall of Fame television presentation *Riding the Bus With My Sister* (Huston 2005). They were excited by the possibilities (not always realized) created by the publicity of movies about people with intellectual disabilities. This image is in color. In bold red lettering, on a background of a soft blue sky and white clouds, the name of the movie occupies the upper left quadrant of the image. Two women—one in brightly colored clothing, the other in dark shades—sit together on a bench. The slightly off-center positioning of the bench draws the viewer's eye to the women sharing it. Group members immediately recognized the colorfully dressed woman on the left as the actress Rosie O'Donnell; the second actress is Andie McDowell, who stares comfortably and confidently at the camera. Yet, pointing in confusion and anger at the image, the group notes that Rosie O'Donnell has been photographed looking up and off to the side, with what they describe as a "dreamy look," unlike that of any persons with intellectual disabilities that they themselves know. Clutching an overly large pink tote bag on her lap, she is staged in marked contrast to Andie McDowell, who is composed and professionally and conservatively dressed. Rosie O'Donnell's t-shirt, shorts, athletic socks, and mismatched running shoes are a fanciful mish-mash of colors—a wardrobe that the group, with some disgust, deems completely inappropriate; better suited to a child than to an adult.

These three original images enact dividing practices, making plain the social distance between people with and without intellectual disabilities. It is readily apparent to the group members that the non-disabled producers of the images possess the power to constitute, by making visible and explicit, social divisions that are believed implicit and readily understood (even if not accepted by people with disabilities). They understand this as political power: the power to make groups and manipulate the objective structure of society (Bourdieu 1989), the power to keep labeled people "in their place" and "out of place" (Kitchin 1998).

The images accomplish this by showing the physical spatial distances—the exclusion from spaces of sociality—that simultaneously construct and reveal labeled persons' social distance from non-disabled others. With much sadness, the group members discern, for example, that the empty, uninhabited, and lifeless space occupied by the man in the diaper—what they understand to be an institution or cell—signifies for labeled people their placelessness, their position outside of human relations. Although the staging of the man's body exaggerates his inability to physically care for himself, there are no indications of care or caring others, no signs of sociality here: He appears to have been abandoned, discarded. In their attention to the physical aspects of this particular space—this room, the floor—they recognize, too, that spaces are places of relationship. The apparent lack of sociality, the placelessness of the man in the image, also indicates the low symbolic status attributed to labeled people in society. The group understands the man as having been tossed aside, unwanted, determined as being of little if any worth:

> He's institutionalized and there's only staff around and they don't seem to care about him and he's locked in this dark room alone, by himself. I think that's what it looks like, an institution. (Bob)

> Where's his mom and dad? Where's his family? Where's his friends? (Donna)

> They're leaving him there 'cause they don't want him. I think he's not wanted and stuff like that . . . because he has a disability. (Robin)

The image inscribes the hegemonic (ableist) consensus that this is an un-lived and un-livable life (Butler 2004). It does not invite the viewer to consider inclusion but only reinforces exclusion.

Far from being a neutral imaging, the wheelchair in the second image defines the girl as un-able, delimiting her to her physical dependence: She needs this medical place, equipment, and intervention; she needs others to provide care, to do *for* her. For Bob, the image says, "because the person just can't function like you can, like normal, can't function as normally as you can, she has to be in a wheelchair and cared for all the time." The exaggerated staging of the girl's body, in contrast to the diminutive frame of the carer holding her, further constructs her as a burden, a task unmanageable except by professionals. Donna picks up on this: "to me, I would find it very difficult; I don't think that I could do it." For the group, the wheelchair both constructs the girl as "different" and reinforces for the non-disabled viewer that this particular place, this medical room, is where she belongs. There is no suggestion of a (lived or even imaginable) life outside of this room, no likelihood of relationship outside of a caregiving relationship.

The spaces and positionings of the figures in these images are restricted. No other possibilities exist for them and, unable to leave, they are entitled to belong to no other spaces. Both the institutional and medical spaces and their related narratives and social positionings are understood by the non-disabled hegemony as "normal" spaces and places for *all* people with intellectual disabilities. Individuality and individual action and agency are limited by the rules governing these spaces (Ferrier and Muller 2008).

The group understands something different as taking place in the Hallmark movie poster. This image exposes the social distances that exist even when people with intellectual disabilities occupy the same physical spaces as non-disabled people. While seeming to share the physical space of the bench at the bus stop, Rosie O'Donnell's character is staged so as to mark her as not belonging in this "normal" public space. She stands out and draws the viewer's attention; she is clearly "out of place" (Kitchin 1998). In contrast, the other woman appears very much to belong, her presence unlikely to elicit comment or challenge. As a character with an intellectual disability, the Rosie character can occupy this space only when her difference, her un-belonging, is clearly marked. While upsetting to the group members, they know, too, that none of this would likely seem out of the ordinary to non-disabled viewers. As that which is "unthought," it is necessary to the maintenance of ableist hegemony and its constructions of "normal"; reinforcing ableist ontological divisions, it thus shuts down other possibilities for being, appropriating, and moving about daily life spaces or spaces of being for people with disabilities (Kumari Campbell 2008). Marginalized as they are, kept so outside of more typical lived spaces, labeled people occupy almost none or very little of the social space available to non-disabled others, and so possess very little power.

The group's critique of these three images articulates the ways in which the original images enact a symbolic violence against the place of people with intellectual disabilities in the world. Bourdieu (1989) understands symbolic violence as the dismissing of the legitimacy of particular subject positions and the views that go along with those positions. Wounded by the experience of viewing and working with these images, the group members are greatly troubled that their views and experiences are not represented: "I just don't know why that the picture would have to look like this . . . Well, this honestly tells a bad story about people with disabilities, it is very bad" (Sam). They worried that they (and all labeled people) would be/had been identified by non-disabled viewers as being the "same" as the people in the images: dependent, unable, frightening, unrecognizable, not human or only barely human. Not only would this identification define and delimit the possibilities for their own lives, but it was also strongly at odds with their own senses of self, their own meanings of "intellectual disability." Nor does it reflect their own very livable lives and the spaces in which they live. These are not their "truths." Refusing these images, refusing to be located and identified thus, the group members "remix" (Bishop 2004) the original images: by inserting contexts and multiplying the spaces the figures occupy in daily living, they "distort" these (un)accepted spaces and attributed subjectivities (Chouinard, Hall, and Wilton 2010).

REWORKING SPATIAL ATTRIBUTION

Bob suggests the first transformation of the image of the man in the diaper. Using *Photoshop*, a soft blanket is draped over the man's body, signifying both the provision of care to the man and the presence of people who love him. It turns a hostile, cold, lifeless space into one of gentleness, comfort, and caring relation. Robin chooses to remove the man's body from the institutional scene and re-place him on a beach—a more typical setting that reflects life, sociality, and adventure, and one where his nakedness is not so out of place.

As a group, they also enact a more complex transformation: The man's body is straightened, fully clothed, and positioned upright beside the front door of what appears to be a middle-class home. Regarding the home as a place of safety and comfort that modifies the socio-economic status of the man in the image (both his economic and cultural capital), it indicates a more meaningful presence; a life (well) lived in a home of one's own. For one group member who has always lived with his family, this has always been his place. The other three members have had experiences of institutional types of living, although their current situations are different. Yet, due to their own poverty, their homes (like those of many people with intellectual disabilities) are not nearly of the same status as that depicted in their transformed image, suggesting that their transformation risks the erasure of the lived realities of many labeled people. Nonetheless, the group members are speaking here to the question of value, of how labeled persons deserve a decent place to live. And, while one might read the re-posturing of the man—standing him up—as an act of normalization designed to make his body (and the man, or labeled people in general) more acceptable to non-disabled viewers, the group intends it otherwise. This manipulation of the man's body reflects that they do not perceive him (or themselves or other labeled persons) as "abnormal"—that he can "stand" on his own as a person with a disability, and "stand up" and take his place as a citizen.[3]

The group's re-imaging of the girl in the wheelchair photograph follows a similar line of reasoning. Altering her body, they reposition her sitting upright in the lap of the woman—a position that the shape of wheelchair suggests is possible for her. Removing both figures from the less pleasurable clinical scene, the group re-places them in a "nicer" setting, like a park, where they could "sit on a bench" and "enjoy the day." In doing so, they counter the medicalized space of the original image and the inference of physical pain created by her original posturing. They counter assumptions of what are acceptable spaces, places, and ways of being for the girl, for them, and, by extension, for all labeled people. The group's selection of a site of recreation, of non-work, like the beach upon which the man with the diaper was placed, does not mean that the girl and the man are placeless, only that the group has chosen sites of pleasure and preference (dispositions or *habitus* in Bourdieu's terms) for these labeled figures to occupy. These "other spaces," or what Foucault (1986) terms heterological spaces, signify special but real spaces that modify the terms of relation.

Reacting to the "mis-placement" of Rosie O'Donnell's character in this ordinary space of a bench at a bus stop, to her staging as not belonging there, the group members' transformation of the image similarly reflects their opposition to how this photographic representation mis-represents persons with an intellectual disability. They know nobody with an intellectual disability who looks "like that," who would dress like this. To counter the exaggeration they read in the original, they go online to search for another image of Rosie O'Donnell as a replacement, one that allows them to alter the character's style of dress (professional shirt and slacks), making it better suited to her age and more like that of the non-disabled woman seated beside her—more like how they themselves would choose to dress. The replacement also enacts a repositioning of the character: With face forward, eyes gazing directly at the camera, and her body more composed and controlled, the transformed Rosie character closely resembles both her non-disabled counterpart and the group members themselves. Using *Photoshop*, they cut the troublesome Rosie from the original image and insert the replacement Rosie in her place. The transformation is intended to demonstrate that most people with intellectual disabilities tend to look more "like" non-disabled people than "unlike" them. Further, by eliminating the staged markers of difference, she no longer looks out of place. Now she looks as if she belongs.

These alternative images enact political strategies of spatial (re)definition that implicitly suggest that, like non-disabled persons, labeled persons also engage in the pleasures of pleasurable spaces. The sharing of space implicates the shadow presence of the non-disabled audience in those spaces, (potentially) bringing the two groups in close proximity and leaving open the kind of relational interaction that could occur. Institutional and medicalized spaces are transformed into spaces of everydayness (at home, in the community); spaces of pain, suffering, and a limited life are transformed into spaces of pleasure; and spaces of exclusion are transformed into relational spaces—spaces of belonging, of being with others, and of being-in-the-world. No longer kept "in their place" and "out of place," the disabled figures in the images are now "in place"—in our shared/same place.

Philosopher Michel De Certeau (1984) writes of the everyday tactics and quasi-invisible ruses by which those who do not occupy positions of power work to appropriate and make the everyday—and everyday spaces—their own. In their transformations, the group members move into and embody these everyday spaces in (perhaps) unexpected ways. Refusing outright the supposition that the imaged "lives" of people with intellectual disabilities stand for the whole of a life (Bal 2004)—both that of the person in the image and of *all* labeled persons—the counter-representations construct people with intellectual disabilities as more fully realized and embodied characters, as "inside" rather than "outside" social spaces and relations. Through these counter-images we gain a sense not only of the difference experienced when people with intellectual disabilities are placed in spaces "they had played no part in shaping" (Chouinard et al. 2010, 2), but also of the possibilities that might be realized in representing the spaces of their real lives—and of their own choosing.

AN AGONISTIC SPACE OF OPPOSITION

Organized around the creation of two sets of images, the project as a whole enacts a visual strategy of creating a simultaneous point and counterpoint, exposure and counter-exposure, and, through the process of publicly exhibiting the work, an address to the (non-disabled) viewer that includes the point of reference of the initial, and wounding, representations. In the exhibits of the work, the group members mounted the transformed images on large sheets of white foam board with quotations from their critique accompanying each. These boards were hung from the ceiling. Resting on tables positioned underneath each board was the original image—available to viewers to pick up, look at, and read the accompanying captions and/or text. This juxtaposition of the two sets of images is an intentional curatorial project, the creation of an installation relying both on an active audience and a relational aesthetics of opposition (Bishop 2004).[4]

Bourdieu (1989) argues that symbolic power has the ability to consecrate or reveal. It is this notion of revelation that is at play in the group's exhibition of the work. Their juxtaposition of these two sets of images creates a palpable contrast between, on the one hand, the spaces represented in the original images and, on the other, *the group members'* actual lived-in spaces in the world (e.g., the park, the beach, at home) along with their possible places in society (e.g., as loved, cared for, wanted, valued—as, in many ways, the "same" as non-disabled citizens). The juxtaposed sets of images represent two "truths" of intellectual disability that are so very far apart. This visual strategy makes plain that the visible—the hegemonic truths of intellectual disability seen in the original images—make *in*visible the ableist power relations that determine them.

Revelation, as achieved through opposition, subverts the assumed consensus. In this sense, the group members' participation in this research is neither innocent nor a romanticized tokenistic participation by labeled people in research. It is, instead, a kind of agonistic or conflictual participation (Mouffe 2006) that intentionally works to disturb the existing (non-disabled) consensus about intellectual disability. The work is addressed to a particular community of viewing subjects—non-disabled people—that understands itself to have nothing in common with labeled people. It does not "smooth over" but, rather, emphasizes the awkwardness and discomfort of non-disabled viewers confronted by the fragility of that which they thought they knew (Bishop 2004, 79). The radical apartness of the two truths of representation opens a space of questioning, contestation, and debate—a space of agency for the group members, and of dissensus that is the very aim of democratic existence (Mouffe 2007). Arguably, both the transformation of original images and the juxtaposed sets of images in the exhibits risk perpetuating the violence of the originals. But to understand these transformed images as dissensus—and to defend against the forgetting of the violence in and of the original images, along with those who suffer(ed) it (Baer 2002)—necessitates the recall of the originals. By referring to the "originals," the participants demonstrate that, while outside of and in opposition to the non-disabled consensus regarding intellectual disability, they *are* part of the social world and its hegemonic instantiations; they are not "outsiders" to this discourse and, in fact, they are wounded by the discourse because they are part of society and cannot/should not be considered otherwise.

Writing about the (re)positioning that can take place in visual re-presentations and performance, Luis Carlos Sotelo-Castro (2009) draws on Emmanuel Levinas (1991) to argue that, through the presentation of the self in public and in spatio-temporal terms, the disabled subject produces a truth about herself as both a relational and spatial human being. As insiders, the group members thus take up the possibilities of speaking out—what Foucault (2001) terms "free speech" and contesting—and putting forth a different perspective than the consensus would allow. Focused on the Greek notion of *parrhesia*, or "frankness in speaking the truth," free speech requires speaking the truth in the face of danger, as necessary criticism, as the duty of a citizen (Foucault 2001, 19). In the critique, production, and juxtaposition of the two sets of images, the group members speak a dissenting truth, (re)positioning themselves as both "writers" and "readers" of the disabled self. As writers, they use the transformed images to (re)position themselves and labeled people in particular spaces. As readers, they position themselves symbolically in relation to the representational space of photographic imagery and exhibit, to the social order and relations that are disrupted and those that are created (Sotelo-Castro 2009). Their acts (re)write disabled subjectivity.

Using what art historian Claire Bishop (2004) refers to as a *relational arts approach* that confronts the viewer with its distorting referent and the imagined spaces of a different type of relationship, the group members demand a re-thinking of how intellectual disability and labeled persons are understood and responded to. In her notion of agonistic plural democracy, Mouffe (2007) suggests that this is a space for opposition among adversaries (rather than enemies). It is constituted by a manifold of critical artistic practices that create friction and foment dissensus by giving a voice to those who are silenced within the framework of the existing (ableist) hegemony. Following Mouffe, we would proffer that in provoking dissensus, the work done in and through this research project does much more than just give voice to labeled people. Considered in terms of their historical and contemporary devaluation and relative socio-political powerlessness, it allows for a redefinition of labeled persons, in Mouffe's term, as "adversaries." We find this intriguing and appealing in that the term *adversary* implies the attribution of (at least some if not equal) power, some symbolic capital. Certainly, the images—as a counter-hegemonic intervention (Mouffe 2007)—seem to be powerful: They demand that "disability" be understood as a product of the dynamic interactions between minds/bodies and particular social and spatial configurations (Freund 2001; Holt 2007; Kitchin 1998; Power 2010). These counter-hegemonic practices are disturbing, even threatening, for non-disabled viewers because they are not familiar, not comfortable, not the "accepted" or "preferred" way of performing disability (Chouinard et al. 2010; Power 2010). As achieved by the group's work then, agonism can be understood as a "constructive form of political conflict" (Mouffe 2007, 5) between people with and without intellectual disabilities—one that subverts the dominant hegemony and contributes to the construction of new subjectivities.

These micro-tactics of dissensus become what Foucault (1986) terms a *dispositive*: a mechanism for inciting responses from non-disabled viewers of the images. The transformed images and exhibits are an open questioning that disturbs and are, in themselves, *the group's* response to the open wounding inflicted by and through the original images, by the repetitive staging of people with intellectual disabilities as less-than. This, then, is a political strategy achieved through the process of viewing images, responding, exchanging views, and, finally, relocating selves and positioning otherwise—both spatially and socially. By becoming agents in social questioning, by pointing to possibilities that can be realized in everyday spaces, and by becoming citizens who partake in the larger societal debate, the group members enact a transformative politics. In that this action disrupts the hegemonic consensus, it works toward a rethinking of intellectual disability not as biologically determined, but as "a socially and spatially produced form of exclusion and oppression" (Chouinard et al. 2010, 3). The project makes plain the capacity of people with intellectual disabilities to challenge, subvert, and transform disabling spatial structures and social relations. The reworking of spatial attribution incites people with and without disabilities to think in different terms, to think that what exists in terms of disabled/non-disabled relationships is not the "truth"—and that another world *is* possible (Mouffe 2006).

NOTES

1. This research project was conducted by Ann Fudge Schormans toward completion of her PhD in Social Work. Adrienne Chambon was Ann's thesis supervisor. For more details about the project's structure, please see Fudge Schormans (2011) and Fudge Schormans and Chambon (in press).
2. In conversations with the photographer, the man's dress and positioning on the mattress are explained as an effort to keep him cool and comfortable on a hot day. This information is not provided to the viewer of the image through the caption or the accompanying text, nor was it available prior to the group members' work with the images. My sharing of this information with them after the work was completed did not change their interpretation of the image.
3. The question of the group's concern with notions of "normality" will be taken up in another publication.
4. The responses of audiences to exhibits of these two sets of images will be taken up in another publication.

REFERENCES

Baer, U. (2002). *Spectral Evidence: The Photography of Trauma*. Cambridge, MA: MIT Press.

Bal, M. (2004). Light Writing: Portraiture in a Post-Traumatic Age. *Mosaic, 37*(4), 1–19.

Bishop, C. (2004). Antagonism and Relational Aesthetics. *October, 110*(Fall), 51–80.

Bourdieu, P. (1989). Social Space and Symbolic Power. *Sociological Theory, 7*(1), 14–25.

Butler, J. (2004). *Precarious Life: The Powers of Mourning and Violence*. London: Verso.

Chouinard, V., Hall, E., and Wilton, R. (2010). "Introduction: Towards Enabling Geographies." In V. Chouinard, E. Hall, & R. Wilton (Eds.), *Towards Enabling Geographies: "Disabled" Bodies and Minds in Society and Space* (pp. 1–21). Farnham, UK: Ashgate.

de Certeau, M. (1984). *The Practice of Everyday Life*. Berkeley: University of California Press.

Ferrier, L. and Muller, V. (2008). Disabling Able. *M/C Journal, 11*(3). http://journal.media-culture.org.au/index.php/mcjournal/article/view/58 (accessed January 14, 2011).

Foucault, M. (1986). Of Other Spaces. *Diacritics, 16*(1), 22–27.

Foucault, M. (2001). *Fearless Speech*. Los Angeles, CA: Semiotext(e).

Freund, P. (2001). Bodies, Disability and Spaces: The Social Model and Disabling Spatial Organisations. *Disability & Society, 16*(5), 689–706.

Fudge Schormans, A. (2011). The Right or Responsibility of Inspection: Photography, Social Work, and People with Intellectual Disabilities. PhD diss., University of Toronto, Toronto, Canada.

Fudge Schormans, A. and Chambon, A. (2010, November 19–20). Representational (Un)Wounding in Public Space: Visual Responding by Persons with Intellectual Disabilities. Paper presented at the *Health, Embodiment, and Visual Culture* conference, McMaster University, Hamilton, Ontario, Canada.

Fudge Schormans, A. and Chambon, A. (in press). "Please Don't Let Me Be Like This!": Un-wounding Photographic Representations by People with Intellectual Disabilities. In S. Brophy & J. Hladki (Eds.), *Embodied Politics in Visual Autobiography*. Toronto: University of Toronto Press.

Garland-Thomson, R. (2001). Seeing the Disabled: Visual Rhetorics of Disability in Popular Photography. In P. K. Longmore & L. Umansky (Eds.), *The New Disability History: American Perspectives* (pp. 335–374). New York: New York University Press.

Hevey, D. (1997). The Enfreakment of Photography In L. J. Davis (Ed.), *The Disability Studies Reader* (pp. 332–347). New York: Routledge.

Holt, L. (2010). Young People with Socio-Emotional Differences: Theorising Disability and Destabilising Socio-Emotional Norms In V. Chouinard, E. Hall, & R. Wilton (Eds.), *Towards Enabling Geographies: "Disabled" Bodies and Minds in Society and Space* (pp. 145–164). Farnham, UK: Ashgate.

Hornecker, E. (2008). "I don't understand it either, but it is cool": Visitor Interactions with a Multi-Touch Table in a Museum. *Proc. of IEEE Tabletop*, 113–120.

Huston, A. (Dir.) (2005, May 1.). *Riding the Bus With My Sister*. USA: CBS.

Kitchin, R. (1998). "Out of Place," "Knowing One's Place": Space, Power, and the Exclusion of Disabled People. *Disability & Society, 13*(3), 343–356.

Kumari Campbell, F. (2008). Refusing Able(ness): A Preliminary Conversation about Ableism. *M/C Journal, 11*(3). http://journal.media-culture.org.au/index.php/mcjournal/article/view/46 (accessed January 14, 2011).

Levinas, E. (1991). *Otherwise Than Being: Or, Beyond Essence* [Translated by Alphonso Lingis]. Boston: Kluwer Academic Publishers.

Mouffe, C. (2000). Deliberative Democracy or Agonistic Pluralism. *Political Science Series 72*. www.ihs.ac.at/publications/pol/pw_72.pdf (accessed January 14, 2011).

Mouffe, C. (2006). Articulated Power Relations: Markus Miessen in conversation with Chantal Mouffe. Roundtable: Centre for Research Architecture, Goldsmiths College, University of London. London, UK. http://roundtable.kein.org/node/545 (accessed January 14, 2011).

Mouffe, C. (2007). Artistic Activism and Agonistic Spaces. *Art & Research: A Journal of Ideas, Context and Methods, 1*(2), 1–5.

Power, A. (2010). The Geographies of Interdependence in the Lives of People with Intellectual Disabilities In V. Chouinard, E. Hall, & R. Wilton (Eds.), *Towards Enabling Geographies: "Disabled" Bodies and Minds in Society and Space* (pp. 107–122). Farnham, UK: Ashgate.

Sontag, S. (2003). *Regarding the Pain of Others*. New York: Farrar, Strauss and Giroux.

Sotelo-Castro, L. C. (2009). Participation Cartography: The Presentation of Self in Spatio-Temporal Terms. *M/C Journal 12*(5). http://journal.media-culture.org.au/index.php/mcjournal/article/view/92 (accessed February 12, 2011).

Tonkiss, F. (2005). *Space, the City and Social Theory: Social Relations and Urban Forms*. Cambridge, UK: Polity.

The Narrator Witness: Dis/Connections Between Disability and Death

Nicole Markotić

DYING TO TELL

In the Spanish film, *Mar Adentro* (*The Sea Inside;* Amenábar 2004), protagonist Ramón Sampedro (Javier Bardem) petitions his nation's courts for the right to die. He argues that, because he is paralyzed from the neck down, he does not enjoy the "choice" of death available to able-bodied citizens. I open with this scene because the film's depiction of Ramón as a noble hero fighting against church-infused bureaucracy calls out for sustained critique. The shot of Ramón arriving at the court steps is a complexly telling one. Contrasting the scene inside the building—where Ramón's lawyer eloquently argues for the right of someone like Ramón Sampedro, "who deems his condition as degrading," to take his own life—the scene outside serves as a tribute to euthanasia. As Ramón approaches the building, reporters surround him and the camera pans to the crush of demonstrators, which consists entirely of able-bodied people, many holding signs that demand "Decriminalize Euthanasia Now." As the reporters lionize Ramón by giving him a public forum, the backdrop re-establishes what Ramón's petition is actually about: not, as the film (and Ramón) constantly reiterate, the right of an individual to kill himself—for not once does Ramón challenge Spain's actual suicide laws—but, rather, for the right to *assisted* suicide. The challenge, then, is for the courts *not* to prosecute friends and family members who assist in the death of a (usually disabled) friend or family member.

In Amenábar's film—Oscar and Golden Globe winner for Best Foreign Language Film in 2004—the protagonist is "heroically" determined to kill himself. This highly crafted biopic manages to embody the ideal self that real-life Ramón purportedly strived to achieve. Besides members of his family, the single character who contradicts his standpoint is a wheelchair-bound priest, a caricatured figure who leaves audiences convinced that the official stance of the church on such matters has become obsolete and that the *only* contradictory standpoint on assisted suicide is a religious one. Interestingly, the film portrays Ramón's attorney, Julia, as suffering from the degenerative disease CADASIL. At one point, she decides to join Ramón in suicide, but later changes her mind. Unlike

Ramón, who is not sick, Julia has a disease that is progressive; she will continue to experience a series of strokes and, eventually, succumb to dementia. Her role in the film is to act as Ramón's love interest and to represent a fearful foil to his unwavering determination. The film ends not with Ramón's suicide (the penultimate scene) but, rather, with Ramón's friends visiting Julia at her lovely seaside home. They bring a final letter to her from Ramón. Julia turns a blank face to her visitors and tragically asks, "Ramón who?" Her words reinforce the by now obvious point that she has made the *wrong* choice in refusing death. By conflating these two "choices" and their ultimate ramifications, the film not only conflates illness and disability, but also suggests that all able-bodied people should react to any variety of physical conditions in exactly the same way. Julia is an able-bodied character living through ongoing strokes, while Ramón is a disabled character who does not suffer physical pain or a cognitive disability. By the end of Amenábar's film, however, Julia has become the visual representation of Ramón's unchosen fate. She literally embodies the tragic result of his failed "heroic" crusade.

The Sea Inside can be productively juxtaposed with Julian Schnabel's *Le Scaphandre et le papillon* (*The Diving Bell and the Butterfly*; 2007). The protagonist, Jean-Dominique Bauby (Mathieu Amalric), is a character who has become disabled because of a life-threatening stroke. Based on Bauby's memoir of the same name, *The Diving Bell and the Butterfly* received much critical attention, winning Best Foreign Language Film and Best Motion Picture Director at the Golden Globes in 2007. *The Sea Inside* ostensibly presents the story of a Spanish man who decides that his life is so unliveable that he would, to use media-driven parlance, be "better off dead." Conversely, *The Diving Bell and the Butterfly* presents its French protagonist as a noble "super-crip" who faces a trying life with no control over any of the muscles in his body, with the exception of his left eye. The film moves between scenes that emphasize Bauby as "trapped" in a body that cannot move and flashbacks that celebrate Bauby's former self as a charismatic rogue. I find it illuminating, in turn, to bring these two film narratives into dialogue with a prose memoir that is politically, culturally, and ethically engaged with the everydayness of living with the disabling effects of terminal illness. Canadian poet Frank Davey's *How Linda Died* (2002) recounts one woman's dying year through the narration of her husband's notes and recordings of her ideas, ideals, and wishes, all celebrating Linda's body, however diminished, due to an invasive and inoperable brain tumor. In contrast to Ramón and Jean-Dominique, Linda does not rage against the lack of sexual activity her new body enables; rather, she rages against dying, against the feared future loss of sensual delight.

THE NORM IN DIS/EASE

In *How Linda Died*, Linda initially reads her cancer diagnosis as a vehicle guiding her toward disability; yet, as the memoir progresses, readers see her eliciting more and more pleasurable sensations from her body and rejecting her own earlier interpretation of illness as somehow dishonorable. Both *The Sea Inside* and *The Diving Bell and the Butterfly* depict paralyzed middle-aged men, devoid of physical sexual activity but, at the same time, sexually attracted to the beautiful women who visit them. To establish these two characters as sexually appealing, the films construct them as *potentially* virile, ironically convincing audiences of the protagonists' normative heterosexuality even as the films depict their bodies as having "lost" an essential masculinity.

Disability critic Robert McRuer (2002) points out that queer characters are often understood as somehow disabled in "an ongoing medicalization of identity" (94). Similarly, healthy disabled characters are typically "understood" as ill or sick. Just as Laura Mulvey (1975) argues that the paradox of phallocentrism is that the symbolically castrated woman gives order and meaning to its world (6), McRuer argues that the prominent figure of the whole and healthy male depends on the equally strong yet often invisible image of the immobile, dependent, and "castrated" male. Invoking Adrienne Rich's vocabulary, McRuer proposes the term *compulsory able-bodiedness* (89) to argue that disability and queerness are similarly invoked to both challenge and reaffirm the white heterosexual male. Not surprisingly, this compulsory identity revolves around the notion of "normal" and its insidious twin, "abnormal." McRuer draws on Michael Warner's *The Trouble With Normal* (1999): "nearly everyone wants to be normal. And who can blame them, if the alternative is being abnormal, or deviant, or not being one of the rest of us? Put in those terms, there doesn't seem to be a choice at all" (Warner quoted in McRuer 2002, 90). For McRuer, the *compulsion* toward normality comes not only from its appeal as the perfect and desirable opposite to abnormality, but also from the positioning of both as "choices" within a system of bodily extremes. Such an appearance of choice, McRuer says, is really about reconfiguring homogeneity: "A system of compulsory able-bodiedness repeatedly demands that people with disabilities embody for others an affirmative answer to the unspoken question, Yes, but in the end, wouldn't you rather be more like me?" (93).

Drawing on McRuer's notion of compulsory able-bodiedness, along with the idea that "people with disabilities are often understood as somehow queer" (94), I argue that Ramón presents himself as a *somewhat* or *sort-of* queer man. That is, he performatively takes on the stigma of queer, though with neither the culture nor the politics of a reworked notion of queerness. Ramón is heterosexual; he longs for a romantic relationship with his lawyer, Julia, but he eliminates even romantic fantasy from his life because he is physically unable to perform what he considers to be the normative male sexual act of penetration. If he cannot achieve heterosexual manhood, he decides, then he must be nothing at all. But the economy of queerness is not simply about sexuality per se. Rather, it potentially intersects with multiple forms of embodiment and social positioning—intersections that complicate and reconfigure the boundaries of social, political, or ethical arenas.

TELLING, AND TELLING ABOUT

Although both films are "based" on actual historical persons, neither *The Sea Inside* nor *Diving Bell* is a documentary; indeed, both subjects died before the directors began filming. Yet, in order to heighten their fictional authenticity, both films rely on audiences to accept their subjects as people from "real life." Who, exactly, in *The Diving Bell and the Butterfly*, conveys Jean-Dominique Bauby's life? His *story* emerges from his autobiographical book, from interviews with friends and family and from hospital records, but the film makes use of visual details that entice and enthral audiences. The film opens with a camera imitating the visual abilities of a man emerging from a coma, along with an accompanying voice-over that signifies his "true" voice (i.e., not the *authentic* voice that gargles in his throat, but an imitation of how his voice sounds in his head). Much filmic verisimilitude comes from the suspension of disbelief that any performance invites from audiences. However, in a visual medium more and more dominated by "reality," the fictionalized life still does—despite the crafted nature of cinema—invite from audiences the expectation of a narrating self, even when audience members understand that the voice-over, for example, could not possibly be the actual historical person speaking.

The Diving Bell and the Butterfly depicts Jean-Do's growing awareness that he must organize his idea of body around new criteria, and that he also needs to re-organize and re-categorize what he has previously thought of as his "life." Once the editor of *Elle* magazine, he fondly remembers his days of sexual promiscuity and social success. For nearly a quarter of the film, the camera's point of view is Jean-Do's, and audiences *see* what his character purportedly sees as he learns to adapt to a body he cannot command. Yet, as the film continues, the camera shifts from its exclusive position as the single eye of the protagonist to various shots that present Jean-Do being washed by hospital staff, waiting on the porch for visitors, wheeled along corridors, or spending time with his family on a nearby beach. The director, then, has made the decision to expand the visual scope of the film beyond the point of view of the protagonist but, as the narrative develops, this technique also distances audience members from that initial identifying-spectator position. The film conveys more than just the idea of how it feels to look with immobile and blurred eyesight; it also conveys Jean-Do's developing awareness and acceptance of his new physical reality. By positioning and re-positioning audience spectatorship, the director manages an identification that is more than mere character-recognition: the shifting point of view becomes a filmic device that entices viewers to follow Jean-Do's thoughts about his own body—*not* as he distances himself from his changed corporeality, but as he begins to "see" himself as *this* person who now lives in *this* body.

In the opening scenes, the camera mimics the blurred eyesight of someone who has suffered major corporeal damage. Jean-Do's entire body is paralyzed except for his left eye, and the muscles of that eye do not focus easily. Audiences experience a room through the visual stimuli of a roving camera, disembodied voices, and the effect of a blinking eye. Jean-Do narrates a perspective, the intimate details of which the audience likely does not know, and the film promises to supply such intimacy. Thus, we "overhear" doctors say that the character has experienced a stroke and that he has been in a 3-week coma. We begin to understand that, although the narrator thinks he is speaking and responding to the medical staff, they do not react to his questions and comments, indicating that although *we inside his head* can hear him, none of the other characters can. As the opening scene continues, doctors, nurses, and medical therapists emerge as characters newly important to Jean-Do's post-stroke life. Surveying his situation, he says, "I'll be patient," claiming his new identity and reassuring himself and the audience of his willingness to live in this—what he hopes at the beginning of the film is a temporary—state. The film's projection of Jean-Do as roaming camera eye has a two-fold effect; the cinéma vérité technique introduces and reinforces the narrator's point of view but, as the film continues, the roving camera also visually enacts the male gaze: As a once "normal" heterosexual male, Jean-Do is expected and *encouraged* to gaze at his (mostly female) caregivers and visitors.

In *The Sea Inside*, there is no welcoming of the in-between, no recognition that Ramón has *survived* a paralyzing diving accident that occurred 28 years earlier. Instead, the film makes a capricious connection between disability and illness by, in effect, denying that a disabled person's identity can ever be healthy. Amenábar's film endeavours to bring about viewer identification with the perspective of the disabled protagonist to the point of presenting his "death wish" as the only reasonable course of action. (For example, when picking Sampedro up for a court date, the driver of the van declares: "You're Ramón Sampedro right? I was hoping I'd get to drive you, man!" His words reveal him as a someone whose job entails conveying disabled people from one location to another; yet he is full of admiration for Ramón's suicidal intentions). In the process, the film minimizes the socio-political contexts informing the protagonist's circumstances. Unusually, the film's point of view is focalized through a character who stays in bed, wishes to die, and views himself as a shut-in *because* he remains alive. Ramón interacts comfortably with his family, reads, and daydreams about his sexual prowess as an able-bodied man. But he refuses to consider his everyday existence as a form of "life." To Ramón, life is what he used to live when he was young and strapping. Not walking, not being able to approximate normative masculine conventions, is disability itself.

Ramón Sampedro's notion of self is either wrapped around a body that moves freely and strongly, as it did in his early twenties, or is permanently trapped in a body so useless that his only option is to die. The film's pro-euthanasia stance entices spectators to cheer for Ramón's "activism." In direct contrast, *The Diving Bell and the Butterfly* insists on chastising even the consideration of the thought of suicide. Early in the film, Jean-Do's speech pathologist demands, "How dare you?!" when he spells out the word "death." Although viewers may feel sympathetic toward Jean-Do's initial desire, the camera also lingers on Henriette's caring face and focuses on the considerate actions she performs for her client, leading viewers to experience and share her shock at his suggestion. Henriette's attitude stems from an adherence to Catholic dogma. Nevertheless, her reaction is not conveyed as dogmatic, but as a genuine (and growing) appreciation of what Jean-Do extends to her as a patient and as a man.[1] In this way, the film depicts Jean-Do as having confronted an obstacle in his imagination and, once past what Todd Davis and Kenneth Womack (2001) call the ethical turn, he never revisits the idea.

Conversely, in *How Linda Died*, Linda begins her treatment repeatedly asking "how" she will die and declaring that she "didn't want to linger as an invalid"

(Davey 2002, 86). Yet, as her illness progresses (and she herself behaves in ways that, earlier in the narrative, she would have thought demonstrated a demeaning loss of physical control), neither she nor memoirist Frank Davey ever refers to her increasing symptoms as a form of past-her-due-date "lingering" again. Both Linda and Jean-Do transform and adjust their senses of self to fit within the bounds of what their bodies *can* do rather than holding onto a nostalgic definition of life based on what their bodies *used to* be able to do. Though Jean-Do's key survival strategies—his memory, imagination, and creative talent—are infused with normatively organized desires premised on his success as a man, he uses them, however nostalgic they are, as a way of propelling himself into the future, *his* future. In contrast, Ramón, who is a quadriplegic, chooses to remain fixed in his bed for nearly three decades because accepting mobility with a wheelchair would be "accepting the crumbs of what used to be my freedom."[2] Each of these narratives presents viewpoints that have dramatically distinct consequences for the rights and options of the disabled to witness and narrate their lives—and to have their lives witnessed, reviewed, and narrated by and through others.

In *How Linda Died,* Davey depicts his wife's last year and explores how her diminishing mobility influences the way he tells her story so that, in effect, the story organized around his wife's dying becomes his own. His role as spectator defines Linda's story not just as a remarkable narrative of a body growing ever more unruly, but also as one of bereavement *before* the fact, of the telling of death by the still-living narrator. While, at times, Davey's memoir indulges in a narcissism of the healthy, he nonetheless manages to translate his personal account of Linda's life into one of his own role as bystander, participant, and spectator of her dying. Susanna Egan (1999) argues that most "death memoirs" (201) rely on the failing other to provide a narrative of an "undoing, and unbecoming" (245), nostalgically attempting to summarize the subject's life and disregarding the death itself. Instead, Davey renders Linda's dying in a way that challenges her life's outcome by focusing on her final year. This is not to say that biographers ignore the deaths of their subjects; on the contrary, biographers are meticulous about providing important dates such as birth and death, often listed on a separate page. But rarely does a biography focus exclusively on the person who is dying, yet who is *not* telling her own story.[3]

Tracing the interpretive, pedagogic, and theoretical concerns of ethics in literary texts, Davis and Womack (2001) write, "Part of being human involves the daily struggle with the meanings and consequences of our actions, a struggle most often understood in narrative structures as we tell others and ourselves about what has transpired or what we fear will transpire in the future" (ix). Each of these three texts proposes its protagonist as a realist character formation and expects audiences to react positively to such a mediated formation. *The Sea Inside* presents a "right to die" activism as if in support of disability rights while hastily sweeping aside larger, more complex social issues impacting disabled people. Meanwhile, *How Linda Died* becomes—unwittingly—an argument *against* the "right" to die. The stereotypical point at which the "better off dead" notion usually claims a narrative is the very point at which this memoir convinces readers that Linda has made an "ethical turn." Davis and Womack argue that narrative itself can be "witness" to the representational truth of what happens in people's lives. Today, they argue, "the ethical consideration of a given work of literature ranges from the close reading of the text itself . . . to the ethical questions that the story raises in the reader's own life beyond the margins of the text" (x). The narrating character, Frank Davey, has no novelistic agenda other than to present diary entries concerning his wife's last year of life. Yet the story moves—as do he and Linda—from a determination at the beginning of the year to maintain "dignity" to an eventual celebration of the body's sensual demands.

SHOW-AND-TELL

Late in *The Sea Inside*, Ramón lies in his bed and conjures an image of himself flying toward the coast. The camera follows his fantasy, imagining a bird's route to the salty water. In his fantasy, Ramón has achieved his ultimate desire: no present, no telling, no body. Ramón loves the ocean, yet hasn't seen it since his accident. He feels he is too much of a physical burden on his family, yet makes no effort to live on his own or to leave his room to go out into the world. He will not even come downstairs to debate a visiting priest who is also paralyzed at the neck. This scene offers a parody of Roman Catholic doctrine, with the priest shouting up the stairs: "Freedom that costs a life isn't freedom," and Ramón shouting back: "A life that costs freedom isn't a life." Freedom, dignity, autonomy: for Ramón, these lofty terms, represented by his flying, all have to do with ambulatory mobility. He scoffs at using a wheelchair, detesting the very idea until he has the chance to go to court to argue for his right to be killed.

Throughout, Ramón comes across as an attractive and compelling character. He is witty, well-read, intelligent, inventive, caring toward his family members, and fatherly to his nephew. Two women fall in love with him in the span of 1 year. One of them will ultimately help him achieve his goal of suicide, not because she wants to, but because he has told her that "the person who really loves me will be the one who helps me die. That's love." As a viewer, it is hard not to be swayed by such an articulate and eloquent character. He understands his own life better than anyone, and he has lived in a paralyzed body for a longer period of time than he lived in an able-bodied one. His single desire is so strong that one feels compelled to empathize with his ultimate goal.

As with other narratives promoting what many people glibly term *euthanasia*, *The Sea Inside* presents Ramón's paralysis as an obscene symptom of a horrific and debilitating illness,[4] an "illness" so drastic that he has been consigned to bed for three decades. But Ramón is disease-free. He chooses to remain in bed because accepting mobility in a wheelchair means accepting that he will never return to the body he nostalgically longs for. Instead, Ramón's fight is for a person other than himself to legally assist him with his suicide, an important distinction that no characters in the film ever make between the "right" to die and euthanasia. Not once in the film (nor in his actual life, for that matter) does Ramón Sampedro attempt to die by starvation. Paralyzed from the neck down, eating or not eating is a choice he makes multiple times every day. But dying, in itself, is not the point; rather, approval of the desire for death—approval that he and other characters believe will come through state-sanctioned third-person interventions—is Ramón's ironic raison d'être.

For Ramón, anything "less" than a body representing heterosexual male power and hegemonic stability is insufficient—is, in fact, deficient. His existence is trapped, Freud (1920/1989) would say, in the throes of the "death drive" (617). According to Freud, the death drive is not only a biological instinct but is also so intertwined in the human psyche that responsiveness to it is automatic, offset only by the pleasure-seeking instinct. Freud's death drive, then, is a bodily instinct to return to the calm stasis that existed before birth (and, paradoxically, pre-corporealization). For Freud, the death drive explains why human beings feel compelled to repeat (through narrative or in dreams) traumatic events, even though these repetitions conflict with the bodily instinct to seek pleasure. The death drive is a mode of coping. Lying in bed, day after day, Ramón refuses any notion of physical Eros, longing, instead, for the nothing he believes awaits him. Achieving such a nothing-death, for Ramón, would fulfill the only desire he allows himself and the only desire denied him. Ironically, Ramón regards his life as more worthless than death because his body has unnaturally deviated from the very death he concludes should be its current condition. Although it is perfectly healthy, he deems his body to be deformed, grotesque, *sick*.

Patients in books and films often argue for the right to die when facing a terminal and usually painful illness based on the fact that death is imminent and that, in their final few years or weeks (or days, or minutes), they will experience unmanageable, unimaginable, extreme, and/or inhuman pain. When Ramón demands a form of "euthanasia" based on the inhuman existence he feels he must endure, he equates disabilities—especially those depicting extremely limited mobility—with the powerful and evocative image of a dying body. In this way, the film trades on an implicit understanding that imminent death promises a much-deserved relief from unbearable life and that visible disability necessarily implies that death is imminent.[5] In fact, Ramón's death is far from imminent, hence his need to petition for the right to hasten it. His argument is that ongoing life in a disabled body is worse than dying of a disease, any disease (he even jokes with Julia about smoking to bring about a quicker death). Both *Sea Inside* and *Diving Bell* shift viewers' focus away from the power of the death drive and refocus on the everyday and its pleasures, but both films remain implicated—imaginatively and politically—in regulatory norms of gender, age, and sexuality. In these films, notions of dignity and human worth are intricately tied to masculine pride and self-sufficiency.

HOW LINDA DIED

Davey (2002) writes his diary to record Linda's dying and his own coping. He is narrator and witness, caregiver and spectator. He is participant and, strangely, biographer. In *How Linda Died*, readers are not going to "learn" how to cope with cancer; rather, this particular narrative presents the social terrain within which Frank and Linda negotiate their individual actions and reactions to her dying. This narrative, then, is not so much operating in the confessional mode of conjuring a so-called "self" as it is presenting a daily journal, the entries of which record everyday resistance to an obvious impending conclusion.

Both Linda's cancer and its treatment cause physical symptoms of illness: hair loss, weight loss, puffy face, leg weakness, leukemia development. And because it is a tumor attached to her brain, the cancer also steals her vocabulary, her ability to move certain parts of her body, her balance, her vision, and her ability to communicate. In spite of being a character constructed within a narrative of ultimate death, Linda adamantly resists any such "drive." Her death is both imminent and unpreventable, yet her instinct for pleasure remains potent. At times, Davey records her as "risking hope" (125), as having "guts" about dying (135), and as impatient to be "healed" (163). Though she does not heal, she stubbornly reaches towards Eros and embraces her remaining days. Always assured that she deserves the "good things" in life, Linda has consumed the best wines, hung the best carpets, displayed the best show dogs. After being given a life expectancy of about 1 year, she throws herself back into the life of pleasure that she and her husband had so assiduously built and maintained. She rearranges the kitchen so that she can more easily find ingredients and cooking utensils, and she indulges in elaborate meals accompanied by very fine wine. Paradoxically, Linda is exactly the character "type" that films display when they wish to present a formidable and remarkable hospitalized character who would rather be dead than accept permanent invalidism and physical dependency.[6] Frank repeatedly tells the reader about Linda's fierce independence: for example, how "troubling" Linda's wish to keep her illness secret has become, or the incident when Linda continually tries, unsuccessfully, to "launch" herself from the bed all the while refusing the narrator's help (Davey 2002, 59, 218). She does not like to be helped; she does not like to be pitied; and she does not want to be needy, or reassured, or taken care of.

Adapting, once again, the phrase that McRuer (2002) adapts from Adrienne Rich, Linda's insistence on self-sufficiency and autonomy registers as a form of what I call *compulsory independence*. Repudiating any construction of herself as needy, Linda refuses to tell friends and family that she is sick, let alone dying, and does not allow her husband to discuss death. She clings passionately to self-sufficiency as confirmation that she is still alive and still very much in control. Visually compelling representations of such "compulsory independence" reinforce the disabled character as stuck between total self-sufficiency and absolute deterioration. At the same time, in a prose narrative that details virtually every aspect of Linda's physical "decline," her pleasure-seeking never waivers, never lessens. Her last year alive is one of determination, humor, intensity, purpose, and pleasure, as is her entire life.

Early in the memoir, Davey reflects that, for Linda, physical dependence is "perhaps even more of a disaster" than death (2002, 222). He documents Linda as announcing to her doctor that she doesn't want to "be a burden" by having the hospital put her on a respirator to extend her life (86). Such a sentiment not only fits her furiously autonomous character, but also reflects the fears and desires of many still-healthy readers: no, I don't want to be kept *artificially* alive; no I don't want to *burden* anyone with my dying. Yet, as the narrative progresses, Davey details numerous occasions when Linda—while maintaining a forceful sense of independence and freedom—makes use of her surroundings and caregivers to enhance a life that has become, physically, more and more complicated. Some examples include asking her husband to set the alarm clock so that she can tell when the angel food cake she is baking is ready (173); allowing her husband and children to set up an invalid bed table that was originally a dog-feeding table (238); and using the base of her wine glass as a spoon when it becomes too complicated to hold a glass of wine and cutlery at the same time (257). The "old Linda" (44) may well have been horrified to regard herself inelegantly spooning food into her mouth with the base of a wine glass, but the ingenuity of her utensil vividly demonstrates Linda's voracious appetite—for food and wine, and for the days and minutes left to her; for the pleasures embedded in everyday physical yearnings and gratifications.

DYING TO BE TOLD

Jean-Do begins the film as a man who understands himself to have lost his sensual enjoyment, his sexual measure, his culture itself. He constantly imagines and yearns for his girlfriend, Inès, who never visits. He longs to embrace his children and to care for his father. The film offers a spectator's montage of his memories with his children, with his lovers, at his job. In addition, audiences experience Jean-Do's (and others') repeated learning of the alphabet-dictation his speech therapist has developed to aid his communication. She repeats and repeats the French alphabet, from most-used letter to least-used: "E-S-A-R-I-N. . . ." She—and others—speak the letters of the alphabet in this particular order, and they (and audience members) stare at Jean-Do's left eye, waiting for him to blink a letter choice. As the camera closes in on Jean-Do's one mobile eye, a single blink is recast as a climactic action, the film relying on inner monologue and out-of-focus shots to convey the internalized protagonist Jean-Do has become.

Diving Bell also cuts several times to the image of a deep-sea diver: a man separated from the world by the ocean, encased within his diving suit, the diving bell pulling him deeper. Director Schnabel chooses not to repeatedly contrast this image with the other titular image that Jean-Do Bauby-the-author used as his alternative self: able to roam his imagination and the world as lightly and as delicately as a butterfly. Rather, the visual stimulus is the anticipated brush of eyelashes against camera lens. Putting aside his project of rewriting *The Count of Monte Cristo* (with the Count rewritten as a contemporary female character), Jean-Do calls his publisher to continue with the book deal, but proposes, instead, that he will compose and dictate his autobiography. "A text doesn't exist until it can be read," he informs his father in a flashback scene. The author-subject needs the reader; the character-subject needs the audience. Rewriting a French classic was an intriguing and playful option. Rewriting his own life onto the page, he now understands, is the story that needs to exist through others' readings.

In her medical consultations, Linda seeks a cure or, at the very least, treatment. Ramón believes the only "cure" for his disability is death, and so denies himself any form of assisted living. And Jean-Do becomes the speaking subject, the disabled writer who can compose his own story only when he is literally frozen into the present. The difference is not merely a semantic one between different conceptions of what it means to be "cured" but indicates how narratives conflate representations of disability with those of disease, often imposing ideas of disability as necessarily terminal and termination as necessarily desirable. Within such narratives, the medicalization of disability points toward physical deviance: narratives of rehabilitation seek to "cure" difference. These cures—or, worse, the inability to "cure"—proliferate. Refusing to conform to other people's ideas of who Linda should be, to the construction of an ill woman, is one of the reasons why Linda is such a compelling character—and why *The Sea Inside* spends so much time on Ramón's unique personality. Meanwhile, Jean-Do's individuality is entirely beside the point *until* he is paralyzed and his story is no longer a clichéd filmic tableau of yet another contemporary middle-aged lech but, more and more, embodies this particular story about this particular life.[7]

Just as "disability" cannot entirely define or embrace numerous bodily realities, so too does the term illness fall short of encompassing a range of medical ailments and remedial disorders. Each of the primary characters I have discussed is attractive and compelling. One, entirely healthy, wishes for death; the second, hospitalized, literally struggles to compose himself; and the third, dying of cancer, grasps at every tidbit of life she can. Ramón portrays a character whose "use," in the film, is to preserve an ideology of superior masculinity and assumed wholeness. Linda, in dying, strikes at readers' appetites. Her story epitomizes the value of and demand for what is still her life, even as Frank is the character who seizes the first-person pronoun. And Jean-Do himself? Jean-Do epitomizes the culture of change: his shift is not so much from able-bodied to disabled as it is a profound conversion from superficial scoundrel to tender personality. Of the three, Jean-Do has "lost" the greatest mobility, yet Schnabel's film envisions him as throbbing within the jubilant swirl of all he has gained.

NOTES

1. In the visual narrative, Jean-Do makes gentle ridicule of how Henriette encourages her fellow parishioners to pray for him, whereas in the textual autobiography, Bauby writes (1997) that such emotional attention, although mostly "unremarkable" in terms of physical results, lifts his spirits and has a direct connection to his body (12–13). He also says that once his daughter sends up her prayers every evening, "I set out for the kingdom of slumber with this wonderful talisman, which shields me from all harm" (13).
2. The film makes much of Ramón's insistence—when he does, finally, leave his home to argue his case in court—that he not simply plonk himself into a "ready-made" wheelchair, but that he modify the chair to his specifications. Such a scene implies that other wheelchair users do not have the inventive impulse to cater to their "impaired" needs, but must accept a pitiful situation, regardless of how inadequate. This not only disregards the fact that most wheelchair users customize their chairs, but it also suggests that only a willful character such as Ramón Sampedro has the determined individuality to fight for "what's right" and that his strength of character with respect to the right to die is exemplified by his imaginative creativity with respect to individual mobility.
3. Egan (1999) provides a long list of texts wherein an author tells of his or her own imminent demise. But, in *How Linda Died*, the story of the end of the subject's life is seen only through her husband and caregiver's perception.
4. As the film plays and replays the scene of Ramón's diving accident, the narrative suggests that his paralysis is a symptom resulting from an interrupted "normal" trajectory of death. He dives, he breaks his neck, he feels the pull of death, and then a hand drags him out of the water. When

Ramón commits suicide, the film repeats the exact same shot of him drowning, but this time no hand intervenes to halt his "natural" flow toward death.

5. Julia, the lawyer character in the film who has the degenerative and terminal illness CADASIL, confesses to Ramón that she "can't take it anymore; this isn't a life," and resolves to join him. When she does not show up on their appointed date and the film ends with the scene of Julia so debilitated that she can no longer remember Ramón, the implication is that (unlike Ramón) Julia has missed her chance to die "with dignity." Here, the conflation of illness with disability is especially insidious in that Julia embodies both: her illness causes disabilities, but also *prevents* her from fulfilling her original (and thus depicted as her "true") desire to end her life.
6. For a particularly saccharine example, see John Badham's *Whose Life Is It Anyway?* (1981), and Paul Darke's (2010) argument that demedicalization demands often conflate with claims against keeping disabled patients alive (97–107). In speaking of that same film, Paul Longmore (2003) writes that he and "disabled friends have had people say to us, 'if I were you I'd kill myself'" (121). Films that propose the nobility of a disabled character "fighting the man" in order to be allowed to die often perpetuate the idea that a life lived at any level other than fully-abled participation is not worth much. Few of those people Longmore quotes are, I believe, actually urging Longmore or his friends to commit suicide as much as they are declaring their own panic about the possibility of facing what they assume is an either/or "choice."
7. Jean-Do constantly jokes that *if* he were able to move, he would re-establish his Casanova role. In the visual field of the film his observation is emphatically empowered: the highly sexualized point-of-view shots of the women who visit him perpetuate the dominance of his (extremely heterosexual) male gaze. Whereas Ramón repeatedly insinuates that he will look up women's skirts or that he will go to bed with them, the film's "punchline" is the suggestion that such conduct on his part is preposterous.

REFERENCES

Amenábar, A. (Dir.) (2004). *The Sea Inside* [DVD]. USA: First Line Features.

Badham, J. (Dir.) (1981). *Whose Life Is It Anyway?* [DVD]. USA: MGM.

Bauby, J.-D. (1997). *The Diving Bell and the Butterfly* [Transl. by Jeremy Leggatt]. New York: Knopf.

Darke, P. (2010). No Life Anyway: Pathologizing Disability on Film In S. Chivers & N. Markotić (Eds.), *The Problem Body: Projecting Disability on Film* (pp. 97–107). Columbus: Ohio State University Press.

Davey, F. (2002). *How Linda Died*. Toronto: ECW Press.

Davis, T. and Womack, K. (Eds.) (2001). *Mapping the Ethical Turn: A Reader in Ethics, Culture and Literary Theory*. Charlottesville: University of Virginia Press.

Egan, S. (1999). *Mirror Talk: Genres of Crisis in Contemporary Autobiography*. Chapel Hill: University of North Carolina Press.

Freud, S. (1989). Beyond the Pleasure Principle. In P. Gay (Ed.), *The Freud Reader* (pp. 594–626). New York: W.W. Norton. (Originally published in 1920.)

Longmore, P. (2003). *Why I Burned My Book and Other Essays on Disability*. Philadelphia: Temple University Press.

McRuer, R. (2002). Compulsory Able-bodiedness and Queer/Disabled Existence. In S. Snyder, B. Brueggemann & R. Garland-Thomson (Eds.), *Disability Studies: Enabling the Humanities* (pp. 88–99). New York: Modern Language Association of America.

Mulvey, L. (1975). Visual Pleasure and Narrative Cinema. *Screen, 16*(3), 6–18.

Schnabel, J. (Dir.) (2007). *Le Scaphandre et le papillon (The Diving Bell and the Butterfly)* [DVD]. France: Pathé Productions.

Warner, M. (1999). *The Trouble With Normal: Sex, Politics, and the Ethics of Queer Life*. New York: Free Press.

Crip Excess, Art, and Politics: A Conversation with Robert McRuer

Danielle Peers, Melisa Brittain, and Robert McRuer

A book, article, or theory might be judged not only by the insightfulness of the claims it makes, but also by the connections, possibilities, and politics that it fosters. By these criteria, Robert McRuer's publications, of which the most widely known is *Crip Theory: Cultural Signs of Queerness and Disability* (2006), are crucial. He weaves together an array of theories, cultural productions, and socio-historical contexts with great care, wit, and generosity. The result is a complex analysis of the role of compulsory able-bodiedness in the context of globalized neoliberal capitalism. McRuer's work is as generative as it is insightful, and as creative as it is political. He provokes his audiences to foster new crip connections, and to explore new crip possibilities and practices, whether academic, artistic, activist, or otherwise.

It was with great pleasure that we, Danielle Peers (DP) and Melisa Brittain (MB), met up with Robert McRuer (RM) for a video interview at the Health, Embodiment, and Visual Culture Conference at McMaster University in November 2011. The conversation has been transcribed and expanded on here.

DP: Robert, for those who have not yet read your work, can you explain what crip theory is?

RM: I think crip theory is a collective practice. First of all, I think that it is a practice that has been generated by a lot of queers, in one sense, partly because the workings of compulsory heterosexuality and compulsory able-bodiedness have been so intertwined for more than a century. And it's really queer crips, crip queers, who have understood those workings really well. And hence, crip theory is this critical cultural practice that has been developed in a lot of queer communities, by artists, activists, and academics, writers of all kinds, poets, painters; many different kinds of cultural workers have put into practice what I think we can call crip theory.

That said, I wouldn't say there is an absolute consensus on what crip theory is. I would say that in many ways it is something that's very much about excess. Compulsory heterosexuality and compulsory able-bodiedness generate sites of containment, where disability and queerness are managed, contained, kept quiet, kept silent. And crip cultural production has been about saying, "we're not going to stand for that," so to speak. "We are going to generate visions of the body and desire and community that are in excess of attempts to contain and manage us." And there is not absolute consensus about what crip theory is, because that generative excess has been so incredibly varied.

MB: Can you offer us some specific examples of crip cultural or artistic practice, and discuss how this excess plays out in the work?

RM: When I think about, say, the work of actor, performance artist, and writer Terry Galloway, with the Mickee Faust theatre company in Florida, in their film, *Scary Lewis Yell-a-thon* (Nudd and Wilkins 2004), there is an inhabiting of exactly the worst ableist stereotypes that are played out by the Jerry Lewis Telethon. In and through the longstanding queer cultural tradition of camp, there is an implosion of able-bodied ideologies in this beautifully excessive way. Galloway performs in drag as Jerry Lewis and parodies Lewis' pathos and sentimentality. "Do we have any of my cripples here?" he asks the audience, and then one of his "kids" (actually an adult man seated in a wheelchair) is asked to stand for a round of applause. The man half-heartedly hoists himself up on the arms of the chair. The parody later shifts to, and luxuriates in, the "true-to-life" story of Little Teensy Weensy Tiny Teena (played by disability theorist Carrie Sandahl), who walked *all by herself* to appear at the Yell-a-thon with Scary Lewis on a conspicuously inaccessible stage. Sandahl plays Tiny Teena with over-the-top cutesiness, with a big bow in her hair, and a huge smile on her face. All Tiny Teena wants to do is please Scary Lewis who, at the end of the parody, decides to stuff cash in her mouth (and kill her!) because she fails to perform "cure" adequately by taking a few steps without her crutches.

DP: As you offer this description, I can't help but think about how similar these themes and parodic elements are to those Melisa and I utilized in our first short video, *G.I.M.P. Boot Camp* (Brittain and Peers 2008): the conspicuously inaccessible stage, the patting on the head, and the violent repercussions of failing to perform "disability" in the expected way. Whereas I think it is easy to read these filmic parallels in terms of similar experiences of disability, I think that it is more theoretically and politically useful to consider that they stem from shared experiences of what you so aptly describe as "compulsory able-bodiedness" (McRuer 2006, 8). In reading the parallels in this way, the humor in these videos becomes readable not only as a shared in-joke amongst crips, but also as a (celebratory and excessive) critique of both able-bodiedness and the social construction of disability.

RM: Yes, it's not at all surprising to me that these two crip parodies share so much! I think a lot of crip theory and cultural production has been about generating a wide range of strong affects, of crip emotions, that are then shared. And I would say shared across communities, shared across bodies, and shared across borders. When you think about Loree Erickson's work in *Want* (2005), that film just gives us over and over again that verb: "I want to be a girl you picture naked, a girl you fuck in public... I want to be a girl you laugh with, a girl you have fun with... I want to be the girl you make come so hard she can't even scream." I want, I want, I want, I want, I want. And it's that sense of affect that she wants to share with her lovers, but also share with her viewers. As Erickson (Erickson, Peers, and Brittain 2010) said in the roundtable at the Health, Embodiment, and Visual Culture Conference at McMaster University, she *wants* because she didn't *have* images that were femme-gimp images. She went into a lesbian store in San Francisco, didn't find those images, and so decided she was going to be a porn star. And what a lovely example of crip theory on the ground: "I don't see what I want here; I'm going to be a porn star."

So there's this sense of sharing that emerges, and a yearning, and I think that crip theory is also about those kinds of affects. I think that crip theory is also, in a more strictly theoretical sense, about recognizing that heterosexuality and able-bodiedness, for more than a century and a half, have instituted themselves as intertwined and invisible norms.

People often ask me: "Why queer studies and disability studies?" "Why queer theory and disability theory?" "Why were those two so uniquely linked?" And I say, well, the history of heterosexuality—a relatively specific form of loving that became a norm and identity over the past century and a half—was really closely intertwined with another form of normalcy that, like heterosexuality, was also made invisible. And that's the norm of able-bodiedness—also, when you think about it, a relatively specific and non-representative way of moving through the world.

And so I think queer-crip practices have worked to expose the invisibility of these normative identities, and the larger naturalization of normalcy.

DP: What brought you to studying this intersection between compulsory able-bodiedness and compulsory heterosexuality?

RM: People make various assumptions about why I do crip theory. My mother, for instance, when my father was dying after living for more than a decade with Parkinson's, said to me, "Do you do disability studies because of Dad?" She didn't say do you do crip theory because of Dad, because she's a fundamentalist Baptist woman and doesn't even know that I wrote a book called *Crip Theory: Cultural Signs of Queerness and Disability*. However, she did ask me once, "Did you do disability studies because of Dad?"

So, there are always these assumptions about, you know, how did you get here? But really, the easy answer is that, as a gay man of a certain age, I came to crip theory because of the AIDS crisis. And when I began doing my own work in graduate school, and with young queer communities in the late 80s and early 90s, it was all about thinking about how the institutions of media, government, medicine, etc., were failing us. And that the structures of oppression were exactly that: *structures* of oppression. Not just sort of incidental prejudice, but institutions that were defined to, again, contain and manage the body, desire, gender, race. The heyday of AIDS activism was exactly when I was going to school, exactly when I was studying queer theory for the first time. I was all involved in that in the late 80s and early 90s, and so I was already doing AIDS cultural theory when I began work in disability studies.

And then, there is this really sweet personal story. I was in a reading group on the body with Rosemarie Garland-Thomson, and we all would bring readings to the group at different moments of the group's existence. When it was my turn I, of course, brought stuff that was about stigma and HIV and the AIDS crisis: I had the group read selections from John Nguyet Erni's (1994) important book on deconstructing the language of "cure." Although I could have brought many AIDS cultural theorists who really, I'd say, represent crip theory *avant la lettre*: Paula Treichler (1999), Jan Zita Grover (1987), Douglas Crimp (2004)—and certainly filmmakers like Gregg Araki or Marlon Riggs as well. So in this reading group, as we were going up the elevator to talk about Erni's text, Rosemarie Garland-Thomson said, "you know, this is really disability studies." So at that moment, *Crip Theory*, the book, was born. And she called me a month later and said, "Would you write something on the intersections of queerness and disability?"

I started to write it, and I said, "This is not an essay, this is a book, this is a career, this is a culture, this is multiple people's careers and lives." I mean it really opened a door for me in terms of thinking and in terms of my own being-in-common with other people.

So one path is AIDS cultural theory, one path is that really sweet story with her, and another path would be various journeys in my own life. My own queer family life or kinship network has been saturated with issues of disability. So those are among the paths that generated that personal work.

DP: It is interesting to me that you structure your answer through paths and relationships that generate your work, rather than as an articulation of a disabled or gay experience or identity. It strikes me that a politics built on such diverse paths and relationships enables crip theory (the book, the theory, and the practices) to explore some of the more complex, overlapping, and/or intersecting aspects of different forms of marginalization, in ways that are not always enabled by identity politics. Do you think this is true of crip theory?

RM: For me that is particularly true of crip theory, and queer theory as well. I think that both forms of thought and cultural practice have often been concerned with thinking the limits. Sure, the LGBT community has pretty clearly defined senses of identity and pride, and so does the disability community. And that's all really important and world making. But I'm also really interested in locations where there may not automatically be the assumption that a person is a member of X, Y, Z community. Or there may even be suspicions about that person's inclusion.

In thinking about crip theory, I've often been concerned with disabilities that are not what have sometimes been cast as "the representative disabilities." So thinking about HIV, and trying to think about that through the lens of disability community and culture, has been really important to me. But also, other kinds of non-visible disabilities have been really important in my thinking and in my work.

In the book *Crip Theory* (2006), I worked and talked a lot with my former partner, who is my family. It was really important, when we talked about our life, to have a picture of him in there, because the picture doesn't really look "predictably disabled." And yet, our lives were shot through, and *are* shot through, with all sorts of intersecting queer, crip, immigrant, and labor issues. So we wanted to capture in this photo—this, sort of, standard tank top gay pride photo—that this is also the face of what it is to be crip and to be an immigrant and a worker, and all those things, even if that is not so obvious without, again, what you name as an understanding of paths and relationships. So, my relationship to crip theory is often concerned with who is at the margins, and with paths to those margins, with who is not necessarily a candidate for the face of the movement.

MB: It also seems vital to think about the ways in which crip theory, as you articulate it in your book, insists that compulsory able-bodiedness and compulsory heterosexuality are normative institutions that bear on *all* bodies, not just those interpreted, by themselves and/or others, as queer and/or disabled. In my own teaching of queer and crip theories, I've noticed the real ease with which people who consider themselves "outside" of crip and/or queer cultures (or identities) dismiss the effects these institutions have on their own subjectivities. The danger of this dismissal, as I see it, is that a failure to consider how we are *all* constituted in and through these institutions enables the reinforcement of compulsory heterosexuality and compulsory able-bodiedness, and their attendant violences. It seems to me that maintaining a critical stance that focuses on the political implications of marginalization, whilst not always focusing on the marginalized body itself, is an important cultural project—one that the artists you talk about above do through camp and parody, and one that you take on overtly in your book, *Crip Theory*, through your analysis of films like *As Good As It Gets* (Brooks 1997), and television shows like *Queer Eye for the Straight Guy* (2003–2007).

Can you tell us what direction your work has been heading in since you published *Crip Theory*?

RM: In the direction of thinking as globally and transnationally as possible. I think that the disability rights movement, often of necessity, has been a very state-based one, around the globe. That has often been because disability has been managed at the level of the state for more than a century. Sharon Snyder and David Mitchell talk about this in *Cultural Locations of Disability* (2006). They talk about how, during the modern era, states were exchanging ideas about how to best "manage" disabled populations. For that reason, disability movements have often struck back at the level of the state and demanded both rights and inclusion at the level of the state. The 1990 U.S. civil rights bill is, of course, the *Americans* with Disabilities Act (emphasis added).

DP: Similarly, in Canada, we can look to the inclusion of Disability into the Canadian Charter of Rights and Freedoms, which was enacted in 1982.

RM: And that's all very good, but it brings me back to where crip cultural production is excessive and just cannot be contained by borders. I think of the work of queer-crip filmmakers and painters and performers—like Leroy Moore and Krip Hop Nation, or Sins Invalid out of San Francisco.[1] These are performing artists and groups who centralize the work of disabled people of color, in particular, and Sins Invalid (2010) definitely reaches across borders for what they call their "unashamed claim to beauty in the face of invisibility." Even the painting of Riva Lehrer,[2] as she puts forward beautiful and enigmatic portraits of individual disabled activists and artists, often has this sort of queer-crip, moving-across-borders valence to it.

These works are definitely not prioritizing inclusion in the state. Again, as with Loree Erickson, there is this sense of, "Damn, we want so much more than that, and we want to create an overflowing movement out of this desire to spread all this excess around." And new global affinities have been generated from all that, a sense, for instance, of, "Hey, we have so much in common with disability movements everywhere; we can't be stopped at, and by, the state." I'm very interested in that generation of a global queer-crip consciousness, because I think that is in some ways really rather new. It's so exciting, and it suggests that the movement's heading in completely unexpected but wonderfully overflowing directions.

MB: You use the term "queer-crip consciousness," which I think can be understood in a number of different ways. In the current neoliberal context, the concept of political consciousness seems largely grounded in identity politics, which requires one to identify as a particular kind of marginalized subject—"gay" or "disabled" for instance—in order to struggle, collectively, for equal rights within the state (for example, contemporary LGBT movements for gay marriage and inclusion in the military). This identity-based consciousness often effaces how subjects are marginalized in complex and interdependent ways by specific state apparatuses, and by the structures of neoliberal global capitalism. As many have argued, identity-based movements that focus on state inclusion often fail to critique the ways in which buying into normative structures, like marriage or inclusion in the military, might further marginalize and reduce the life chances of some of the most vulnerable members of our communities.[3]

It seems to me, however, that while you see usefulness in political movements grounded in identity, you're also trying to get at something quite different in your thinking about a global queer-crip consciousness. I wonder if what you're talking about here is a kind of consciousness that is in excess of identity categories: a kind of political desire that stems from diverse locations, yet is generated under similar global and state-based constraints, such as neoliberalism and global capitalism?

RM: I'm interested in thinking about global queer-crip movements because I'm writing about neoliberalism, and the generativity of what Michael Hardt and Antonio Negri

(2000, 2004) call "the multitude," which I think queer crip movements are part of this productive and global multitude. Neoliberalism constantly checks and contains and stops bodies and desires at borders, in the interests of safeguarding the free flow of capital. So I'm very interested in thinking through the question of what are the ramifications of the global spread and sedimentation of neoliberalism? What are the ramifications of that for disabled bodies, queer bodies, disabled desires, crip desires and queer desires? So, I'm thinking about that right now, and largely thinking about it in film and filmic representations that are shared across borders.

For example, in an article I've written with Nicole Markotić (Markotić and McRuer 2012), via an analysis of *Murderball* (Rubin and Shapiro 2005), we look at the ways in which national borders get reconstituted on the court. They're made to seem as though they're so significant in terms of the battle that is being played out: but only on that court, because the relatively privileged players in the film actually cross borders with relative ease.

In contrast, in our article, Nicole and I theorized our own bodies moving across borders, because I almost came to Canada. I was offered a job at the University of Toronto, which would have been great for the partner I was talking about who would have papers much more easily through me in Canada than he does through me in the United States, or doesn't, as the case may be.

But, ironically, given our conversation thus far, there's this "excessive demand" clause in The Canadian Immigration and Refugee Protection Act that says if one is deemed to potentially, at some point in the future, be someone who might make excess demands on Canadian health and social services, you might be denied landed immigrancy, or permanent residency.[4] Maybe... might...It's all these "ifs," right? And the U of T lawyers said, "Well... that may in the future apply to you." And so it was interesting, because I had colleagues on the US side saying, "We don't want you to leave, but from a queer perspective we can understand how you would go to Canada." On the Canadian side they're saying, "We want you to come, but we can understand how from a disability perspective you wouldn't want to face that question mark." And so, in the end, we didn't go.

Margaret Price has this beautiful moment in her book, *Mad at School: Rhetorics of Mental Disability and Academic Life* (2011), where she defines disability as a kind of reaching across spaces of difference (20)—somewhat akin, I'd say, to the paths and journeys we were talking about earlier. But (and I'm sure Margaret would agree with this), as we reach, or travel, or cross borders, we're in a moment right now that is particularly dangerous. First, as I just suggested, there's that obvious moment where some are denied entry. But another, perhaps reverse, danger raises the serious question of cooptation. For instance, a certain "global gay" (usually male and able-bodied) community is clearly catered to now as an identifiable market. And that target marketing, as it first constructs and then capitalizes on the pink dollar/pound/euro, paradoxically encourages the crossing of borders but domesticates all that crip and queer excess we've been talking about.

Hence, we constantly need to be as rigorous in our thinking as we are expansive in our sharing: What forces stymie the kind of inventiveness we've been discussing? How do movements cross borders in complex and sometimes contradictory ways? What new questions are raised when the issues activists and artists and theorists have been working with at the level of individual states overflow across borders? I hope that the sorts of containments I just gestured toward will be resisted by all of us, in whatever ways we can think of to resist them.

DP: The excessiveness of these crip movements that you describe is particularly interesting to me. You evoke imagery of this creative mobilization spilling out of these locations of containment, over the borders of states, and across the boundaries of identities and movements. It strikes me that a fruitful way to think about the potential excessiveness of these movements is through the diverse, interrelated, and transnational resistance strategies that have emerged and spilled over within and against common sites of containment.

Take medicine as a site of containment. Feminist, trans, queer, impoverished, and crip communities have all, at various times, come up with really interesting strategies for accessing denied or controlled medical care without having to rely on the state, or at least without having to connect to the state in certain problematic ways. Some of these strategies happened at a more local level than the state (for example, abortion vans, and early independent living movements). Others involved receiving or fighting for care beyond state borders (for example, international trans surgeries, ACT UP). Many of these strategies can be seen as excessive, in that the strategies and their effects spilled over between movements, across bodies and borders, and creatively challenged common sites of containment. Some of these strategies, however, can be seen as antithetical to the kind of excess you describe. For example, both local and international capitalist markets have increased the forms and availability of certain medical interventions (abortions, gender surgeries, treatments), but only for the privileged few with the right income bracket and/or citizenship status.

RM: Exactly. We're talking again about open-ended dangers and the multi-faceted workings of cooptation. But, again, in the midst of what Gramsci called our pessimism of the intellect, there is optimism of the will, and what I would term the critically disabled or crip read of neoliberalism that is being communicated transnationally right now reflects that optimism of the will. Whether it's "Wheelers Against Walker," a group in Wisconsin that joined with thousands of other workers resisting Governor Scott Walker's efforts to eliminate collective bargaining rights in the state, or the Hardest Hit March in London, which brought out thousands of disabled people (perhaps the largest disability protest ever) to protest the Tory-Liberal coalition's cuts to vital social services, we could argue that crip responses to local conditions of oppression are animated by a transnational sharing of critical strategies for resistance.

MB: You offer these great examples of the "on the street" disability work that we normally associate with activism. Your writing also, however, deals with crip art as a really vital and generative form of disability activism, and as a central component of contemporary crip movements. I wonder, though: what do you think the role of academic theorizing is within the transnational crip movements that you describe?

RM: Theory is a form of activism, too. Sometimes there's this sense with theory, like, what do we do with it, right? I think sometimes it's more productively thought of in the other direction: How have all these amazing artistic and political and activist efforts generated these really complex ways of thinking about norms and institutions and structures? It's not like *Crip Theory*, or any other disability text, should be a handbook for a movement. Rather, in some ways, it's a document of all of this energy that has been going for decades at this point, and it's not showing any signs of stopping soon.

REFERENCES

Brittain, M. and Peers, D. (Dir.) (2008). *G.I.M.P. Boot Camp* [DVD]. Canada: KingCrip Productions and Vtape.

Brooks, J. L. (Dir.) (1997). *As Good As It Gets* [DVD]. USA: Columbia TriStar.

Crimp, D. (2004). *Melancholia and Moralism: Essays on AIDS and Queer Politics*. Cambridge: MIT Press.

Erickson, L. (Dir.) (2005). *Want* [DVD]. www.femmegimp.org.

Erickson, L., Peers, D., and Brittain, M. (2010, November 18–20). Disobedient Bodies: Video Artistry and Activism. Roundtable discussion presented at the Health, Embodiment and Visual Culture Conference, McMaster University, Hamilton, ON, Canada.

Erni, J. N. (1994). *Unstable Frontiers: Technomedicine and the Cultural Politics of "Curing" AIDS*. Minneapolis: University of Minnesota Press.

Grover, J. Z. (1987). AIDS: Keywords. In D. Crimp, *AIDS: Cultural Analysis, Cultural Activism* (pp. 17–30). Cambridge: MIT Press.

Hardt, M. and Negri, A. (2000). *Empire*. Cambridge, MA: Harvard University Press.

Hardt, M. and Negri, A. (2004). *Multitude: War and Democracy in the Age of Empire*. New York: Penguin.

Markotić, N. and McRuer, R. (2012). Leading with Your Head: On the Borders of Disability, Sexuality, and the Nation. In R. McRuer & A. Mollow (eds.), *Sex and Disability* (pp. 165–182). Durham, NC: Duke University Press.

McRuer, R. (2006). *Crip Theory: Cultural Signs of Queerness and Disability*. New York: NYU Press.

Nudd, D. M. and Wilkins, D. (Dir.) (2004). *Scary Lewis Yell-a-thon* [DVD]. USA: Mickee Faust.

Price, M. (2011). *Mad at School: Rhetorics of Mental Disability and Academic Life*. Ann Arbor: University of Michigan Press.

Puar, J. (2007). *Terrorist Assemblages: Homonationalism in Queer Times*. Durham, NC: Duke University Press.

Queer Eye for the Straight Guy [Television show]. (2003–2007). New York: Bravo.

Rubin, H. A. and Shapiro, D. A. (Dir.) (2005). *Murderball* [DVD]. USA: MTV Films.

Snyder, S. and Mitchell, D. (2006). *Cultural Locations of Disability*. Chicago, IL: University of Chicago Press.

Sins Invalid. (2010). *Sins Invalid: An Unashamed Claim to Beauty in the Face of Invisibility*. http://www.sinsinvalid.org (accessed April 22, 2010).

Treichler, P. (1999). *How to Have Theory in an Epidemic: Cultural Chronicles of AIDS*. Durham, NC: Duke University Press.

The Specials Meet the Lady Boys of Bangkok: Sexual and Gender Transgression and Smashing Intellectual Disability[1]

Michael Gill

People are supposed to act in ways that line up with their presumed sex. That is, we expect people we think are females to act like women and males to act like men. People hold other people accountable for "doing gender" correctly.

—C.J. Pascoe (2007, 13)

Reality shows are not new. What seems to be new is a reality show choosing to broadcast the everyday lives of a group of individuals with intellectual disabilities on the web. This article explores patterns of gender and sexual transgression in *The Specials,* a web-based reality show that *The Guardian* describes as a "docusoap" (Mahtani 2009). *The Specials* follows five white young adults with intellectual disabilities living together in Brighton, England. Imagined as *The Real World* meets *Friends,* it offers up selections of everyday events in these young adults' lives that are deemed worthy of circulation and consumption.[2] *The Specials* was originally conceived as a traditional television broadcast reality show, but, after the pilot was created, the broadcaster decided not to pursue the series.[3] Despite the lack of institutional funding and support, producer/director Katy Lock and web developer Daniel May continued the series as a web-based reality program in 2009. My analysis of *The Specials* is informed by the critical premise that, as Marc Andrejevic (2004) put it, reality television operates with a "promise of interactivity" that "functions increasingly as a form of productive surveillance" (2). *The Specials* uses "the promise of the internet" not only in allowing the housemates to gain celebrity status by having their lives documented and broadcast, but also by "gain[ing] greater participation in and control over the mediated version of reality in which they are immersed" (5).[4]

More specifically, this article engages with Margrit Shildrick's (2009) observation that "the interweaving of disability, subjectivity, and sexuality constitutes a dangerous mix" in light of both the reality genre and new media (6). Here, I explore the productive potential of that "dangerous mix" while simultaneously considering how gender and sexualized desires are reified in the process of being exhibited online. At various moments in the series, Sam, one of the housemates, expresses his attraction to and love of women, often within earshot of the object of his desire. Sam also transgresses expected patterns of relationships by actively courting women without intellectual disabilities, albeit unsuccessfully. Yet, the sexual desire of men with intellectual disabilities is often constructed as deviant if not potentially threatening (Cambridge and Mellan 2000; Cuskelly and Bryde 2004; Kempton and Kahn 1991; Thompson 1997), and, though Sam tries quite hard to live up to traditionally masculine norms of gender and sexuality, he is often shown failing to do so, a failure that could be read as negating any potential threat associated with men with intellectual disabilities. How are sexual desire and gender trouble—crafted through Sam's gendered identity and his repeated expressions of desire—politicized through intellectual disability in this web-based serial? How does the show valorize the gender transgressing performance of "The Lady Boys of Bangkok"—a cabaret of Thai *kathoey* drag performers featured in the episode on which I focus—as it is perceived by these young adults with intellectual disabilities who are, in turn, navigating their own sexualized desires? By addressing these questions, I discuss the limitations and possibilities of this series in expanding an articulation of intellectual disability, sexuality, gender, and desire.

My analysis focuses on the portrayal of sexuality in the third episode of the first season of *The Specials*, in which the housemates attend a show by the Lady Boys, a travelling, UK-based performance group. Here, Sam is particularly vocal about his excitement to see the "sexy ladies" perform. During the show, one of the performers sings Frank Sinatra's "My Way" while removing a wig and all makeup. At the end of the song, the camera closes in on Sam's face as he appears at the very least surprised, if not disappointed or shocked, at the transformation he has just witnessed on stage. Of particular interest is the contrast, visually constructed through alternating camera shots, between Sam's reaction to and interpretation of the performers' comment on the mutability of gender on the one hand, and other audience members' presumed understandings and endorsement of the event, as indicated by their applause, on the other. This momentary gender trouble is quickly resolved for Sam as new performers in drag take the stage and the spectacle of the show continues, leaving him to believe that they are indeed Thai women. The statement by Pascoe that I have taken as my epigraph highlights the persistent and particular tensions attendant on gender and performance. Outside of drag shows, there appears to be very little cultural room for ambiguity around gendered performances, especially in a reality show in which male participants are portrayed as intellectually disabled and sexually normative.

Of course, the draw of the Lady Boys depends on a deployment of the colonial gaze—that is, on a type of ethnicized imagination. Edward Said (1978) reminds us that, "the relationship between Occident and Orient is a relationship of power, of domination, of varying degrees of a complex hegemony" (5). Anne McClintock (1995) updates Said by remarking that imperialism has to be understood through the interconnectedness of race, class, gender, and sexuality (4–5, 14). In the analysis below, I trace the interlocking representational and relational implications of the Lady Boys' performance as well as Sam's gendered desire for the performers. It is questionable if, within the bounds of ethnicized entertainment for an audience presumed to be white, drag and a playful parody of gender provide sufficient theoretical ground to illuminate the transformative potential of intellectual disability and sexual desire.

DRAG, THE LADY BOYS, AND A REIFICATION OF OTHERNESS?

In their ethnographic examination of drag queens at The 801 Cabaret, a popular tourist attraction in Key West, Florida, Leila Rupp and Verta Taylor (2003) remark that:

> Drag embodies ambiguity and ambivalence. When straight women exclaim that they are attracted to the girls and they aren't even lesbians, when straight men are aroused by gay men in dresses, when lesbians find it erotic to see two drag queens doing the lesbian number "Take Me or Leave Me" from the Broadway show *Rent*, the conventional divisions between female and male, straight and gay, become almost meaningless. (5)

For Rupp and Taylor, the ambiguity around gender binaries and labels of sexual identity, desire, and orientation that the drag show offers—to performers and audience members alike—creates a type of "protest" not only against traditional gender and sexual scripts, but also against bodily expectations, a "subtle questioning of the meaning of gender and sexuality as we normally understand them. It is in that sense that the drag queens 'perform protest' " (116). This protest against gender norms and hegemonic power has the potential to highlight the artificiality of presumed continuities between genitalia, desire, and sexuality (Connell 2005). On-stage ambiguity and ambivalence are intensified when Western intellectual disability and non-Western eroticization complicate visibility and attraction through the mode of a reality show.

On the website advertising the Lady Boys' 2010 *Fantasy and Feather* travelling performance, the description of the performance foregrounds ethnic difference interlaced with gender and sexual diversity:

> It's non-stop entertainment all the way... In a flamboyant extravaganza combining the heady spice of Bangkok's exotic nightlife with the glamorous showgirl appeal of Las Vegas... Performed by 16 of the world's most beautiful show-girls (who just happen to be men!)... The fantasy starts as soon as you enter the fully carpeted Sabai Pavilion. You have left behind your daily existence and are transported to Bangkok's exotic nightlife. Inhale the aroma of freshly prepared Thai food—then choose from a range of mouth-watering dishes... Direct from the heart of Bangkok's exotic nightlife, you will be entertained—like no one has entertained you before!—by 16 of the world's most stunningly beautiful representatives of the Third Sex (Kathoey)—the sensational Lady Boys of Bangkok. It's the best party night in town!

From Vegas to Bangkok, from Thai food to showgirls, the *Fantasy and Feather* performance is advertised as a night to remember. Audience members are invited to consume a constructed version of Thailand mediated through costuming and cuisine. Echoing the imperial display, eroticization, and consumption of ethnological wonders, the show promises a narrative of tourism through food and costume while simultaneously exalting difference (McClintock 1995, 4–6). Significantly, this representation of Thailand is completely devoid of the "realities" of the sociopolitical and economic conditions in 21st-century Thailand. The recent coup d'état by a military junta and subsequent violent (and often deadly) struggles for power are visibly absent from the fantasy and feathers. The representation of Thailand is sanitized for the Western audience, and entertaining performances gloss over any discomfort that could be caused by addressing political instability.

Yet, though it erases a certain type of political difference, the show does advertise an education in the limits of dichotomous gendered thinking, or, rather, hints at the limits of this type of thinking with the mention of *kathoey*, a type of "third gender" within Thailand. *Kathoey* refers to a male-to-female transgendered person or an effeminate gay man, although no one of these categories necessarily maps out completely onto the individuals who embrace one or another of them. Han ten Brummelhuis (1999) argues that *kathoey* have to be seen as women, regardless of genitalia, and that definitions of *kathoey* remain fluid because there is not one universally accepted definition (124). One Thai saying describes *kathoey* as a person born physiologically male but possessing a "female heart" (Beech 2008). Nevertheless, the category of *kathoey* most often connotes an alignment with femininity either through dress, mannerisms, or body modifications such as breast enhancement surgery or hormone-induced alterations. In English, *kathoey* is most often translated as "lady boy," and thus the gendered mix of the Lady Boys of Bangkok is embedded in the title of the group as well as the advertisement of the event.[5]

The Lady Boys of Bangkok are a well-travelled group, often performing on multiple dates in cities, and catering to groups and "hen parties." A BBC article describing the Lady Boys at the 2010 Edinburgh Fringe Festival reports that the ratio of men to women in the audience is 40:60, and that 75% of the audience is made up of individuals not specifically attending the Fringe Festival ("Lady Boys," August 9, 2010). These demographics indicate that the mainstream appeal of the Lady Boys is well established. How do mainstream audiences encounter the intersecting gender, sexual, racial, and ethnic differences that structure the Lady Boys' performances? And, with respect to my focus in this article, how do disability and desire complicate such encounters?

In Asian North American Studies, David Eng (2010) explores queer liberalism and the emergence of a queer agenda that "works to oppose a politics of intersectionality, resisting any acknowledgement of the ways in which sexuality and race are constituted in relation to one another, each often serving to articulate, subsume, and frame the other's legibility in the social domain" (4). Eng's analysis of queer liberalism allows me to problematize the Lady Boy performance as a seemingly progressive location where gender performativity automatically challenges dichotomous gendered thinking. Interactions between the largely white European audience and the Thai performers might complicate notions of sexuality and desire in ways that depend on constructions of ethnicity and exoticness. Admittedly, the Lady Boys of Bangkok put on an entertaining show. That is clearly part of the appeal. The reliance on costuming, lighting, pop music, and

Thai food that caters to an English palate, along with a simultaneous decontextualization of the economic, social, and political realities of Thailand, most likely does not challenge many of the previously held perceptions of audience members. In the next section, though, as I explore the episode in question from *The Specials*, I will be proposing that Sam's reading of the Lady Boys as women potentially has the ability to challenge gendered scripts and expectations of sexualized desire for men with intellectual disabilities. Additionally, borrowing from Eng's formulation of queer diasporas as a response to queer liberalism that "offers a critique of modernity and its forgetting of race that calls attention to unauthorized subjects and to unacknowledged structures of feeling beyond an empirical tradition of liberal rights and representation" (15), I theorize the unruly patterns of affect, kinship, and desire that the interaction between the housemates and the Lady Boys generates.

GENDER, SEXUALITY, AND DESIRE IN *THE SPECIALS*

In the third episode of *The Specials*, Sam and his housemate Lewis are discussing the upcoming Lady Boys show with their support-staff member, Robbie. Sam and Lewis are, respectively, 22- and 19-year-old white males. Robbie is also white, and is older than both housemates. At the beginning of the scene, Robbie remarks to Sam and Lewis: "You do realize, and you, Lewis, that what we are going to watch tonight—the show—the Lady Boys of Bangkok are not actually girls, they're boys pretending." Sam emphatically responds: "I already told you! They are real girls. Trust me." Robbie again tells Sam that the Lady Boys are good performers, are very pretty, and do good impressions but are not actually girls. Sam, in a moment of dramatic desperation, gets down on one knee and says, "Please, I beg you. They are just real girls." The exchange concerning the "realness" of the performers' sex—boys or girls—becomes an anatomy lesson when Robbie tells Sam that the Lady Boys have "willies." In a last-ditch effort to convince Robbie that he is in fact mistaken, Sam says, "Well, A: They've got a vagina. B: They are real girls." Sam's emphatic insistence that the Lady Boys are women centers partially on his assertion that the performers have vaginas, presumably as opposed to "willies." It would appear that gender, as imagined by these two men, is conferred purely through the presence or absence of particular genitals. Sam is quite vocal during this episode about the sexy ladies he is going to see. To help explain his desire to see these performers as women, he has to categorically deny Robbie's reading of the performers as boys—a reading that, I would speculate, is shared by the majority of those attending the Lady Boys' shows. Lewis, sensing Robbie and Sam's inability to come to an agreement, suggests that they ask the performers themselves. His suggestion, a motion to a type of standpoint epistemology around gender, embodiment, and self-identification, makes the experiences and self-knowledge of the Lady Boys central in this discussion of sex and anatomy. Unfortunately, the experiences of the performers are not shared in the episode.[6] In her foundational work on the topic of drag, Judith Butler (1993) remarks that "the impossibility of reading means that the artifice works, the approximation of realness appears to be achieved, the body performing and the ideal performed appear indistinguishable" (129). Quite possibly, Sam's struggle to articulate his desire to see the performers as women against the dominant narrative that they are not points to his own ambiguity and inbetweenness.

In his discussion of lady boys, Brimmelhuis (1999) comments that "sexual excitement is about images, the presence or absence of a penis can be bargained about or accommodated" (130). Brimmelhuis is interested in explaining how European men, who do not necessarily identify as gay or queer, find lady boys sexually attractive and enter into sexual relationships with them, either as customers in a sex work arrangement or as long-term dating partners. Part of the success of lady boys working in European locations, especially in sex work, centers on what Brimmelhuis considers as "the impression that [*kathoey*] attraction works best in Western environments because of the heavily dominated two-gender system" (133). Because of rigid gender systems in which bodies "ought" to be coded as male or female, the outward appearance of femininity can confirm gender identity for a Westernized audience not willing to accept or entertain ambiguity. Anne Fausto-Sterling (2000) discusses how bodies that do not live up to a dichotomous sex/gender system because of the appearance of a non-average phallus have to be controlled, often through violent and unnecessary corrective surgery, in order to maintain gender divisions that do not "blur the borders" of gender (5). Although the Lady Boys of Bangkok blur the borders of gender in their stage show, the discussion between Sam and Robbie attempts to reify gender borders. Even as the discussion about whether the performers are "real" women re-inscribes normative binary gender categories, the conversation also registers varied expressions of desire, regardless of biological genitalia and disability status, that reflect the ambiguity of gender and sexual desire. According to Butler (1993), "the phallus functions as a synecdoche, for insofar as it is a figure for the penis, it constitutes an idealization and isolation of a body part and, further, the investment of that part with the force of symbolic law" (139). Sam's desire to see the Lady Boys of Bangkok as women, despite Robbie's insistence on the "truth" of a phallus, can be read as disrupting the normative alignment of gender with genitalia.

In representing young men labeled as intellectually disabled discussing desire, *The Specials* challenges gender normative declarations of attraction. In their study of images and how participants labeled genders, Kessler and McKenna (2006) note that if the image had a penis, participants identified the images as male 96% of the time, regardless of other characteristics, including breasts and long hair. The presence of a vulva resulted in the figure being labeled female only 64% of the time (171–172). They comment that "penis equals male but vagina does not equal female... [G]ender attribution is, for the most part, genital attribution; and genital attribution is essentially penis attribution" (172–173). Kessler and McKenna continue, "the cultural genital is the one which is assumed to exist and which, it is believed, should be there. As evidence of the 'natural sexuality,' the cultural genital is a legitimate possession. Even if the genital is not present in a physical sense, it exists in a cultural sense if the person feels entitled to it and/or is assumed to have it" (173). Sam's affectively motivated reading of the Lady Boys as female secures them as objects of desire and himself as a desiring subject, and Sam's reasoning to Robbie is based on a linking of femaleness to what he calls vaginas. Sam's desire to see the "sexy ladies" can be considered queer in that it validates the Lady Boys' temporary and performative self-expressions of gender outside a biological linking of genitalia to gender. According to José Esteban Muñoz (1999):

> Disidentification is about recycling and rethinking encoded meaning. The process of disidentification scrambles and reconstructs the encoded message of a cultural text in a fashion that both exposes the encoded message's universalizing and exclusionary machinations and recircuits its working to account for, include, and empower minority identities and identifications. (31)

Sam's insistence on femaleness, in the term's both sexed and gendered meanings, enables the Lady Boys' self-identification process to rewrite the narrative of gender within the reading of their bodies as "boy." Both Sam's reading of gender and the Lady Boys' gendered presentations challenge normative social identities "bound to a hegemonic structure of whiteness" that are "circumscribed by a homosexual prohibition bound to a racialized position" (Eng 2001, 13–14). The minoritarian subject positions of both the Lady Boys and Sam illuminate the limits of recognizing desire solely within normative constructions tied to dominant racial, ethnic, sexual, gendered, and disability identities.

In an interview with *.net*, an Internet magazine for web designers, Katy Lock, producer and director of *The Specials*, comments that part of the reason the broadcaster withdrew support for the series was because of the uncertainty of the show's success given the content:

> To be honest, *The Specials* does make for challenging viewing at times, such as when Sam falls in love with the ladyboys of Bangkok or Lucy sings an ear-splitting karaoke version of Greased Lightning. Scenes like these can be confusing for the viewer. Is it okay to laugh or not? But we thought it was important to show the guys' lives as honestly as possible. Like anyone else, they have good times and bad times and sometimes the joke's on them! However, maybe these kinds of scenes made the broadcasters nervous. ("The Brains Behind: *The Specials*" 2010)

By her own admission, Lock considers Sam's expressions of love (or temporary sexual attraction and arousal) for the Lady Boys challenging. Her comment raises the question: To what extent does the dynamic of surveillance inherent to the reality genre render Sam's sexualized desire and the Lady Boys' gendered self-expression unthinkable or inappropriate—and perhaps deviant? Overall, these scenes create a sense of ambiguity and nervousness, especially around intellectual disability, sexuality, and gender queerness. Even so, the apparent "honesty" of representation challenges the narratives of intellectual disability that are pervasive in television and Hollywood cinema. Part of an emerging genre of reality television programs that address disability, *The Specials* presents a certain type of narrative that changes the landscape of intellectual disability and sexual desire. It becomes important to interrogate how such images can be used as "raw materials for representing a disempowered politics or positionality that has been rendered unthinkable by the dominant culture" (Muñoz 1999, 31). The interaction between disability and non-Westernness, with inflections of the erotic and desire, complicates the commodification of a certain type of gendered representation for consumers that capitalizes on a sense of otherness, if not freakishness.

GEOGRAPHIES OF DESIRE: OTHERNESS ON DISPLAY?

Now let me connect the categorization of the Lady Boys and Sam's queer desire to Anne Anlin Cheng's (2001) contention that, "with phenomena such as segregation and colonialism, the racial question is an issue of *place* (the literalization of Freudian melancholic suspension) rather than of full relinquishment. Segregation and colonialism are internally fraught institutions not because they have eliminated the other but because they need the very thing they hate or fear" (12, emphasis in original). The Lady Boys' performance depends on a construction of *place*—a place of ethnographic promise that constructs the performers' bodies and Thai culture as consumable goods. Jacqui Alexander (2005), in exploring the contours of gay-themed tourism, wonders, "what kinds of geographies of desire and pleasure are possible, and necessary, in light of the conflation of the erotic and the exotic?" (69). Alexander is particularly concerned with the ways that a "queer fetishized native" gets commodified through the development and promotion of gay cruises, queer-friendly airlines, travel-themed credit card offers, gay-themed guide books, and travel specifically marketed toward gay men and lesbians—all of which promote a narrative of orientalized fetishes that, in essence, recolonizes tourist destinations through the promotion of "friendly" natives for the largely white Western travelers (70). Along with Cheng's point about *place*, Alexander's questions about constructing solidarity communities and geographies of desire and pleasure help me to tease out postcolonial, feminist, queer, and critical disability studies approaches to the representation work at play in *The Specials*, especially given the promise of tourism and travel foregrounded in the advertisements for the Lady Boys. Moreover, Eng (2010) complements Alexander by wondering if queer diasporas can attend to a "retheorization of family and kinship relations" (16). The *place* of the Lady Boy performance on English soil, *mediated through* reality television, points to the potentiality of affective kinship—outside of normative constructions of family—as geographies of desire.

After the above-mentioned discussion between Sam, Lewis, and Robbie, the episode of *The Specials* shows but a brief glimpse of the Lady Boys' performance. In a quick succession of shots, the camera captures the housemates entering the performance tent. Once inside, it cuts from shots of Sam dancing as he takes his seat to large banners of various Lady Boys hanging on the walls. Next, we see the stage as the curtain opens. A voice announces: "Welcome, to the Lady Boys of Bangkok!" The Lady Boys are shown on stage, enveloped in fog and pink stage lights. Almost immediately, we see a group of performers on stage dancing to the Pussycat Dolls song, "Don't Cha," the lyrics of which add an element of irony to the performance: "Don't cha wish your girlfriend was hot like me? Don't cha wish your girlfriend was a freak like me? Don't cha?" In the middle of the performance, Sam comments to the camera, "The girls are sexy!" Although the rest of the housemates are clearly enjoying the show, Sam is particularly vocal about his pleasure, both in direct dialogue with the camera and through his active participation.

Sam's direct dialogue about the sexiness of the performers functions as a kind of "inside joke" for viewers. Most viewers "know" that the Lady Boys are not "girls" in a biological sense; that is, they "know" the truth of gender and sex, while Sam does not. Katy Lock's suggestion that the joke, at times, is "on" the housemates is clearly at work in this episode, illustrating Andrevejic's (2004) claims around the connection between reality television and surveillance (103). Robbie interprets Sam's apparent unwillingness to read the Lady Boys as men as naïveté, and the scene prepares viewers to come to the same conclusion. Yet, such a dismissive reading depends on denying both Sam's and, perhaps, the Lady Boys' own understandings of gender.

Social scientists have demonstrated that intellectual disability is often associated with naïveté and acquiescence to suggestion (Jenkins 1998; Rapley 2004), and, at face value, Sam's vocal expressions of desire within the space of a drag performance by a group of Thai nationals certainly has the potential to invoke anxiety about his credulity. Yet, Shildrick's comment that, "if any coming together of bodies, and more specifically the intercorporeality of much sexuality, is encompassed with an implicit anxiety about the loss of self-definition, then that body of the other already breaches normative standards of embodiment" (84), allows me to fashion a critical reading of spectatorial anxiety. Sam's repeated denials of Robbie's reading of the Lady Boys as men also entail the possibility that, at some point in the near future, and perhaps off camera, Sam will "get it." And when he does "get it," he will be ashamed and disappointed—perhaps embarrassed.[7] Anxiety is not only the property or problem of the spectators, then, for Sam's potential loss of self-definition is also at stake.

Homophobia and ableism often work together not only to deny the disabled subject the ability to express sexual agency and desire, but also to actively redirect queer sexual desire. In this context, what I particularly emphasize is that the gendered exoticism of the Lady Boys, combined with Sam's disability status, creates a conflation of contentious images—images that are simultaneously problematic and violent as well as transgressive to dominant narratives of gender, ethnicity, disability, and "intelligibility of sex" (Butler 1993, 139). The non-Western, gender-queer bodies of the Lady Boys become the occasion for a meaning-making process that generates multiple identifications as well as multiple anxieties.

Regardless of what "we" might assume to "know" about the bodies (and, more specifically, the genitalia) of the Lady Boys, their embodiment is mitigated through self-preservation and presentation. What theatre audiences, as well as audiences tuning in to the web broadcast of *The Specials*, see on the stage is a constructed version of the Lady Boys' bodies as well as their nationality. The offer of traditional Thai food in the fully carpeted pavilion has the potential to, in Alexander's terms, recolonize individuals through native fetishes (79). Cheng's point about *place* and racial melancholy illustrates how racial and ethnic stereotypes contain subjects in order to sustain "the exclusion-yet-retention of racialized others" (2001, 10). The internal anxiety of misreading gender interacts with the recolonizing of Thai bodies, customs, and food for a Western audience.

In turn, reading Sam's sexuality through his embodiment of "disability" creates a disavowal. It is important to note that the sexuality (or sexual appeal) of the Lady Boys is clearly on display in the episode through brief clips of the performers dancing in bikinis to pop music; on one level, then, Sam's desire is visually corroborated. Yet, despite the transgressive potential of validating the queer desires of a disabled man, Sam's sexual expression is renounced as an ostensibly inappropriate object choice based on incorrect understandings of non-normative embodiment. Sam's sexual desire is seen not only as comical, but also as inherently "inappropriate" and queerer. Shildrick (2009) considers that to deny sexuality for those "whose embodiment is non-normative" is to "damage the very possibility of human becoming" (126–127), and Sam's encounter with the Lady Boys shows that there is a certain amount of rhetorical (and actual) violence in denying the sexual agency of individuals with intellectual disabilities. Sam's apparent naïveté has the potential to justify the need to protect those with certain disabilities from becoming sexually active because of concerns about manipulation and abuse.

Tellingly, the segment in the episode about the Lady Boys is book-ended by another narrative of romance, desire, and sexuality, one that both sutures people with disabilities into heteronormativity and negates their ability to inhabit its norms. Two of the housemates, Lewis and Megan, are in a long-term relationship. In the second episode of the season, Megan moves into the house where Lewis and Sam live, along with their other housemates, Hilly and Lucy. During the third episode, as a way to reconnect and move beyond their strained and awkward interactions, Lewis and Megan go out on a dinner date.[8] Commenting on the interactions between Lewis and Megan, Lucy remarks, "I think he's a bit shy, I think. Because Megan moved in. Because they're not talking to each other." By his own admission, Lewis admits to not talking much to Megan either, although he wishes that were not the case. This lack of communication between people in a relationship who are expressly not fighting seemingly illustrates the tentative nature of that relationship.

Sam and Lewis' expressions of heterosexuality and masculinity—grounded in longing for intimacy with Megan or sexual attraction for the Lady Boys—illustrate for the viewers of *The Specials* that men with intellectual disabilities are capable of clear articulation of desires. As Lewis and Megan get ready for their date, the camera shows Lewis putting product in his hair and gargling with mouthwash. Sam's voice-over tells the viewer that tonight could mark the first kiss between Megan and Lewis. Megan, meanwhile, waits patiently, dressed up, coat on, purse in hand at the bottom of the stairs. The camera, in a low-angle shot, shows the empty staircase. We hear Lewis gargling and spitting off-screen. As he finally appears, walking down the stairs, he proclaims, "That mouthwash was awful!" Despite having taken what are the conventionally held steps to ensure a good date, including dressing up and freshening his breath, as Lewis walks down the stairs he walks right by Megan and proceeds to search for a house key, even though Megan announces that she has one. This constructed version of a "dinner date" is in direct contrast with Sam's portrayal as a "typical," rowdy heterosexual man, even though both instances show men trying to inhabit normative heterosexual masculinity. One important difference between Sam and

Lewis' expressions of masculinity and sexuality is that Sam believes and insists that he is succeeding and that his expression is authentic. In comparison, as a couple, Megan and Lewis do not seem to be communicating on multiple levels, and the strained and uncomfortable interaction between the two anticipates the dissolution of their relationship. Later, after an extremely quiet dinner in which Lewis appears to be most interested in getting the last drops of soda from his can, Megan and Lewis are walking back home. Lewis audibly says to himself, "Go for it!" The camera then shows Megan and Lewis holding hands. Lewis questions aloud, "Is she holding my hand? I'm not minding that!" As Megan and Lewis walk back home with the camera behind them, the episode ends. At least temporarily, they have reconnected through physical contact. The two plots of this episode work together to indicate a range of sexual desires and expressions while, at the same time, putting either housemate's ability to attain "real" heterosexual masculinity into doubt.

As a whole, then, the episode seems to comment on the appropriateness of certain types of interactions between people with intellectual disabilities. Given that this show is the first reality show to feature participants with intellectual disabilities, Lewis and Megan's relationship is not threatening or overtly sexual, mitigating concern that they can share a house, with separate rooms, without significant sexual contact. The presumed asexuality of their relationship does not necessarily concern the viewer in the same ways that Sam's expression of desire for the Lady Boys might. Lewis and Megan are seemingly living up to societal standards for their sexuality—as is Sam, as long as he does not actually begin dating a Lady Boy. Shildrick remarks that those outside the corporeal mainstream (those who are transgendered, HIV positive, disabled) have a choice between "apparent asexuality that comforts normative expectations in its very powerlessness to challenge or an expression of desire that will be necessarily exploratory and transformative" (143). The transformative potential of a certain type of sexuality—a sexuality that fundamentally challenges heternormative and ableist norms rather than reconfirming paternalism—can ultimately queer normative expectations of embodiment and desire. However, this potential is not actualized within a representational formula and a spectator dynamic that tends toward the "recovery" of the norm.

DRAG AND DISABILITY: SOME CONCLUDING THOUGHTS

As a way to conclude, I want to look closely at a brief moment during the performance, referred to at the beginning, when one of the Lady Boy performers sings "My Way" while gradually removing makeup, eyelashes, and a wig. This particular moment is in direct contrast to the other brief glimpses of the Lady Boy show, when Sam is a visibly engaged audience member. When the Lady Boy performer transitions from the female costume, the audience, with the exception of Sam, applaud the Lady Boy's playful mocking of the limits and enactment of the fluidity of gender. Sam, however, is directly confronted with the reality that the performer he previously saw as sexy and feminine does not seem to be so any longer. Only after a few dramatic moments in which Sam has a look of wonder on his face does he gradually clap his hands in some show of support for the performer. After this moment of gender trouble, a new group of Lady Boys takes the stage in bikinis, dancing to the lyrics, "I can't wait for the weekend to begin." Sam shifts into the mode of an engaged audience member once again as, with an enormous smile on his face, he dances along to the music and claps his hands.

At the end of the Lady Boy performance, in an interview with Katy Lock that is part of the episode, Sam declares his wish to see the sexy ladies again. His housemates, Hilly and Lucy, again repeat the declaration that the Lady Boys are not women but lady *boys*. Sam's apparent unwillingness to accept his roommates' readings of the performers highlights a rigid reading of the sex/gender system on both sides. Or, a more playful reading of Sam's articulation is that he is purposefully negating his roommates' readings of the Lady Boys in order to illustrate the absurdity of such a desire to label and classify. The Lady Boy doing "My Way" is performing a gendered commentary on the queer potentiality of drag as much as performing a type of disguisability of "real" identity, and Sam could be reading the transition of the Lady Boy into male costume as another type of drag, a particular interpretation on the mutability of masculinity. If drag performers can be understood as "educat[ing] their audiences about the performativity of gender . . . sending different messages about what queer genders and sexualities look like" (Rupp, Taylor, and Shapiro 2010, 286–287), then, no matter his intention, Sam, in this episode, does as much as the Lady Boys to dismantle rigid articulations of dichotomous gender.[9]

NOTES

1. I am extremely grateful to Nicole Markotić for her helpful edits, suggestions, and commitment to my process. I am appreciative to Eunjung Kim for her feedback and helpful discussion as I worked on multiple drafts of this article. I am grateful for the helpful suggestions from the anonymous reviewer as well as for Janice Hladki's and Sarah Brophy's excellent suggestions for improvement and commitment to my work. Finally, I also thank the participants of the Health, Embodiment, and Visual Culture Conference.
2. *The Specials* won the 2010 Webby Award for best reality series as well as the People's Voice Award for the same category. This recognition partially demonstrates the success of the first season of the show. A second season is currently being filmed.
3. In discussing the reality television shows, *The Real World* and *Road Rules*, Andrejevic (2004) points out that "the premise of the show is that the cast members live in a panopticon—not everything they are doing is taped and watched, but they have to live with the knowledge that their words and actions, could at any time, be recorded for broadcast" (103). The housemates in *The Specials* are also subject to this panopticon and surveillance in order to share their lives and experiences.
4. There is an active Facebook group for *The Specials* that facilitates conversations among viewers, the producer, and castmates. There is also a hosted forum on the website for the show.
5. In a 2008 article in *Time* magazine entitled, "Where the 'Ladyboys' Are," author Hannah Beech repeats the narrative of non-Western progress in accepting individuals who transgress gender dichotomies by glossing over any discrimination that *kathoey* face in Thailand. The narrative of progress complements the Western fascination with difference and romanticization of non-Western cultures.
6. Rupp and Taylor (2003) remark that drag "opens a window to multiple and confusing genders and sexualities. By portraying ambiguity and inbetweenness, drag successfully invites audience members to consider what it means to be a man or woman, what it means to desire someone of a particular sex, as more complicated than they would ordinarily think" (212).

7. Sam's reading of the Lady Boys gender is presented as "wrong" because of Robbie's insistence on informing him of the "truth." The scenes of "gender/sex misinformation" mirror another scene in which Sam finally "gets it," though that scene does not appear in the web broadcast.
8. Megan and Lewis' apparent sexual innocence is in direct contrast to Sam's vocal sexual expression of desire in this episode and later in the series. After Lewis and Megan end their relationship, Sam actively flirts with Megan. This flirting places strain on Sam and Lewis' friendship and causes some overall unease in the house between the housemates.
9. Andrejevic (2004) remarks that "reality programming highlights the increasing importance not just of surveillance but of interactive technologies that rearrange the conventional distinctions between work and play and between consumption and production" (17). Sam's productive labor as a reality star and gender theorist is seen through his interactions with his housemates, support staff, and the camera in this episode.

REFERENCES

Alexander, M. J. (2005). *Pedagogies of Crossing: Meditations on Feminism, Sexual Politics, Memory and the Sacred.* Durham, NC: Duke University Press.

Andrejevic, M. (2004). *Reality TV: The Work of Being Watched.* Lanham, MD: Rowman & Littlefield Publishers.

The Brains Behind: *The Specials.* (2010, August). *.net.* 17. http://www.netmag.co.uk/zine/discover-interview/the-brains-behind-the-specials (accessed January 22, 2011).

Beech, H. (2008, July 7). Where the "Ladyboys" Are. *Time Magazine.* http://www.time.com/time/world/article/0,8599,1820633,00.html (accessed October 31, 2010).

Brummelhuis, H. T. (1999). Transformations of Transgender: The Case of the Thai *Kathoey* In P. Jackson & G. Sullivan (Eds.), *Lady Boys, Tom Boys, Rent Boys: Male and Female Homosexualities in Contemporary Thailand* (pp. 121–139). New York: Harrington Park Press.

Butler, J. (1993). *Bodies that Matter: On the Discursive Limits of 'Sex'.* New York: Routledge.

Cambridge, P. and Mellan, B. (2000). Reconstructing the Sexuality of Men with Learning Disabilities: Empirical Evidence and Theoretical Interpretations of Need. *Disability and Society, 15*(2), 293–311.

Cheng, A. A. (2001). *The Melancholy of Race: Psychoanalysis, Assimilation, and Hidden Grief.* New York: Oxford University Press.

Connell, R. W. (2005). *Masculinities,* 2nd ed. Berkeley: University of California Press.

Cuskelly, M. and Bryde, R. (2004). Attitudes Towards the Sexuality of Adults with Intellectual Disabilities: Parents, Support Staff, and a Community Sample. *Journal of Intellectual and Developmental Disabilities, 29*(3), 255–264.

Eng, D. (2001). *Racial Castration: Managing Masculinity in Asian America.* Durham, NC: Duke University Press.

Eng, D. (2010). *The Feeling of Kinship: Queer Liberalism and the Racialization of Intimacy.* Durham, NC: Duke University Press.

Fantasy and Feather. (2010). http://www.ladyboysofbangkok.co.uk/ (accessed September 15, 2010).

Fausto-Sterling, A. (2000). *Sexing the Body: Gender Politics and the Construction of Sexuality.* New York: Basic Books.

Jenkins, R. (Ed.) (1998). *Questions of Competence: Culture, Classification, and Intellectual Disability.* Cambridge, UK: Cambridge University Press.

Kempton, W. and Kahn, E. (1991). Sexuality and People with Intellectual Disabilities: A Historical Perspective. *Sexuality and Disability, 9*(2), 93–111.

Kessler, S. and McKenna, W. (2006). Toward a Theory of Gender. In S. Stryker & S. Whittle (Eds.), *The Transgender Studies Reader* (pp. 165–182). New York: Routledge.

Lady Boys of Bangkok Keep Edinburgh Fringe Party Going. (2010, August 9). http://www.bbc.co.uk/news/uk-scotland-edinburgh-east-fife-10918621 (accessed October 31, 2010).

Lock, K. (Dir.) (2009). *The Specials.* KADA Films. http://www.the-specials.com/ (accessed July 15, 2010).

Mahtani, S. (2009, September 2). "Friends meets Skins" with a difference. *The Guardian.* http://www.guardian.co.uk/society/2009/sep/02/the-specials-docusoap-learning-disability (accessed July 15, 2010).

McClintock, A. (1995). *Imperial Leather: Race, Gender, and Sexuality in the Colonial Contest*. London: Routledge.

Muñoz, J. E. (1999). *Disidentification: Queers of Color and the Performance of Politics*. Minneapolis: University of Minnesota Press.

Pascoe, C. J. (2007). *Dude, You're a Fag: Masculinity and Sexuality in High School*. Berkeley: University of California Press.

Rapley, M. (2004). *The Social Construction of Intellectual Disability*. Cambridge, UK: Cambridge University Press.

Rupp, L. and Taylor, V. (2003). *Drag Queens at the 801 Cabaret*. Chicago: University of Chicago Press.

Rupp, L., Taylor, V., and Shapiro, E. I. (2010). Drag Queens and Drag Kings: The Difference Gender Makes. *Sexualities, 13*(3), 275–294.

Said, E. (1978). *Orientalism*. New York: Pantheon Books.

Shildrick, M. (2009). *Dangerous Discourses of Disability, Sexuality, and Subjectivity*. New York: Palgrave Macmillan.

Thompson, D. (1997). Profiling the Sexually Abusive Behaviour of Men with Intellectual Disabilities. *Journal of Applied Research in Intellectual Disabilities, 10*(2), 125–139.

Intimate Borders: The Ethics of Human Organ Transplantation in Contemporary Film

Donna McCormack

> [Organ donation has] no other limit than incompatibility of blood types (without sexual or ethnic limits, my heart could be the heart of a black woman). . . . Quickly, however, the other as stranger may become manifest: not woman, or black, or youth, or Basque, but the immunitary other, the irreplaceable other who has nonetheless been replaced. It is called rejection: my immune system rejects that of the other.
>
> —Jean-Luc Nancy (2000, 29–30)[1]

The image of the intruder is central to human organ transplantation rhetoric. The external, fleshy other crosses a supposedly definitive and divisive line by traversing and settling inside the epidermal layer of an other's self. While transplant teams make a putative claim that grafting is essential to the continued survival of critically ill patients, they also stress the dangers of rejection, wherein the originary body attacks the unfamiliar presence of an other's organs. The organicity of the rejection process—that the body resists incorporating organs from an other—seemingly shows how the skin marks the limit of the self, making the peaceful cohabitation of self and other an impossibility. The immune system is figured as an army always ready to attack any outside intrusion that may threaten the integrity, and therefore the survival, of the self. Here, outsiders pose risks and should be managed, surveilled, and even destroyed for the sake of protecting the sanctity of the wholesome, healthy body. Yet, in order for the transplant recipient to survive, there must be a repression of this system of defence; it must be weakened to let the other do its life-saving work of pumping vitality into the otherwise waning body. Highly toxic immunosuppressive pharmaceutics prevent the immune system from performing its militaristic duties, allowing the organ of an other to labor away at its everyday functions of keeping the other/self alive.

In this article, I examine three contemporary films that bring together histories of transnational racism and ethical quandaries regarding organ donation: Miguel Sapochnik's *Repo Men* (2010), David Moreau's *The Eye* (2008), and Stephen Frears' *Dirty Pretty Things* (2002). These films are diverse in genre and diegesis, and yet, I argue, they all share a preoccupation with how the biotechnological imperative to cut through bodily borders is intimately tied to state control, surveillance, and protection of geopolitical boundaries. *The Eye* and *Repo Men* are popular Hollywood productions designed to appeal to a mass audience through their emphasis on the spectacle of fear, stereotypical gendered and raced characterizations, and gory, violent visualities. *The Eye* is an American adaptation of a Hong Kong production (Pang and Chung 2002), which was originally concerned less with romantic self-discoveries and more with the deeply disturbing (and very scary) ways in which transplants haunt our imaginaries. In contrast, *Dirty Pretty Things* attempts to paint a more complex picture of precariously legal migrants in London through the social realist genre. Using a grainy visual effect to emphasize the lack of "gloss," and thus the focus on reality, in these migrants' lives, the film nevertheless borrows from Hollywood sensationalism with its images of bloody body parts, scenes of violence toward women, and largely stereotypical national and racialized representations. However, *Dirty Pretty Things* is the sole film on which this article focuses that is, arguably, driven by a political agenda. It is openly concerned with the politics of race and gender in contemporary Britain—a subject that has been of some interest to Frears throughout his career—and with transnational inequalities.[2] Although the other two films may not offer overt political messages, I suggest that slippages between bodily and geopolitical borders open up a critical and political space where the viewer can engage with the intersecting issues of biotechnologies and transnational migrations. I further argue that all three films convey a politics of belonging deeply invested in ethics, and thus in a concern with hospitality.[3] Organ donation is currently carrying the weight of cultural anxieties not only regarding divisions between self and other, but also concerning national boundaries of belonging and whether "different others" are to be welcomed or expulsed.

As Susan Whitman Helfgot's work (2010) illustrates, transplant teams, media broadcasts, and fictionalized representations of organ transplantation draw on an increasingly familiar nationalist discourse to describe this technologically advanced biomedical intervention. Here, self and other are cast as distinct beings that pose a potential danger to each other. Since the events of September 11, 2001, in the United States, along with subsequent bombings in European countries including the United Kingdom and Spain, many nations of the global North have waged a mediatized military and ideological attack on those they readily identify as the enemy. Through a racialized rhetoric in which otherness is readable on the skin of the perpetrator, these nations consistently posit their borders as at risk of attack from outsiders (usually from the Middle East and invariably Muslim populations). Use of a racialized religiosity permits the production of an imaginary being—"the terrorist"—who embodies a threat to the geopolitical boundaries and moral parameters of a supposedly unified

"Western" society. The "transnational production of terrorist corporealities" (Puar 2007, 4) justifies shutting down sovereign borders. To assert that a nation must seal its geopolitical and ideological boundaries to prevent "different others" from entering into this impenetrable and "uncontaminated" space is to forge a notion of citizenship that affirms class, race, ability, sexual, and gender privilege as the means through which one gains membership and rights. The imagined, and threatened, national community is therefore reiterated as a white space infected by and at risk from non-white migrants who, according to this rhetorical logic, spread chaos, violence, and disease.

Increasingly, bodies come to matter within the context of a transnational sociality and morality where organs are posited as scarce commodities, and where modes of belonging are forged through a fear-inducing nationalist rhetoric. In this context, bodily matter accrues value as it migrates from the global South to the global North, from black and brown bodies to white bodies, from poor to rich, and from women to men (Scheper-Hughes 2001, 45). The meaning and viability of the human are at stake in a globalized network of belonging where a class- and race-based national citizenship, particularly in "Western" countries, permits privileged access to border crossing, health care provisions, state protection, and a sense of bodily and communal integrity.[4] Organ donation and transplantation bring to the fore a "crisis of ethics," where the possibilities of being open to the other and of bearing witness to the epistemic limits of self and other are increasingly situated in a desire to procure parts of the other solely to sustain the vitality of the self (Chakravorty and Neti 2009, 196). At issue in my analysis of visual texts in this article is whether ethical modes of being with others are possible now that the human is a biomedical commodity.

MARKET ECONOMIES AND MECHANICAL BODY PARTS IN *REPO MEN*

Repo Men invites viewers to witness the technological advances of organ transplantation in a future when life expectancy is no longer restricted to the precariousness of flesh. Instead, perfectly functioning and constantly improving cybernetic existence is imagined into being through mechanical organs and body parts that are placed inside the human body to perform even better than the most perfect of organic components. Anyone can have access to the all-improved, ever-enhanced, and soon to be immortal body if s/he can maintain the regular, extraordinarily expensive, monthly payments to the medical corporation known as the Union. Failure to pay results in the arrival of repo men who take back the body part(s) owned by the Union; the repo men, Remy (Jude Law) and his best friend Jake (Forest Whitaker), literally rip out the mechanical object, now a visceral cog in the bloody machine, regardless of whether the person lives or dies. The implants that are integral to the individual body are also the property of the Union. What it means to have a body, to own one's body, is here put into question as a failure to make the necessary payments results in the loss of essential body parts, one's well-being, and even one's life.

While evidently capturing the intimately violent effects of privatized health care and biotechnological advances, *Repo Men* also encapsulates a crux of the debate surrounding organ transplantation regarding whether our bodies and their parts are our individual property or that of the "caring" system. Ed Cohen (2008) suggests that "our legal and economic notions of individualism and individual rights (such as right to property) rest on the premise that as embodied persons we possess ourselves. It seems a simple enough formula: *to be* a (legal) person means *to have* a body" (103, emphasis in original). The interrelation of individual rights, legal recognition, and a sense of *having* (i.e., owning) a body conveys how visceral being is always and already enmeshed in economic and state relations and structures. In *Repo Men*, state and corporate ownership over bodies and their parts entails intense surveillance of individuals to ensure they do not miss their monthly payments. Not only is there increased restriction on how bodies move through space, but there is also a prohibition on exiting the area over which the Union holds jurisdiction.

Much of the film takes place in borderland zones, where what "is at issue is the permeability of [both] the boundaries that guarantee the normatively embodied self" (Shildrick 2002, 1) and the putative homogeneity of the geopolitical order. The film's tenuous premise is that Remy, a repo man seemingly devoid of human emotion, goes into heart failure and, unbeknownst to him, receives a "new Jarvik 39 heart module, top-of-the-line." The post-transplant Remy is unable to cut open fellow transplantees, to repossess organs, and therefore to earn money to keep up his payments. In order to avoid certain death, Remy must flee the Union-controlled territory where his best friend, Jake, will soon repossess his organs. With his newly found cyborg lover, Beth (Alice Braga), he heads to a wasteland filled with disused buildings and populated by indebted citizens. Once in debt, these citizens become "less-than-human" and therefore expendable (Butler 2004b, 2). Their legally sanctioned murder, justified and deemed necessary because they have not adhered to the collective contract, exemplifies their status as what Giorgio Agamben (1998) calls "bare life." For Agamben, biological life (*zoe*) is integral to and inseparable from political, legal, and moral life (*bios*). Those who appear to threaten the political, legal, and moral integrity of the nation or of a transnational conglomeration—such as the (European) Union—are always potentially subject to the state of exception, where illegal practices, including torture and murder, are normalized and deemed necessary. One could even suggest that their cyborgian (i.e., not-quite-human) bodies reinforce the illusion that the state of exception is exceptional (Puar 2007, 9). In other words, *Repo Men*'s transplantees have broken the contract and thus, as cyborgian beings, the laws that apply to humans do not protect them.

The transplantee body is an immobilized biomass tied to the economic and health structures that determine the movement of individuals. Those whose fleshy borders have been repeatedly crossed cannot, in turn, traverse the geopolitical boundary that offers freedom from economic duress and panoptic surveillance. The interrelation of territorial borders and bodily boundaries is brought to the fore as battered Remy and Beth attempt to leave Union territory via the sparklingly white airport. The film's representation of the airport as a porous, multi-ethnic, and multi-national space where the boundary between inside and outside is no longer definitive bears witness to the biopolitical scrutinization of migration. As Beth's leg begins to ooze black oil over the white floor, literally leaking the not-quite-human inside out, a swarm of patrol guards leads her and Remy to a private room in which their bodies are revealed as containing antiforgs (transplanted mechanical body parts). Here, we see how the "corporeal cut both fails to solidify the boundaries of self and other, *and* enables a quite literal incorporation of otherness that cannot fail to disturb the dominance in the sociocultural imaginary of a sovereign self" (Shildrick 2008, 41, emphasis in original). In other words, our understandings of the relation between national and individual self and other are at issue when slicing through the skin and replacing originary body parts with those that are not-self. Although Remy and Beth let the non-self inside the self (in the form of technological prostheses), their respective psychic selves are never put into question. Instead, the film's emphasis is on how fleshy crossings are understood as needing to be monitored by an economically motivated biomedical gaze.

Although they manage to briefly escape the clutches of the murderous guards, Remy and Beth realize that "there is no way out." In an attempt to break free from this systematic, all-encompassing, and seemingly all-powerful institutional control, Remy sets out not to achieve personal freedom but, rather, to save all transplantees from the horror of the repo men. The viewer witnesses Remy's determination to reach Union headquarters by killing everyone who gets in his way. The spectacle of blood, gore, and violence in the name of "equality" for transplantees indicates to the viewer that what is being seen may not be the diegetic reality. Indeed, a few "technical glitches," where the screen switches very briefly to paradisiacal images, suggest to the attentive viewer that this reality is only in Remy's head (a suggestion that is confirmed towards the close of the film). Once inside the room that contains the omnipotent "system," in a scene that mimics a heterosexual sexual encounter, Remy and Beth cut through each other's skin, allowing blood, oil, and viscera to ooze out, objects and hands to glide inside each other, and organs to be "returned" to the Union in an attempt to blow up the central system. Perverse sexual intimacy (insofar as intense pleasure and pain are gained by cutting through the body's border) and gory cybernetic bodies are offered as the means through which an embodied system of control can be defeated. Bodies that defy both borders and sexual norms can undo the biomedical power of the transnational conglomeration.

Yet, the dream of change is merely another biopolitical invention of the technologically advanced Union, which can now keep bodies alive in an idyllic, pain-free, and dream-like state for as long as payments are maintained. Remy's utopian overthrowing of the system and freeing of all from the violent constraints of the Union are revealed to be coma-induced visions paid for by his close friend, Jake (who, in his role as repo man, killed Remy). As the head of the Union tells the viewer: "Imagine your loved ones living out the rest of their natural lives where they are always happy, always content and always taken care of. You owe it to your family. You owe it to yourself." Death is the cruel contrast of uninterrupted, coma-induced happiness. *Repo Men* concludes that happiness is the purchase of a wished-for image, where the violence of everyday life is forgotten, and where sensory stimulation comes only in the form of state-controlled biotechnologies. The body is docile and passive, an object of control repeatedly transplanted so as to be kept static and unthinking. The only responsible way to demonstrate one's love is financial investment in the prolongation of life, and life finally becomes the property of the profit-seeking, ever-present Union. Organ transplantation, in this vision, is the means to definitive, capitalist state control. Bodily borders are crossed to create indebted citizens who cannot legally traverse territorial boundaries without being subject to extreme forms of state-sanctioned violence. Transplantation is thus the ultimate form of disempowerment, a literal giving over of psyche and soma to the state. We are left with an image of capitalism controlling minds and bodies by ensuring that citizens want only to purchase the dream of eternal happiness.

WHOLESOME BODIES AND EXPUNGING THE OTHER IN *THE EYE*

Whereas *Repo Men* shows how healthiness and well-being are "biological commodities that can be bought and sold" (Waldby 2002b, 310), David Moreau's *The Eye* emphasizes a "profound sense of ontological insecurity" by exploring how an organ recipient's sense of self is haunted by and merges with the donor's psychic and material existence (Scheper-Hughes 2001, 32). Although littered with horror-like scenes (mainly the sudden appearance of the living dead), the film is also shaped by a typical narrative of self-discovery, in which the disabled character must find her "true" self and her "true" love. This is a simple diegesis about the potential trauma of corneal transplantation, complicated only by nightmare visions and by the belated revelation that the transplantee now sees not her own reflection, but that of her donor. *The Eye* visualizes the spectacular possibilities of being haunted by a donor, such that the transplantee literally sees through the eyes of the now dead other.

Finding her sight miraculously restored after a double corneal transplant, Sydney Wells (Jessica Alba) realizes something is awry. She tells her doctor: "I'm seeing things that aren't real... I'm dreaming things I've never seen. This surgery was supposed to make me normal." Transplantation normalizes able-bodiedness, rendering blindness "abnormal" and therefore a burden to be overcome. The protagonist emphasizes how the organ both contains "some trace of the donor" and brings about "an intense identification with the unknown donor" (Waldby 2002a, 247). Sitting at her computer searching for information her doctors refuse to share with her, Sydney discovers a possible answer to her post-transplant hauntings: "Based on the theory that all living tissues have the capacity to remember, cellular memory explains how energy and information from a donor's tissue can transfer, consciously or unconsciously, to the recipient." The deployment of cellular memory is clearly a sensationalist portrayal of organ donation. Yet, it is also an affective and embodied means of conveying deep-seated anxieties about the presence of Mexicans in the United States. Just as Sydney feels that her donor has literally occupied her body and mind, the film is haunted by a fear of the Mexican other penetrating and dominating the American self.

Nikolas Rose (2007) suggests that, according to the logic of neoliberal biopower, "every citizen must now become an active partner in the drive for health, accepting their responsibility for securing their own well-being" (63). However,

The Eye portrays how a "drive" for "well-being" is intimately tied to a notion of (national) integrity, where the individual body is distinct from other bodily beings, and where the security of the visceral border is assured through a national belonging that actively seeks to expunge different others. *The Eye* conveys a disquieting U.S. nationalism, fearful of difference and afraid of those who inhabit what is represented as the proximal lands on the other side of the geopolitical border. Ana Christina Martinez (Fernanda Romero) is the Mexican "bruja" (witch) who, after committing suicide because of her mistreatment at the hands of this "small town with many superstitions," is now an integral part of the extraordinarily talented concert violinist, Sydney.[5] The film's representation of Mexico as a rural and poverty-stricken space, steeped in an irrational and ignorant mysticism, is in stark contrast to the modern, medically advanced urban landscape of the United States. Space is racialized, with Mexico appearing as primitive and backward in comparison to the United States, which appears to be healthily white and therefore threatened by the prospect of getting too close to—literally occupied by—the non-white other. As José Esteban Muñoz (2006) explains, "whiteness [is] a cultural logic that prescribes and regulates national feelings and comportment. Whiteness is thus an affective gauge that helps us understand some modes of emotional countenance and comportment as good or bad" (680). The presence of "brownness" in the American body produces endless psychic and fleshy perturbations: Sydney experiences constant visual disturbances and even bears the marks on her flesh of the imagined reality that Ana is trying to convey to her. The Mexican other, now inside the American body, manifests herself by pushing the recipient to the brink of madness, where the ability to distinguish between the real and the imagined brings about a loss of everyday normality. In other words, the ordinary sanity and wholeness of the American citizenry fades when parts are removed and replaced with Mexican viscera.

In *The Eye*, just as in *Repo Men*, anxieties around the dissolution of the body's borders and their interrelation with a nationalist sentiment of ethnic and class unity culminate in a scene that takes place at a geopolitical boundary. After visiting Ana's destitute home, where Sydney cradled her already dead donor in her arms to stop Ana's melancholic repetition of daily suicide, Sydney and Dr. Paul Faulkner (Alessandro Nivola) sit at the border of Mexico and the United States waiting to return "home." Finally realizing that her donor has been trying to encourage her to "see" the events that are about to unfold, the protagonist sets out to save everyone who is about to die in a car-chase explosion. Ana had been unable to prevent the many deaths at the factory where her mother worked because no one would believe her occult predictions. Determined to succeed where Ana failed, Sydney saves the crowds of people by insisting that there is a bomb on the bus. When one of the students on board asks her, "Is it like a terrorist thing?" the film asserts a nationalist fear of the American self being violated by a different—and easily identifiable—other who is determined to destroy American unity. Terrorism, Mexico, border migrations, and organ transplants are condensed in a scene where we witness spectacular explosions. When she is caught in a blast, Sydney's final sighted image is that of her own reflection in a car window. In previous mirror scenes, Sydney had only been able to see Ana's reflection. Yet, that which allows her to see her self becomes the very thing that results in the loss of her corneas and, once again, her vision: the car window shatters into Sydney's eyes.

For Jacques Lacan, the mirror stage generates (the illusion of) a recognizable, coherent self, and for Michel Foucault (1986), the mirror facilitates a process of gazing in which "I" "reconstitute myself there where I am" (24). *The Eye* represents numerous mirror scenes in which the glass, and therefore Sydney/Ana's image, is shattered. Although the dispersed reflection functions as a simple metaphor for the protagonist's fragmented identity, it also becomes the means through which the overpowering other is destroyed. Thus, when Sydney finally sees her own reflection, she loses her sight. That which reflects the self (Sydney) and which no longer reflects the other (Ana) only does so in order to finally destroy that which should not be part of the American self: the Mexican other. In other words, the Mexican other is destroyed at the national border, expulsed from the American body so that the integrity of the (national and visceral) self can be restored. There can be no coming together of self and other, of American and Mexican. Order and differences are restored—borders are protected and sealed—as Sydney and Paul return "home." The Mexican other is finally dead, and the American self lives on, distinctly separate and at a great distance from the borderlands of Mexico. Sydney saves everyone, even giving "peace" to Ana, and is the idealized disabled character who excels beyond the normal in her ability to perform national belonging, well-being, and wholeness.

STATES OF EXCEPTION AND DONOR HISTORIES IN *DIRTY PRETTY THINGS*

In *The Eye* and *Repo Men*, organ donation, procurement, and transplantation are figured in terms of border anxieties and imaged as violations of supposed natural bodily and community boundaries. Stephen Frears' *Dirty Pretty Things* also takes up these anxieties around the dissolution of national identity, the flesh's vulnerability, and the detrimental effects of a market-based health care system. Yet, rather than focusing on the transplant recipient, as is the case in *The Eye*, or on a future landscape, as we see in *Repo Men*, *Dirty Pretty Things* hones in on the precariousness of migrants—both legal and illegal—in an early 21st-century London. Where the horror genre makes a spectacle out of transplantation and the science fiction genre exceeds the boundaries of contemporary biomedical reality, the conventions of social realism lend a documentary aesthetic to Frears' film. The grainy visual field, in particular, reflects the gritty reality Frears wants to capture and convey.

Dirty Pretty Things takes place in a boutique hotel where precariously legal migrants labor to maintain the inviting image of chic and exclusive hospitality. The film tells the story of Okwe's (Chiwetel Ejiofor) work life as an illegal immigrant who drives a taxi by day and is a hotel receptionist at night, and his growing intimacy with Senay (Audrey Tautou), a Turkish asylum seeker who cleans at the same hotel. Centered on Okwe's discovery of a healthy human heart in a toilet at the hotel, the narrative slowly reveals that the hotel manager, Señor Juan (Sergi López), is "enabling" his staff to donate their healthy organs to rich, dying clients/patients in exchange for forged European passports. What unfolds is a network of vulnerability where sex work, precarious migrations, and organ trafficking are intimately tied together without being determining of or dependent upon the other's existence. *Dirty Pretty Things* illustrates how bodies become molecularized commodities in a democratic "Western" society that institutes a biomedicalized state of exception. The contrast between the shiny, expensive hotel setting and the poverty- and surveillance-ridden lives of Okwe and Senay renders visible not only varying levels of global inequalities and migrations, but also the centrality of illegal labor and trade to the British economy, health care system, and society in general. A systematized state of exception, foundational to the law, keeps economic and social hierarchies in place and ensures that some people matter while others are useful only for their (bodily) matter.

In *Repo Men*, the Union instrumentalizes a state of exception in which all citizens can potentially be mutilated or killed in a process that neither undermines the law nor results in criminal prosecution. In contrast, the creation of bare life through the state of exception in *Dirty Pretty Things* functions somewhat differently from Agamben's complex formulations. On the topic of the sale of kidneys by women in India, Lawrence Cohen (2005) writes, "what is exceptional in these situations is less one's reduction to a zone of indistinction in which political life and bare life collapse together, but a more articulated zone in which one trades in one's bare life—kidneys, other biomatter—in order to remain a political subject of sacrifice and love" (82–83). By sacrificing fleshy parts, these women gain familial and community recognition for their immense generosity, even as they are denied national visibility in a country that legislates against the sale of organs (L. Cohen 2005, 80–81). In other words, these women are figured as exceptions to the law and as pushed to such "extremes" because of exceptional circumstances. The nation refuses to bear witness to both how the law instigates its own exceptionalisms and how transnational economic structures encourage, in this case, Indian women to enter into political subjectivity through the body. Similarly in *Dirty Pretty Things*, the precariously legal migrants commoditize their body parts to become citizens of a European nation and thereby to gain access to state protection. Here, the state of exception entails not only the disposability of bodies without recourse to juridical protection, but also the sacrificing of viscera, the marketing of organs, to become a citizen of a democratic, liberal nation. To this extent, and operating somewhat differently from Agamben's formulations, bare life *enables* political subjectivity.

At one point, *Dirty Pretty Things* visualizes a semi-naked hotel worker in a smart hotel room pleading with Okwe to remove her kidney. In another moment, the camera zooms in on the gaping wound of a Somali man who, we are told, "swapped his insides for a passport." These scenes are testament to how a medical rhetoric of scarcity is being "addressed by 'simply' tapping into and plundering the bodies of the *living*" (Scheper-Hughes 2005, 146, emphasis in original). The desperate desire to undergo the corporeal cut bears witness to how bodies of color both travel precariously across borders and are monitored, not only through technologies of the state but also by medical surveillance networks. A photographic close-up of an 8-year-old girl who will die should an illegal donation not go ahead, along with Señor Juan's voiceover, presents the putative dilemma of organ transplantation to both Okwe and the viewer. Señor Juan tells us, "So, I'm an evil man, right? But I'm trying to save her life. That's weird, eh? The kinda thing that keeps you awake at night." To some extent, the words confirm that transplantation is based on a medical ethics "where death has been deemed unacceptable on any terms" (Brown and Webster 2004, 110). Although Nik Brown and Andrew Webster aim to rethink transplant ethics by exploring how death is increasingly viewed as the unnecessary end to a life that can be almost infinitely prolonged through biotechnologies and pharmaceutics, such an intervention does not capture the essence of Señor Juan's quagmire: who gets to live at the expense of whom. In Judith Butler's (2004a) words: "The subject who is no subject is neither alive nor dead, neither fully constituted as a subject nor fully deconstituted in death" (98). Saving the dying girl is not simply about intervening when medically possible, but also about why it is possible to harm some bodies when attempting to prolong the lives of *certain* others. Not quite subjects, the donors are constructed as exceptions and exceptional. They are exceptions to the law that criminalizes the trade in organs, and exceptional in that their donations are unique "gifts." For these migrants, desubjectivization takes place when crossing the geopolitical border of the European Union; resubjectivization begins once they sacrifice a part of themselves to save the life of a richer other. *Dirty Pretty Things* shows how donor histories fall out of a medical rhetoric that focuses on saving the lives of the ill and the dying at the expense of remembering the origins of the life-saving fleshy matter.

On the one hand, *Repo Men* bypasses the visceral relationship between donor and recipient by creating mechanical organs made in laboratories. On the other hand, any notion of a gift that may be present in this relationship is dependent on a market-based structure. In other words, the (mega-)donor is the profit-making health care company, which rescinds its "gift" of life once payments stop. In contrast, *Dirty Pretty Things* represents the vulnerability of human organ donors and the migratory histories of organ donations. Yet, like *Repo Men, Dirty Pretty Things* focuses on the "happiness" of the biological citizen. Here, ethics is formulated through a notion of happiness that is inseparable from the act of buying goods that ensure a long (healthy) life, regardless of the impact this may have on the lives of others. This is how Señor Juan describes his business to Okwe when trying to persuade the latter to become a transplant surgeon for his illegal, fleshy network: "I sell the kidney for £10000, so I'm happy; the person who needs the kidney gets cured, so he's happy; the person who sold his kidney gets to stay in this beautiful country, so he's happy. My whole business is based on happiness." Señor Juan's words are redolent of those voiced by transplant teams who see no problem in cutting open those who "choose" to donate.[6] Indeed, the right to "choose" is formulated as a democratic act that enables individual and collective happiness. Speaking on the subject of how the claims of collective happiness mask hierarchical structures of labour, Sara Ahmed (2010) poses the following question: "How better to justify an unequal distribution of labor than to say that such labor makes people happy?" (50). More specifically, she adds, "Happiness is imagined as social glue, as being what sticks people together. The mission to put glue back into communities not only suggests that communities lack such glue but that they once had it. . . . In mourning the loss of such a world, migration enters the narrative as an unhappiness cause, as what forces people who are 'unalike' to live together" (121–122). Señor Juan's persuasive life-saving discourse is framed by a notion of collective happiness that is tied to normalizing biopolitical and national structures that seek to conceal unequal distributions of power, wealth, and rights. Even if the unnamed migrants, along with asylum-seeking Senay, "choose" to donate their biomatter in exchange for transnational and national state protection and rights, they do so within a system that initially refuses to protect their bodies from illegal violations simply because they are not British nationals. European nation states do not confer the same rights on precariously legal migrants as they do on legally recognized citizens, and thus illegal migrants become part of a systematized state of exception. Transplant happiness ignores how biological citizenship (which includes the rhetoric of the "gift") institutionalizes these exceptionalisms. As Ahmed makes clear, these migrants are publicly perceived as eroding national happiness even though their labor and body parts are (privately and illegally) central to the continuation of national life.

Human organ transplantation is clearly bringing about a crisis in ethics and thus in hospitality (cf. Derrida 2001). The hotel in *Dirty Pretty Things* is a microcosmic representation of a space of hospitality where one can buy multiple services, including sexual, aesthetic, and gustatory pleasure, and even improved health. The topography of the hotel is a synecdoche for the hopes and failures of individual and national hospitality. The corporeal incisions and deaths that occur within its confines indicate repeated violations of the ethical bind. And although the film offers a glimpse of a potential ethical moment of coming together that exceeds the desire for national biomedicalized happiness, even this glimmer necessitates an epidermal intrusion and a visceral exchange. Despite Okwe's pleas, Senay insists that she will donate her kidney illegally. What is initially presented as Okwe wanting to protect his close friend from being butchered on the operating table turns into an ambiguous undoing of hierarchies that keeps biotechnological controls and state surveillance mechanisms in place. Rather than removing his friend Senay's kidney, as Señor Juan demands, Okwe takes out the latter's organ. Having transformed the hospitable hotel room into a hospital theatre, Okwe, with the help of an asylum seeker (Senay) and a sex worker (Juliette, played by Sophie Okonedo), undermines the power of European nationals to determine which bodies donate and which ones receive organs by placing the Spanish man on the operating table and Senay in a surgical gown. Asserting that "we are the people you do not see," Okwe exchanges the organ for the money that allows him and Senay to leave Britain with their new, albeit forged, European passports. A gift that requires nothing in return, the gift of non-violation and of recognizing the importance of the other to the self, is an instance of the impossible and thus of the possibility of ethical relations. Of course, the impact of this transaction on Señor Juan suggests that the crisis in ethics persists, as he is transported from the tourist place of hospitality—the hotel—to the medical space of hospitality: the hospital. The biomedicalization of citizenship necessitates the violation of the migrant body, except when the migrant employs the tools of the hospitable and caring medical profession. Avoiding the corporeal incision for Okwe and Senay involves hospitably cutting into a more powerful other. Having avoided bodily mutilation by violating an other and protecting each other, Okwe and Senay gain access to the privileges of border crossing and state protection through fictionalized, and yet hugely important, biopolitical documentation.

BIOETHICAL MATTERS AND BEING OPEN TO THE OTHER

When Jean-Luc Nancy (2000) explores how his failing heart, his own ailing body part, comes to feel alien, he demonstrates that intrusions do not simply come from the outside but are also integral to the self (17). Figuring intrusion as external to the self serves only to reinforce the misconception that the self is sealed and contained, at risk of disease or invasion solely from the outside. Immunological studies often confirm the idea that the body is contained matter by representing the immune system through a rhetoric of foreign invasions, defense mechanisms, and intrusive others. What difference means in the practice of transplantation continues to be a subject of heated debate, and one that is often reduced to bodily markers that are said to signify the irrevocable gaps between self and other. The racializing and gendering of these differences serves only to reinforce hierarchies of skin as "real" (material) distinctions. Biotechnological developments continue to normalize the idea that the individual body, the self, is incompatible with and distinct from the different (racialized, stigmatized, and/or queered) other.

Hollywood productions such as *Repo Men* and *The Eye* offer rather complex representations of biopolitical subjectivity. Even with their simple narrative structures, uncomplicated plots, and predictable camera angles, these two films offer points of entry—albeit sensationalist ones—into conversations that remain largely absent from mainstream medical discourses. *Repo Men* is critical of capitalist interventions in medical care and of the increasing intimate and visceral surveillance of transnational mobility. *The Eye* reinforces nationalist ideals, exemplifying how the Mexican other must be blasted out of the American self if the latter is to continue flourishing. Yet, the film still opens up the possibility of a dialogue on how self and other may be intimately connected through organ transfer. *Dirty Pretty Things*, with its gritty aesthetic, offers a multifaceted look at the lives of migrants and the precariousness of contemporary bioethical living. Still, even here, Frears slips into national stereotypes.

All three films raise questions about the functions of biotechnologies in our lives and about medical interventions in a global society that naturalizes inequality. Importantly, the *spectacle* of organ donation—hearts in toilets, livers torn from living bodies, and eyes controlled by another being—complicates any political undertones that may be present in these films. Their critiques of state and medical structures and discourses work in tandem with a valorization of heteronormative relations and, ultimately, the search for romantic, monogamous ideals encapsulated by the dominant notion of happiness. Nonetheless, the crisis in ethics, in what it means to be with others and to care for others, emerges as a central issue, prompting us to address how normative definitions of the human function to create new states of exception. I suggest that the potential for ethics is situated in the persistent and indefinite engagement with how hospitality is possible in a transnational structure that remains attached to national ideals and personal gains. To remain open to the other cannot involve a violation of the psyche or the viscera, but it must involve a reconfiguring of our understandings of the self and our relationship with others. To be open is a vulnerable state of being, but one that constitutes our being for and with each other.

NOTES

1. Translations of Nancy's text are my own.
2. Examples of Frears' films concerned with the politics of race, gender, and sexuality in Britain include *Sammy and Rosie Get Laid* (Frears 1987) and *My Beautiful Laundrette* (Frears 1985).
3. Jacques Derrida (2001) asserts that "*ethics is hospitality*" (17, emphasis in original).
4. It is evident that national belonging does not secure access to effective health care or state protection for all bodies, regardless of the wealth of the state or country. Vulnerability to institutional violence is tied to multiple vectors of power and to one's shifting position within this complex nexus.
5. Sydney's extraordinary talent contributes to a somewhat stereotypical representation of disability, where because one sense is perceived as lacking, the other senses are understood as exceeding normative expectations.
6. R. R. Kishore, a previously high-ranking medical bureaucrat who was involved in the development of the 1994 Transplantation of Human Organs Act in India, argues, "allowing for an exchange of one man's surplus money for another man's surplus kidney is not really traffic [. . .] but 'life for life.' Everybody wins" (quoted in L. Cohen 1999, 137).

REFERENCES

Agamben, G. (1998). *Homo Sacer: Sovereign Power and Bare Life*. Chicago: Stanford University Press.

Ahmed, S. (2010). *The Promise of Happiness*. Durham, NC: Duke University Press.

Brown, N. and Webster, A. (2004). *New Medical Technologies and Society: Reordering Life*. Cambridge, UK: Polity Press.

Butler, J. (2004a). *Precarious Life: The Powers of Mourning and Violence*. London: Verso.

Butler, J. (2004b). *Undoing Gender*. New York: Routledge.

Chakravorty, M. and Neti, L. (2009). The Human Recycled: Insecurity in the Transnational Moment. *Differences: A Journal of Feminist Cultural Studies, 20*(2–3), 194–223.

Cohen, E. (2008). A Body Worth Having? Or, A System of Natural Governance. *Theory, Culture & Society, 25*(3), 103–129.

Cohen, L. (1999). Where It Hurts: Indian Material for an Ethics of Organ Transplantation. *Daedalus, 128*(4), 135–146.

Cohen, L. (2005). Operability, Bioavailability, and Exception. In A. Ong & S. J. Collier (Eds.), *Global Assemblages: Technology, Politics, and Ethics as Anthropological Problems* (pp. 79–90). Malden, MA: Wiley-Blackwell.

Derrida, J. (2001). *On Cosmopolitanism and Forgiveness*. London: Routledge.

Foucault, M. (1986). Of Other Spaces [Translated by Jay Miskowiec]. *Diaeritics, 16*(1), 22–27.

Frears, S. (Dir.) (1985). *My Beautiful Laundrette* [DVD]. UK: Channel Four Films.

Frears, S. (Dir.) (1987). *Sammy and Rosie Get Laid* [Video]. UK: Channel Four Films.

Frears, S. (Dir.) (2002). *Dirty Pretty Things* [DVD]. UK: Miramax.

Moreau, D. (Dir.) (2008). *The Eye* [DVD]. USA: Lionsgate.

Muñoz, J. E. (2006). Feeling Brown, Feeling Down: Latina Affect, the Performativity of Race, and the Depressive Position. *Signs: Journal of Women & Culture in Society, 31*(3), 675–688.

Nancy, J.-L. (2000). *L'Intrus*. Paris: Galilée.

Pang, D. and Chun, O. P. (2002). *Gin gwai (The Eye)* [DVD]. Hong Kong: Palm Pictures.

Puar, J. K. (2007). *Terrorist Assemblages: Homonationalism in Queer Times*. Durham, NC: Duke University Press.

Rose, N. (2007). *The Politics of Life Itself: Biomedicine, Power, and Subjectivity in the Twenty-First Century*. Princeton, NJ: Princeton University Press.
Sapochnik, M. (Dir.) (2010). *Repo Men* [DVD]. USA: Universal.
Scheper-Hughes, N. (2001). Commodity Fetishism in Organs Trafficking. *Body & Society*, *7*, 31–62.
Scheper-Hughes, N. (2005). The Last Commodity: Post-Human Ethics and the Global Traffic in "Fresh" Organs. In A. Ong & S. J. Collier (Ed.), *Global Assemblages: Technology, Politics, and Ethics as Anthropological Problems* (pp. 145–167). Malden, MA: Wiley-Blackwell.
Shildrick, M. (2002). *Embodying the Monster: Encounters with the Vulnerable Self*. London: Sage Publications.
Shildrick, M. (2008). Corporeal Cuts: Surgery and the Psycho-Social. *Body & Society*, *14*(1), 31–46.
Waldby, C. (2002a). Biomedicine, Tissue Transfer and Intercorporeality. *Feminist Theory*, *3*, 239–254.
Waldby, C. (2002b). Stem Cells, Tissue Cultures and the Production of Biovalue. *Health: An International Interdisciplinary Journal for the Social Study of Health, Illness and Medicine*, *6*(3), 305–323.
Whitman Helfgot, S., with Novak, W. (2010). *The Match: Complete Strangers, A Miracle Face Transplant, Two Lives Transformed*. New York: Simon & Schuster.

"The Most Famous Brain in the World": Performance and Pedagogy on an Amnesiac's Brain

Katherine W. Sweaney

Project H.M. was just the sort of thing one might expect the Internet to latch onto: it was a live streaming video of a frozen human brain being slowly sliced apart. Users who clicked the link on Twitter or Facebook between the 2nd and 4th of December 2009 were immediately confronted with a close-up shot of the brain's interior, which was parchment-colored and framed by a block of ice. In this video, a machine called a microtome slid the brain's halved surface across the screen, shaving off layer after layer of translucently thin tissue—like prosciutto, in the words of the project's Italian director. As each completed slice crumpled against the microtome's blade, it was wiped up by a gloved human hand bearing a large paintbrush and whisked off-screen so the process could begin again. To the left, a smaller video feed featured an aerial view of the lab, showing white-coated scientists tending the machine and the trays of fresh brain slices. Project H.M. became a small sensation for its 3-day duration. Visitors to the link re-posted it enthusiastically, left both admiring and critical comments for the scientists, and surfed through the rest of the website to watch informative documentaries and learn more about the process. During the 53 hours it took to fully section the brain, more than 400,000 people clicked in to watch (Cavanaugh 2009). What narrative was this project performing, and what—if anything—did it intend to teach?

Project H.M. was staged by The Brain Observatory, the neuroscience laboratory of Dr. Jacopo Annese at the University of California at San Diego. The brain itself had until recently belonged to Henry Molaison, an anterograde amnesiac who was left unable to form new conscious memories after undergoing a radical brain surgery in 1957. Anonymized under the moniker H.M., Molaison had spent the rest of his life under clinical observation. Studies of him have contributed more to the science of human memory than any single patient in history, and Annese has more than once referred to H.M.'s cognitive organ as "the most famous brain in the world." When he died in 2008, Molaison's brain was bequeathed to The Brain Observatory, where Annese keeps a comprehensive collection of unusual brains. After sectioning, the brain slices are photographed at high resolution to be examined for the neural substrates of memory, disease, and other features (Palca 2008). An informational pamphlet distributed by the lab uses a textual metaphor:

> The collection is envisioned as a library, each brain likened to a manuscript that contains a unique life story. Each specimen is carefully read, its narrative reconstructed, and its pages are finally digitized to illustrate and immortalize the multiple views and neuroscientific insight that each case study provides. ("The Human Brain Library" 2010)

But Project H.M.'s mode of presentation was not just textual. It was explicitly performative—a performance that used a webcam to put a literal frame around the lab's practices and that predicated its authenticity upon liveness (Auslander 2008). The process of opening the rare book of Molaison's brain for the public in real time was an innovative way of de-sequestering laboratory work, allowing anyone with an Internet connection to see in real time how the daily grind of science gets done—and, importantly, to respond critically to the site. The Brain Observatory's website hosted a blog where visitors could leave comments that questioned or otherwise critically engaged with Project H.M., in theory creating a space for the public to co-author the project's master narrative.

In the research fields that have been termed the public understanding of science (PUS) and the public understanding of research (PUR), a key ongoing discussion involves the need for practical and active engagement with science's knowledge-making practices by the lay population. The goal is to allow public involvement with the *process* of science, rather than simply its *products* (Chittenden, Farmelo, and Lewenstein 2004; Collins 1987). It's a truism that the world in which we live is saturated by the influence of science. In daily social and political life, non-scientists must navigate a world shaped by everything from pharmaceuticals and genetically modified foods to nuclear power and information technologies. According to H.M. Collins (1987), the phrase "public understanding of science" incorporates two differing types of understanding: "the *content* of scientific knowledge [and] the *nature* of science as a cultural enterprise" (690, emphasis in original). It seems self-evident that, in order to navigate our technologized world, members of the lay public should be reasonably literate in scientific content, as this will help them to make decisions as consumers and voters. But what is the layperson to do when two equally reputable scientists offer widely differing views on the same politically and ethically charged scientific issue, like stem-cell research or alternative energy? In these cases, for the layperson to assess the available evidence requires an understanding that scientific knowledge is made through a culturally mediated process, and is not simply waiting to be found in the natural world. It is therefore a central goal of PUS that the public is provided with the resources to develop an understanding of these processes, along with the uncertainty and the multiple, conflicting opinions they often entail. In the broader field of pedagogical practice, this paradigm is what Henry Giroux (2001) has referred to as "performative pedagogy": a democratic teaching practice that affords the public opportunities to intervene meaningfully in the creation of cultural texts.

In this article, I begin from the stance of one seeking strategies to practice and improve performative science pedagogy. While I am not suggesting that Project H.M. was intended to fit into Giroux's paradigm, I will consider the tools for public engagement that the project employed and assess how they fit into and complicate the paradigm. The Brain Observatory is unique in that it allowed real-time public access to an important laboratory procedure and because it harnessed the burgeoning power of social media to do so. The professional spaces of science-making are often thoroughly off limits to the public, and this obstructs the popular view of what laboratory practices really entail. It is therefore useful to the fields of PUS and PUR to examine The Brain Observatory's example and to consider how the tools it uses might be employed in future performative projects. I begin my article by identifying the qualities of performative science pedagogy and some of the difficulties it faces. I then historicize The Brain Observatory within the tradition of anatomical display to introduce the viewing practices upon which these spectacles generally rely, taking note of the fact that these practices may impede active audience engagement and arguing that this is a potential hurdle for pedagogues attempting performative scientific displays. Finally, I turn toward an explication of Project H.M. itself, analyzing the rhetoric its producers employed, its *mise en scène*, and the available data about audience reactions, in an attempt to determine its own pedagogical goals and evaluate its accomplishments. Ultimately, my examination of The Brain Observatory outlines the challenges of, and suggests practices that foster, a critical science pedagogy that allows meaningful engagement with the processes of scientific production. In part, I believe that Project H.M. is a particularly valuable topic for an assessment of the state of public science pedagogy because it deals with medical imaging. While it is unlikely that the Project's viewers will have their own brain sectionings broadcast online in the future, the vast majority of them have had or will undergo an x-ray, CAT scan, or MRI, learning what it is like to have a team of experts use the imperfect processes of laboratory science to assess their bodily interiors and, possibly, disagree about their findings. If they are to become educated scientific citizens when it comes to the resulting (and possibly life-changing) decisions resulting from these knowledge-making practices, it is essential that they get a glimpse of what those practices entail. The question, then, is what kind of glimpse did The Brain Observatory give them?

PERFORMATIVE PEDAGOGY

Performative pedagogy is a mode of teaching and learning that is not merely didactic, but that invites interventions on the part of the learner (Giroux 2001). It aims to go "beyond the institutional boundaries of the disciplinary organization of question and answers" (Grossberg 1996, 145) and "produce critical public spaces, regardless of how fleeting they may be" (Giroux 2001, 7), spaces that transform the pedagogical experience into an opportunity for learners to become aware of their social context, intercede in it, and potentially improve it. In particular, this requires an interpretation of "performativity" that goes beyond simply expressing and interpreting "events as cultural texts" (Giroux 2001, 10). It must move beyond choosing between a right or wrong interpretation of an event as a fixed document and focus, instead, on lived realities; beyond a conception of knowledge as a monolith and toward an involvement of the subjective experiences of each learner in the process of meaning-making.

Though the scholarly sense of "performative" has been divorced somewhat from theater, one of the seminal articulators of the imbrication of deep critical learning with performance is still Bertolt Brecht. In "Theatre for Pleasure or Theatre for Instruction" (1964), Brecht writes that art that focuses on "the strong centralization of the story," making all of its parts seem connected, its morals self-evident, and its conclusions inescapable, is fundamentally failing its audience (70). He goes on, "when something seems 'the most obvious thing in the world' it means that any attempt to understand the world has been given up" (71). Similarly, the hegemonic "cultural texts" to which Giroux refers are presented as self-evident, and if a subject's individual identity does not conform to them, it is the individual, rather than the text itself, that is identified as problematic. Giroux's performative pedagogy seeks to reverse this assumption. Likewise, Brecht's solution was to create a theatre of contradictions of which the spectator says there is, "nothing obvious in it—I laugh when they weep, I weep when they laugh" (Brecht 1964, 71). The performance does not do the cognitive work for the spectator, presenting him or her with a solution at the story's end: Rather, the spectator must actively work to draw conclusions.

What does performative pedagogy look like when applied to the teaching of science? It begins, as Brecht does, with challenging the portrayal of scientific knowledge as self-evident and allowing publics to critically engage with it in a manner congruent with their lived experiences of the world.[1] Practitioners of the sciences are frequently characterized as believing that their work aims for a plane of pure knowledge and is, therefore, neither inherently political nor accessible in its intricacies to the lay public. According to sociologist Steven Hilgartner (1990),

> A two-stage model [of the popularization of science] is assumed: first, scientists develop genuine scientific knowledge; subsequently, popularizers disseminate simplified accounts to the public. Moreover, the dominant view holds that any differences between genuine and popularized science must be caused by "distortion" or "degradation" of the original truths. (519)

Creating a democratic scientific citizenship requires moving beyond the right-or-wrong view of science that Hilgartner identifies and, instead, contextualizing science as a cultural practice continuous with the non-professional world and finding ways to let non-professionals intervene in its established discourses. As science studies scholars have thoroughly documented, professional science-making is just as much a cultural, historically-contingent process as art-making (Daston and Galison 2007; Latour and Woolgar 1986; Shapin and Schaffer 1985), and, despite disciplinary assumptions to the contrary, science can be significantly influenced by popular cultural conceptions of its objects (Dumit 2004; Friedman 2004).

Performative science pedagogy would require accounting for the complex, multi-faceted ways in which laypeople interact with science and scientists.

Sociologists such as Shelia Jasanoff and Bryan Wynne have found that laypeople's acceptance of scientific advice is predicated on their trust of scientists and their institutions, and that this social knowledge is not to be dismissed lightly (Jasanoff 1998; Wynne 1992, 1993). Wynne's (1992) famous study of Cumbrian sheep farmers affected by fallout from Chernobyl found "laypeople capable of extensive informal reflection upon their social relationships toward scientific experts, and on the epistemological status of their own 'local' knowledge in relation to 'outside' knowledge" (281). If scientific institutions wish to improve their communication with the general public and generate better social policy as a result, they should "[express] an equivalent reflexive discourse in the public domain" (Wynne 1992, 281). Such reflexivity would require taking local knowledges, or "lay expertise" (Epstein 1996), seriously and allowing that the "ideal" scientific solution to a problem may not be appropriate in a given local context.

Yet, this raises an important counterpoint, and one that must be accounted for by attempts to use performative pedagogy to improve the public understanding of science: To what extent should laypeople actually be involved in science-making and its resultant policies? This is the point that sociologists of science Harry Collins and Robert Evans (2002) make in their call for a "third wave of science studies." In their view, social constructivism has so permeated science studies that the field is now characterized "by a tendency to dissolve the boundary between the experts and the public so that there are no longer any grounds for limiting the indefinite extension of technical decision making rights" (235). In other words, the Science and Technology Studies impulse to deconstruct and historicize science's political investments and social implications has obscured an important reality: There are, legitimately, certain types of scientific knowledge that an expert's lifetime of specialized work allows her to uniquely grasp in a way that lay communities simply cannot. Allowing Collins and Evans' point opens up a question for the paradigm of performative pedagogy: Is it possible that the "critical space" made available to laypeople would actually foster misinterpretations of rigorously tested scientific information?

Though some critics have contested the apparent call for apolitical normativity in Collins and Evans' article (Jasanoff 2003; Rip 2003), it nonetheless provokes lingering pedagogical questions. Despite arguments such as Hilgartner's that science popularization is much more complicated than facts being "dumbed down" for lay audiences, a potentially wide communications gap between scientists and the public remains because they simply speak different languages. Physicist Richard Feynman illustrates this effectively in a clip about magnets from his 1983 BBC series, *Fun To Imagine*. When the interviewer asks Feynman why magnets repel one another, the physicist responds with 7 minutes of proliferating metaphors that draw on the lived world, using their inadequacy to conclude that such metaphors are simply not sufficient to answer such "why?" questions from a scientist's perspective. He says, "I really can't do a good job—any job—of explaining magnetic force in terms of something else that you're more familiar with, because I don't understand it in terms of anything else that you're more familiar with" (Feynman 1983). Whereas science educators might prioritize giving students metaphorical explanations that they can immediately relate to their own lives, professional scientists would likely find such explanations inadequate, even misleading. Yet, prioritizing accurate technical information of which a scientist would approve is more likely to sacrifice students' sense of personal engagement with the material. If performative pedagogy wishes to create meaningful dialogue between scientists and laypeople, how can it satisfy both groups?

PERFORMING ANATOMIES

As a public anatomical display, The Brain Observatory is a part of a long history. In many ways, it is an Internet-age version of the popular public anatomical theatre of Early Modern Europe, in which members of the lay community paid to witness the surgeons from the local university dissecting freshly executed corpses from the gallows (Sawday 1995). Officially, the demonstration was conducted to teach human anatomy to medical students, but people from all walks of public life flocked to these purpose-built theaters, much as they did to the playhouses. Though the trend of public dissection died out in the 17th century, the public's fascination with looking at the insides of bodies does not appear to have waned. Anatomical museums sprang up around universities and surgeon's colleges, many of which still exist and continue to be popular with tourists.[2] In recent years the controversial anatomist Gunther von Hagens has become well known for his touring *Body Worlds* exhibitions, in which real human (and animal) bodies, preserved and posed via his "plastinating" technique, are arranged like a gallery of statues. In fact, Von Hagens seems so determined to return public anatomical spectacle to its Early Modern roots that, in 2005, he conducted the first dissection aimed at a lay audience in 300 years when he completely dissected the donated body of a 55-year-old man in a televised spectacle for BBC's Channel 4 (Maxwell 2008).

The main benefit of such anatomical displays is that they expose the lay public to real specimens of the human interior, a sight otherwise reserved for professionals. Yet, from a pedagogical standpoint, their drawback is that they tend to lack meaningful opportunities for public engagement in favor of a more passive mode of spectatorship. While few scholars would argue that spectating is a wholly passive endeavor, the standard *mise en scène* of anatomical display is to present the human body as a self-evident, universal text. Unless the dissection being performed is a forensic autopsy—the goal of which is to account for one particular individual's history—the rhetorical framing tends to present *the* human body, a generalized Platonic ideal, rather than *a* unique human body full of variations from the "norm." This universalizing narrative often precludes room to question what a "normal" body might be, in terms of gender, race, size, age, sexualities, and so on (Canguilhem 1978), and the individual identity of the dissected subject is often subordinated to the identities of the scientists.

Renaissance-era public dissections, in which a professor read aloud from a standardized anatomical textbook while helpers performed the actual cutting and indexing of body parts as they were named, exemplified this universalizing impulse. Such practices could result in numerous technical inconsistencies, but this did not matter. Knowledge of the body was taken for granted as pre-existing and was simply imposed on particular specimens. Or, put another way, it was assumed that an authentic knowledge was immanent in the body itself: to see it, and to be in its presence in real time, was to know something fundamental about it. This contact with the "real thing" was understood as the benefit derived from the experience by a general public unfamiliar with the technical intricacies of anatomy, and, in many ways, this perspective persists today. Generating aesthetically motivated wonder, awe, and even repulsion is clearly a primary goal of most anatomical displays. Often, they overwhelm the senses with sheer repetition: body after body, jar after jar, organ after organ. It is difficult to imagine how one might find a space in which to critically intervene amid this sensory onslaught. The possibility of a dialogic relationship between viewer and viewed recedes in such an environment, and while the bodies on display retain their feel of authenticity, the "knowledge" encoded within them begins to seem hermetic, penetrable only by experts. Such displays obscure the reality that scientific knowledge is made, not found. One of the problems with anatomical display is that it particularly tends to emphasize the *products* of medical research—the preserved specimen, the opened corpse—rather than the *process* of making meanings from them. The point is not that wonder and aesthetic appreciation are themselves problematic; indeed, they foster creativity and discovery (Daston and Park 1998), which are vital to the learning process. But creativity will not come about unless learners believe they can have a personal impact on the object of learning.[3]

Finally, anatomical displays have a long history of suppressing the identities of the dissected subjects on display. Because there was a shortage of legal bodies obtained from the gallows, stolen corpses often populated the Early Modern anatomy theatre slabs; and Gunther von Hagens became notorious when the press unearthed possible evidence that not all of his plastinated subjects had agreed to being displayed in their flayed state. To my mind, one way that anatomical display could begin to incorporate the principles of performative pedagogy would be to acknowledge this issue as a pressing one. If the goal of performative pedagogy is to elevate the importance of individual lived experience over the dominance of hegemonic cultural texts, then, in the context of anatomy, it surely must acknowledge that the "specimens" that make up anatomical displays were once human beings whose lived experiences are just as vital as the knowledge scientists hope to glean from their bodies.

PERFORMING IDENTITIES

According to this rubric, Project H.M. is off to a good start. Dr. Annese was explicit that Project H.M. meant to capitalize on the concept of the brain as a biographical document, as indicated by his lab's characterization of "the brain as manuscript" ("The Human Brain Library" 2010). By examining the slides of brain tissue generated during Project H.M. at high resolution, Annese and his lab can look for exactly which cells are missing near the lesions that were removed from Molaison's brain during his original surgery, and thereby learn whether the abilities he lacked are predicated on certain missing cells. Because there are decades of data on Molaison's cognitive abilities, the lab will correlate his cellular anatomy with his documented behavior. In this way, says Annese, he will "write a biography of this person based on the evidence that I find in the brain" (Cavanaugh 2009). Suzanne Corkin, one of the neurologists who worked closely with Molaison during the latter part of his life, arranged for her patient's brain to be bequeathed to Annese's lab specifically *because* of their biographical focus. "Anybody who hears H.M.'s story, I think," she said in a public radio interview, "can connect to it. And one of the—his important contributions is providing a bridge between the science of memory and everyday life" (Cavanaugh 2009). In her scientific publications on Molaison, Corkin has always been an advocate for reminding readers that he was a human being as well as a patient. Though "philosophers, psychologists and neuroscientists have proposed that, without memory, a person lacks an identity," she describes Molaison in an academic journal as having "high moral standards," "a conscience," "good insight into his memory disorder," and "a sense of humour," and includes many humanizing anecdotes about her patient's gentleness and good spirits (Corkin 2002, 158). She concludes that "whether H.M. in fact has a sense of self is a matter for the reader to ponder" (158), but her own opinion on the matter seems abundantly clear.

The rhetoric around Project H.M. expressly focused on treating Molaison and his brain with respect and dignity, and on using his biography as a nexus at which scientific practice and "everyday life" could collide. Annese acknowledges this responsibility in the following rationale for webcasting the brain sectioning:

> It was such a gift, this brain, but also such a responsibility that I really thought we would have to be very candid of what we were doing. And in case anything went wrong, I wanted to show that we were not unprepared or we were not being reckless or we were not being, you know, incompetent. So now we were at the judgment of my peers, my colleagues. (quoted in Cavanaugh 2009)

The original inspiration for making the whole process public was the spirit of scientific transparency, which, in this case, provides Annese with a kind of professional insurance in case something went awry during the process. This discourse of accountability is common to the scientific performance of self, and here, by deliberately representing themselves in real time for an online audience, the scientists of The Brain Observatory were not just doing but literally "performing" their work. They explicitly invited scrutiny of their lives as scientists.

Three video feeds on The Brain Observatory's site during the live sectioning of Molaison's brain reinforced this explicit invitation to outside observers to scrutinize the labworkers. In addition to the central feed featuring a close-up of the brain, there were two smaller flash videos included on the website. One was a shot of the microtome's control panel, the dials of which were covered with messages from the lab team, scrawled on post-it notes, providing updates on which parts of the brain's anatomy were currently visible, how many sections they had collected, how many hours they had all been awake, and what music they were currently listening to (usually it was The Beatles). Below the console video was a shot of the whole lab provided by a camera mounted in the ceiling. This aerial view resembled nothing so much as video surveillance. Given Annese's statement that the live streaming video was to allow for instant peer review, the sense of surveillance can be taken as deliberate. Moreover, it can be taken as implicitly including the lay public among those whose opinion he values. Verbally and visually, the rhetoric of Project H.M. focused on allowing the public to evaluate the in-process narratives of science-making.

The Brain Observatory also made an effort to create an open space for critical public engagement. Before the actual sectioning began, the lab set up a blog detailing the technical and ethical specifications of the project on which anyone, after registering a username, could comment. It also set up an extensive social media presence via Twitter and Facebook, both of which allow instantaneous global response and debate, the course of which can never be entirely controlled. On the one hand, new media are firmly embedded in the everyday world of social relations (Kellner 1995), granting them the potential to host an engaged performative pedagogy. They can also provide a space for the curated expression of self-identity, a performance of self in which users "modify their behavior for a specific imagined audience" (Westlake 2008, 23). On the other hand, these privately owned social media forums are not only regulated by the companies who own them, but the expressions of individuality they host may also be closer to the neoliberal idea of self-identification through consumption, so identity claims made in these settings must be taken with a grain of salt.

It is true that Project H.M.'s digital mode of display allowed people to talk back and, though much of the feedback was overwhelmingly positive, The Brain Observatory made a point of cataloguing a selection of what it called "The Good, The Bad, and The Ugly" responses on its site in the days after the webcast. It is worth considering the tenor of the negative responses for the alternative narratives of the project to which they gesture, especially where ethics are concerned. Many who raised objections were disturbed by what they perceived as the exhibitionist nature of exposing someone's body online:

> I found out about the slicing of the brain of 'H.M.,' which you are pursuing right now. I am the sister of a 31 year old Australian man who donated his own brain following death due to a brain tumour. I find this quite a bizarre way to carry out research, and it disturbs me that you feel the need to stream the cutting on the internet. I question any value this could have, other than self-promotion. It's sad that people's morbid curiosity can now be satisfied by projects like this.[4]

Connecting Molaison's brain to his life story and making them both public was intended to personalize the experience for viewers, but this anonymous visitor indicates that making bodies public can also collapse an important aesthetic distance between viewer and body, and may deny dignity to the subject on display. Moreover, though none of the visitors raised this issue, this comment also suggests the problematic ethics of getting permission for brain donation from a man who would never remember making such an agreement.[5]

Indeed, The Brain Observatory's webspace had problems beyond the ethical quandaries around permission and the intrinsic limitations of social media. The sign-in mechanism for the supposedly open blog was permanently faulty,[6] meaning that even looking at the archive of posts was difficult. The visitor who wished to learn about brain tomography in detail could do her own external research via the pre-assembled series of links on The Brain Observatory's homepage; but these all led to a range of newspaper articles and television segments on Project H.M. that, for the most part, were PR-managed by the lab and restated its narrative about honest science and honoring Molaison. And, crucially, it was only by clicking on these external links that a visitor could discover Molaison's identity. Nowhere on The Brain Observatory's site itself is there an explanation of who "H.M.," whose name flashed on the banner above the videos, might be. The homepage refers to him as "the most famous medical patient in the history of science," a decidedly vague, albeit grand, designation. Amnesia and neurology are not mentioned; instead, Molaison (never called by his full name) becomes the ur-patient of all medicine—indeed, of the whole "history of science." Consequently, even though the project's surrounding rhetoric emphasized Molaison's individual identity, the staging of the broadcast itself leans toward the classic problem of suppressing the identity of the subject of an anatomical performance.

Project H.M. inherits many difficulties from the history of anatomical display. The primary experience The Brain Observatory created was simply about looking at the brain: clicking back in hour after hour to see a new cross-section exposed, watching the hypnotic, regular motion of the machine, appreciating the aesthetic value of the organ on display. Svetlana Alpers (1991) has identified this as "the museum effect," which causes any object under the spell of display—whether it is a man-made painting or an object from nature—to appear to have been deliberately crafted for the sole purpose of contemplation by the onlooker. It gives viewers a sense of automatic connection with the displayed object, because even if it is foreign or startling or mysterious, it has been domesticated, held still, and offered up for visual consumption.

The fact that Project H.M. clearly emphasized the aesthetic value of the laboratory process is not, in itself, a problem. As someone who was glued to the screen during the live broadcast, I can assert that the spectacle was truly fascinating. I was excited by the rare opportunity to see inside this lab and to watch the impossibly strange sight of a brain being shaved like a ham in a butcher's machine. And the knowledge that I was not watching an old recording, but a live webcast, exerted a strong pull on my attention. When, I wondered, would I ever see something like this again? Likewise, the idea of the brain's pure presence and liveness seems to be what struck the majority of Twitter commentators during Project H.M.: "wanna watch a brain get sliced? i know i do"; "Fascianted [*sic*] and grossed out. Watching a LIVE dissection of a human brain"; "Live brain slicing! Hard to pull away but must go to 4 year old's birthday party"; "World's most famous amnesiac donated his brain to science. They're slicing it RIGHT NOW."[7] The project combined the perceived authenticity of live performance with the museum effect—the sense that this object was there just for its audience—and its draw was magnetic for many.

Part of Project H.M.'s appeal for lay audiences was indeed the chance to see the process of science. But it might also be said that the perspective on the scientific process afforded by the project was mainly superficial—that is, in the literal sense of being limited entirely to surfaces. The Brain Observatory relied heavily on the scientific "promise of the visible" (Maxwell 2008): the idea that seeing an object at the greatest possible level of accuracy and resolution allows viewers to truly know it. Audiences were provided with little insight into exactly how knowledge would be generated from the brain slices after they had been created. A complex understanding of the process of science would require a window into the culture of the lab (Latour and Woolgar 1986), an understanding of the uncertainties involved in interpreting evidence (Collins 1987), and knowledge of the ways that institutional structures help determine what will be studied. On the one hand, granting audiences such insights might entail following Wynne's suggestion that scientific institutions develop greater self-reflexivity about their practices and how they relate to the public. On the other hand, gaining this complex understanding of scientific processes could involve a serious investment of time and might risk overwhelming viewers with technical information and driving them away. It is admirable that The Brain Observatory encouraged feedback from its audience through its blog and various social media; however, it called little attention to the structures that influence science-making outside of this publicized moment in the lab. The critical public space the lab built was limited to a discussion of the 3 days of sectioning. From The Brain Observatory's standpoint, this is understandable: making a more prominent space for a public counter-narrative about the sectioning of Henry Molaison's brain might result in an unfavorable framing of Annese or his colleagues, and this could limit their funding or prevent further donations of important brains.

Yet, for advocates of performative pedagogy, this is a real stumbling block. How can scientific institutions do their work while opening meaningful spaces for public engagement? One solution might be for the pedagogical work to take place via intermediary institutions like museums or science centers, where the main focus of the endeavor can be forming dialectical encounters that take the concerns of both scientists and lay publics into account. But such a suggestion evades one of Project H.M.'s unique contributions, which is that it showcased a real laboratory engaged in all the everyday processes of science-making—and that it allowed over 400,000 people to access it in the space of 3 days, a number that would be impossible without the Internet or television.

If something like Project H.M. were to be repeated, a performative pedagogical strategy that deals competently with these forms of mediation would need to be developed. The fascination inspired by the repetitive nature of brain sectioning would need to be channeled into a more complex form of engagement—one that relates the viewer's identity to the project on a more critical level than, simply, a sense of possession over the scientific object facilitated by the "museum effect." Simple changes to the digital *mise en scène* might push the project in this direction. For instance, a comments section, or even a live moderated chat with a lab worker, could be included on the same webpage as the video feeds, lending the acts of watching and discussing an equal status. Certainly, more details about who Henry Molaison was and why his brain was extraordinary enough to warrant this public display would have to be a priority. Above all, I believe that for members of the lay public to meaningfully reshape their identities through performances like this one, the point of personal connection cannot be that we all have human brains (or bodies) and, therefore, that we can all "naturally" relate to the one on display. This falls back too easily on what Brecht would call the "centralization of the story," indicating that we should all be assessing our bodies against some Platonic ideal of the human. Instead, audience members must be afforded opportunities to reflect on whether or not they agree with the narrative of humanness being offered to them, to realize that their own subjectivities are always central to that narrative, and to incorporate their phenomenological experiences into that narrative. For performative science pedagogy more broadly, this means that audiences must be given the chance not just to watch real experiments, but also to experiment themselves.

NOTES

1. For discussions of the possibilities and problems of educating critically engaged scientific citizens, see Elam and Bertilsson (2003), Hagendijk (2004), and Hilgartner (1990).
2. To name just two examples: The Mütter Museum in Philadelphia displays the livers of Cheng and Eng, the original Siamese Twins, in a vat, and also owns the body of the famous Soap Lady; and the Hunterian in London keeps the bones of Irish giant Charles Byrne, a man who specifically requested that he be buried at sea in order to avoid public gawking at his body postmortem but whose undertaker was ultimately bribed by a "collector."
3. Two contemporary science museums that do excel at fostering critical audience engagement are the Exploratorium in San Francisco, where the "displays" are all hands-on experimentation machines, and the Wellcome Collection in London, which houses commissioned art and scientific artifacts in equal proportions, with the goal of allowing a broader interpretation of what it means to be human.
4. This page of the website is no longer online.
5. In terms of legalities, Corkin (2002) is careful to note that "[Molaison] and his court-appointed conservator have both signed his brain donation form" (159). But, philosophically, the question of Molaison's consent to Project H.M. could still be considered an open one.
6. Users complained about this on Twitter during the webcast, as documented in one of the responses The Brain Observatory includes at http://thebrainobservatory.ucsd.edu/the_bad.php.
7. I have quoted users @MrNorth, @jinal_shah, @katejinx, and @Moriah_, whose Project H.M.-related tweets are catalogued at ScienceBlips, accessed March 2010, http://scienceblips.dailyradar.com/story/the-most-famous-brain-in-memory-science-h-m/tweets/.

REFERENCES

Alpers, S. (1991). The Museum as a Way of Seeing. In I. Karp & S. Lavine (Eds.), *Exhibiting Cultures: The Poetics and Politics of Museum Display* (pp. 25–32). Washington, DC: Smithsonian Institution Press.

Auslander, P. (2008). *Liveness: Performance in a Mediatized Culture*. New York: Routledge.

Brecht, B. (1964). Theatre for Pleasure or Theatre for Instruction. In J. Willett (Ed.), *Brecht on Theatre* (pp. 69–77). New York: Hill and Wang.

Canguilhem, G. (1978). *On the Normal and the Pathological*. Boston: D. Reidel Publishing Company.

Cavanaugh, M. (2009, December 10). First Complete Brain Sectioning Also a Social Media Experiment. San Diego: KPBS.

Chittenden, D., Farmelo, G., and Lewenstein, B. V. (Ed.) (2004). *Creating Connections: Museums and the Public Understanding of Current Research*. Walnut Creek, CA: AltaMira Press.

Collins, H. M. (1987). Certainty and the Public Understanding of Science: Science on Television1. *Social Studies of Science*, *17*(4), 689–713.

Collins, H. M. and Evans, R. (2002). The Third Wave of Science Studies: Studies of Expertise and Experience. *Social Studies of Science*, *32*(2), 235–296.

Corkin, S. (2002). TIMELINE: What's new with the amnesic patient H.M.? *Nature Reviews Neuroscience*, *3*(2), 153–160.

Daston, L. and Galison, P. (2007). *Objectivity*. New York: Zone Books.

Daston, L. and Park, K. (1998). *Wonders and the Order of Nature, 1150–1750*. New York: Zone Books.

Dumit, J. (2004). *Picturing Personhood: Brain Scans and Biomedical Identity*. Princeton, NJ: Princeton University Press.

Elam, M. and Bertilsson, M. (2003). Consuming, Engaging and Confronting Science: The Emerging Dimensions of Scientific Citizenship. *European Journal of Social Theory, 6*(2), 233–251.

Epstein, S. (1996). *Impure Science : AIDS, Activism, and the Politics of Knowledge*. Berkeley: University of California Press.

Feynman, R. (1983). Magnets. *Fun to Imagine*. BBC. http://www.bbc.co.uk/archive/feynman/ (accessed April 2011).

Friedman, L. D. (2004). *Cultural Sutures: Medicine and Media*. Durham, NC: Duke University Press.

Giroux, H. A. (2001). Cultural Studies as Performative Politics. *Cultural Studies/Critical Methodologies, 1*(1), 5–23.

Grossberg, L. (1996). Toward a Geneaology of the State of Cultural Studies. In C. Nelson & D. P. Gaonkar (Eds.), *Disciplinarity and Dissent in Cultural Studies* (pp. 131–148). New York: Routledge.

Hagendijk, R. P. (2004). The Public Understanding of Science and Public Participation in Regulated Worlds. *Minerva: A Review of Science, Learning & Policy, 42*(1), 41–59.

Hilgartner, S. (1990). The Dominant View of Popularization: Conceptual Problems, Political Uses. *Social Studies of Science, 20*(3), 519–539.

The Human Brain Library. (2010). *The Brain Observatory*. http://thebrainobservatory.ucsd.edu (accessed April 2011).

Jasanoff, S. (1998). The Political Science of Risk Perception. *Reliability Engineering and System Safety, 59*, 91–99.

Jasanoff, S. (2003). Breaking the Waves in Science Studies: Comment on H.M. Collins and Robert Evans, "The Third Wave of Science Studies." *Social Studies of Science, 33*(3), 389–400.

Kellner, D. (1995). *Media Culture: Cultural Studies, Identity, and Politics Between the Modern and the Postmodern*. New York: Routledge.

Latour, B. and Woolgar, S. (1986). *Laboratory Life: The Construction of Scientific Facts*. Princeton, NJ: Princeton University Press.

Maxwell, I. (2008). "Who Were You?": The Visible and the Visceral. In M. Bleeker (Ed.), *Anatomy Live: Performance and the Operating Theatre* (pp. 49–66). Amsterdam: Amsterdam University Press.

Palca, J. (2008, December 12). Examining an Amnesiac's Brain. *Talk of the Nation*. Washington, DC: National Public Radio.

Rip, A. (2003). Constructing Expertise: In a Third Wave of Science Studies? *Social Studies of Science, 33*(3), 419–434.

Sawday, J. (1995). *The Body Emblazoned: Dissection and the Human Body in Renaissance Culture*. New York: Routledge.

Shapin, S. and Schaffer, S. (1985). *Leviathan and the Air-Pump: Hobbes, Boyle, and the Experimental Life: Including a Translation of Thomas Hobbes, Dialogus Physicus de Natura Aeris by Simon Schaffer*. Princeton, NJ: Princeton University Press.

Westlake, E. J. (2008). Friend Me if You Facebook: Generation Y and Performative Surveillance. *TDR, 52*(4), 21–40.

Wynne, B. (1992). Misunderstood Misunderstandings: Social Identities and the Public Uptake of Science. *Public Understanding of Science, 1*, 281–304.

Wynne, B. (1993). Public Uptake of Science: A Case for Institutional Reflexivity. *Public Understanding of Science, 2*, 321–337.

Ending Fat Stigma: *Precious*, Visual Culture, and Anti-Obesity in the "Fat Moment"

Scott Stoneman

"A KIND OF IDENTIFICATION," OR FAMILIARIZING FATNESS

Audiences marveled at previously unknown actress Gabourey Sidibe's performance in *Precious: Based on the Novel* Push *by Sapphire* (Daniels 2009). The seemingly endless commercial buzz the film generated through celebrity endorsement (talk show host Oprah Winfrey encouraged everyone to see it, despite describing the trauma the film represents as an unbearable viewing experience) almost served to drown out a recurrent characteristic of the media coverage it received: Few, if any, reviews and articles could comment on the film without sensationalizing actor Sidibe's fat proportions. Across the board, writers reiterated her weight and dimensions as though they were describing a piece of furniture, a characterless piece of the *mise en scène*. Betsy Sharkey (2009) in the *LA Times* even glibly declared that "there is little that seems precious about Precious, whose 330 pounds and constant scowl is cross-the-street intimidating."

The "audacity" of *Precious*, as the *New York Times*'s Lynn Hirschberg (2009) titled the phenomenon, consisted in director Lee Daniels' brazen disregard of the fact that his general audience might not be "ready" for the story of "an obese Harlem girl" whose family and community unrelentingly terrorize her. Hirschberg supposes that "the audience's initial rejection of Precious, even repulsion at the sight of her," as she puts it, "slowly gives way to a kind of identification" in which audiences work past their initial shock at having to relate to the character in order to become more sympathetic readers of her body.

It is all the more outrageous, then, that in popular reception of the film Sidibe's body has been subjected to a battery of beratement centered on the intersection of her body size and ethnicity. In a scathing indictment of what he sees as the film's racist and opportunistic denigration of its impoverished characters, Armond White (2009), chief film critic of the *New York Press*, had no qualms about degrading Sidibe, who, he claimed, is "so obese her face seems bloated into a permanent pout." Anthony Lane (2009) wrote in *The New Yorker* that Sidibe is "grimly overweight, her face so filled out that the play of normal expression seems restricted." Like Hirschberg, Lane identifies Sidibe's fatness with the coercion of Precious into silence, while at the same time assuming that the perceptive viewer gradually "learns to spot the flare of anger" in Precious' eyes as the film unfolds. A. O. Scott (2009) followed a similarly fatphobic line in the *New York Times* when he called Precious's "massive body at once a prison and a hiding place," adding with an unclear mixture of compassion and disdain that Sidibe seems "inarticulate and emotionally shut-down." And, in *New York* magazine, David Edelstein (2009) remarked hatefully that the actor's "head" is like "a balloon on the body of a zeppelin, her cheeks so inflated they squash her eyes into slits." Edelstein echoes Lane's assumption that "normal expression" is debilitated by fatness when he writes that Sidibe's expression is "either surly or unreadable. [That] even with her voice-over narration, you're meant to stare at her ebony face and see nothing." What these critics share is the conviction that, to see and be susceptible to the particularity of Precious' trauma, viewers have to "push through" entrenched dispositions toward size that are far from neutral to the implications of body size.

While Daniels' film and Sapphire's (1996) novella are fundamentally concerned with surviving sexual violence, AIDS, and the late 1980s attack on public education by the white solipsism of the Reagan–Bush era, *Precious* has come out, today, at a time when fatness is more than ever a marker for racial and class division. I argue that, given our current context, in which fatness is unprecedentedly medicalized, politicized, and stigmatized, the interpretation of *Precious* could not help but be constrained by the fatphobically coded images manufactured through authoritative talk of an obesity crisis. Confronting Precious' own sense that she is, as Sapphire puts it, merely "ugly black grease to be wipe away, punish, kilt, changed" (31) implies the need to address the film in terms of fat stigma because contemporary hostilities to fat bodies coextend with what Ange-Marie Hancock (2004) calls a "politics of disgust" that vilifies Black people as parasitic of a white mainstream.

Hancock delineates four principal aspects of the politics of disgust, and while all are relevant to the current discussion, the fourth aspect of disgust/intolerance—"a distinct lack of political solidarity between citizens who are and citizens who are not part of the target population of the legislation at issue" (6–7)—is particularly useful for linking a reading of *Precious* with the cultural dynamics of the obesity epidemic. Images play a decisive role in limiting the possibilities for political solidarity in both the racial context of rendering welfare recipients as a needless bane on state funds and in constructing "the obese" as a homogenous group whose shared characteristics vex public health. For example, images of the "headless stomach" (or fat bodies represented in popular culture with heads cropped under the pretense of protecting the subject photographed) circulate as reminders that the visual culture of obesity represents fat as a reprehensible identity requiring some form of cover-up. The effect of fatphobic stereotypes and judgments brought to bear on these images, and the reality of being fat to which they refer, is that the possibility of acting individually or collectively within available democratic modes of public-making and public-shaping becomes increasingly to be seen as a "negative right" (Roberts 1997, 309). The persistence of unequally distributed social opportunities and the misdistribution of wealth are permitted within the democratic framework of liberty as freedom from state power. In contrast, what Dorothy Roberts describes as "positive" liberty is constituted through the active responsibilities of governments to foster self-determination through rigorous protection from "degradation" (309). Especially in the United States, then, emerging policies that medicalize the consumer lifestyles of Black people, framing them as problems for the management of obesity, may ultimately lessen the drain on health care to some extent, but this still amounts to blaming the social condition of disadvantaged groups on the individual choices of those within those groups.

The combination of culture and biology in the discourse on social contagion, especially as it is applied in visual culture to the representation of fat bodies, exposes a central, self-evident, yet frequently mystified fact of the obesity epidemic: that the public defended in the "war on obesity" is a public that summons the authority of public health and preventive medicine to marginalize fat bodies and voices more generally. After all, the war on obesity is not imagined as necessitated by a spreading contagion in the sense of something like the 2003 outbreak of SARS in cities like Toronto and Hong Kong. Instead, it is imagined as the contagious spread of *habits* through the density of the social. In a 2006 speech laden with the neoliberal rhetoric of "empowering individuals" to take responsibility for their health, former UK Prime Minister Tony Blair said that, rather than being an epidemic in the strictly biological sense, obesity represents the costly outcome of "millions of individual decisions, at millions of points in time" (quoted in Rawlins 2008, 136). The answer, in this context, becomes effecting weight loss at the population level by educating populations to make a different set of choices. But how does it become possible, without prescription or presupposition, to address racialized populations in terms of their agency in constructing a healthy (read: thin) body?

At their first Summit on Weight Bias and Discrimination, members of the Canadian Obesity Network and media outlined the project of working through how "a deeply ingrained stigma against obesity" affects "individual Canadians, the health system, employers and the economy" ("1st Canadian Summit" 2011). Asked, after delivering one of the conference keynote papers, whether concerned experts can ever really have it both ways—calling for the eradication of obesity while at the same time advocating for tolerance of fat people—Rebecca Puhl suggested that what needs to change is not the population prescription to reduce obesity, which she maintains is a sound and urgent project, but, rather, the nature of the "causal attributions" assigned to overabundant body weight. These tend to individualize the cause, indicting heavy people as "architects of their own ill health" (quoted in Kirkey 2011). "Healthism" is Robert Crawford's (2006, 2011) term for the ways in which, especially over the last 40 years, the pursuit of health has begun to operate as both an indicator and determinant of social capital. Crawford's seminal concept is useful here, in the sense that it helps clarify the elevation of thinness to what Nikolas Rose (1999) calls a "super-value," or a "norm of civility" that establishes a scale of subjectivities based on valuing bodies according to their perceived degree of discipline or self-care (69).

As a public health project, can the worldwide effort to reduce fat populations mean anything other than protecting the public from the burden and the blight of "the obese"? In looking at the cultural politics of obesity, my sense is that anti-obesity has made fat embodiment an increasingly untenable subject position by reinforcing a fatphobic "disposition of the visible" (Butler 2004, 306). The effect of this visual disposition is the creation of what Eve Sedgwick and Michael Moon (1994) have called a "privileged narrative understanding" of the fat person's individuality, "will," "history," "perception," and "prognosis" (240). This sizeist projection happens according to the same logic of stereotyping by which images of racial or ethnic otherness are made "overscrutable," in Sianne Ngai's (2005) terms (93). But what are the specific implications of considering race here? How does being both a person of size and a person of color heighten a vilifying visibility and differently affect social stigma? Ngai describes the ways that stereotypes of affect and intellect are inscribed on the body, substituting firsthand knowledge of the other's habits, routines, and styles of self-care with a presumed history overdetermined by "the always obvious, highly visible body" (95). Ngai's insistence that stereotypes have "symbolically violent effects"—that the limits of stereotype analysis are not as important as the cultural power that is at stake in the paralyzing circulation of stereotypes—offers an important insight for producing a dialogue between critical race studies and fat studies. Taking Ngai's thoughts on stereotypes as a point of departure for understanding how Sapphire's protagonist battles against multiple regimes of visuality that frame her body as either pitiable or completely abject, I will examine the particular disdain with which "superfluous" mass is treated and represented today (as the indicator of a "lack of self-control, leading to disease" [Kent 2001, 134]), arguing that concepts like social contagion, which depict images of fat bodies as pathogenic, inherently reinforce fatphobic stereotypes. In this sense, the intersection of the war on obesity with a continuing class antagonism toward racialized ethnic others is a consequential part of understanding the construction of the normatively healthy body, harnessed as it is to a privileged notion of whiteness.

In an October 2009 article in Canada's newspaper of record, *The Globe & Mail*, Sarah Boesveld suggests that rising body mass index (BMI) values among North Americans, combined with the sudden appearance of images in a variety of cultural registers that "suggest it's okay to be fat," has created a cultural climate of fat acceptance that verges on the displacement of thinness as a "super-value." In a more recent case of the *Globe* representing an overtly fatphobic perspective, columnist Judith Timson (2011) laments "the proliferation of overweight kids," waxing nostalgic that "it used to be that most kids *looked the same*" (emphasis added). This, Timson insists, "is where the outrage should be directed": at the slow generational slide of Westerners into overnutrition, idleness, and illness. Her purpose, in other words, is to recount the "familiar story of Western decadence and decline" (2011). This trajectory will become increasingly desperate unless, in the words of American pediatrician Dr. Stephen Ponder, we "get proactive" and declare war against obesity (quoted in Sealey 2003). In "Fat Kid in Class No More" (2003), Geraldine Sealey's exposé for ABC News on the possibility of relaxed standards of body morphology in the face of widespread BMI increases, Ponder asks, "*what will be normal* in 20 years if something doesn't change" (emphasis added). Underlying these sentiments is a powerful fear that fat is on the verge of becoming entirely naturalized, a concern that "letting oneself go" has invaded the mainstream.

The assumption that the representation of fat subjects in visual culture is neutral toward the issue of body size is patently false. Assessing the rhetoric surrounding the fading power of norms regarding body shape and body care alongside obesity documentaries, in particular, exposes the ways in which the "obesity epidemic" contains a kernel of repulsion that denigrates fat people. If, in certain research communities, the familiarization or inoculation of fat is thought to be socially viral, then the focus of the cultural study of corpulence should be, in part, developing a way of assessing how fat as an image of the "revolting" is equally culturally "viral." Anthropologist Tina Moffat (2010) notes that stigma is occasionally endorsed in terms of its medical utility (9). In the words of Sally Satel (2007), if obesity and whatever "behaviors" are seen to cause it are understood to "portend humiliation," then individuals will be faced with a powerful societal imperative to more closely control their weight (149). Anti-obesity projects employ stigma, I contend, as a kind of visual antivirus, a defamiliarization of fatness in the service of preventing the perceived collapse of physical standards for body size. The reason we should interpret the function of stigmatizing images of the fat body as a characteristically liberal means of replacing a dangerous complacency about fat with intolerance is that they are not meant to evacuate voluntariness from the fat subject: on the contrary, stigma employed as a kind of antivirus protection functions to emphasize that obesity is "a truly autonomous biological condition," and to stereotype it as such (Satel 2007, 149).

BBC's *Dead Fat* (Ferguson 2011), a documentary invested in undermining acquiescence to fat, emphasizes the material's inherent morbidity and abnormality. At the center of the film is the autopsy of an unnamed obese woman who had died from a stroke 4 days before filming: Her body is shown floating in formaldehyde before being dissected and inspected, to the disgust of the documentarian who arranged the needlessly lurid spectacle. In the scene, witnesses to the procedure are palpably unsettled, commenting on the overpowering smell of her body—the "thick, heavy layers of yellow fat"—while listening anxiously to a description of how fat has "played a big part in killing her." An analogous example of the medical morality that enables the conflation of fat with social death, Steven Greenstreet's reactionary 2008 documentary, *Killer at Large*, narrates the epidemic as a "mystery of our civilization" and even a "crime on the body." The film opens with the dilemma of Brooke Bates, a 16-year-old in Texas who, after "struggling many years with weight problems" and dealing with the "emotional scars" of being fat, opts, under the guidance of her parents, to have liposuction. Gratuitous shots of Bates nearly naked and manipulating her flesh to show her surgeon particular "trouble areas" give way to disturbing scenes of the procedure itself. While we are left wondering what could possibly necessitate this extreme response to adolescent adiposity, Greenstreet flashes through a litany of medical problems associated with obesity, juxtaposing it with images of outbreak maps, pictures of appendages lost to diabetes, and images of expert talking heads who describe how "shocking" and "shameful" the scale of the problem has become.

What are the politics of intolerant and itinerant concerns over the perceived normalization of fat, a normalization emphasized in many mainstream news sources and reinforced by carefully commissioned "expert" opinion? I am especially concerned with the intolerance for fatness that views the representation of fat bodies in popular culture as reinforcing fat's banality in ways that erode norms of body shape. Looking to critical race studies as a means of understanding the ways that a "racist organization and disposition of the visible" (Butler 2004, 306) mediates in determining cultural power, I seek to refute arguments that posit fatness as a threat to the public sphere. In his work on fear, securitization, and the need for radical democracy, Zygmunt Bauman (1999) points out that "the perception of crisis precedes the awareness of the norm. And so . . . it is the perception of a crisis that prompts the search for a theory of the 'normal'" (142). If the image of what counts as normal is not just defined, but created and contained in opposition to the abject object it is protected against, then Sarah Boesveld's (2009) sense of the perils of the "fat moment" take on a different significance. Far from becoming suddenly more banal through the accumulation of supposedly fat-neutral images, what Sarah Boesveld terms our current "fat moment"—a time when fat is meant to appear extraordinarily ordinary—is instead defined by a culture of anti-obesity that uses techniques of shock and disgust ostensibly meant to address the social and economic drain posed by obesity.

"CATCHING" THE SOCIAL

In presenting a particular type of body with a particular set of habits as healthy and normal (or at least salutogenic and unproblematic), the concept of social contagion is especially emblematic of the way obesity not only politicizes medicine and medicalizes politics, but also creates new subject positions with regard to what is acceptable within the ideal, healthy public sphere. Beyond just employing the same "privileged narrative understanding" (Sedgwick and Moon 1994, 240) of the fat subject's risky behaviors, social contagion authors see the "obesity epidemic" as the potential result of a declining intolerance or disgust toward fat, a diminished fatphobia. And as Boesveld's sense of the perils of the "fat moment" helpfully illustrates, there is a specific and recurring visual bent to anxieties around fat's coming banality.

Social contagion is significant for the way it makes problematic populations intelligible as danger zones where fat and black pathologies are seen by a dominant culture to be fomented through a normalized set of cultural practices. For example, Greg Critser (2000) has argued that a degree of fat stigma "may serve to control obesity among white women," inferring that young black women are exposed to a dearth of fatphobia and that "a few more Black Kate Mosses wouldn't be a bad thing" (4). Here, the administrative imperative of health as a form of social regulation makes finding motivation for weight loss (no matter the potential harm of anti-obesity discourse) an adequate justification for undermining community autonomy and healthfully pro-fat standards for beauty and body size. Moreover, the depiction of the power of social contagion to spread health or illness through representation has a determining role in constructing "the epidemic."

The social contagion framework for understanding the genesis of the obesity "epidemic" is not just a convincing one; it is also an infectious one. Michael Gard's *The End of the Obesity Epidemic* (2011) attempts to document both the ebbing of obesity statistics (so the conclusion of the BMI-increase saga dubbed the "obesity epidemic") and an end to the need for further intervention, making the case that there can "never be a scientific answer for why the obesity epidemic happened" (169). Tracing obesity's etiology means identifying the spread across media and scientific argument of what Gard aptly names "rhetorical viruses," or models for interpreting the manifestation of fatness in populations that demonstrate a disposition toward body size that relies heavily on "underlying social and cultural currents" to constitute anti-obesity as a broad social movement (167).

Social contagion is a concept-metaphor that flourished as a model for obesity's primary cause following a presentation given in 2000 by William Dietz and Ali Mokdad, representatives of the Center for Disease Control. In an avowed effort to publicize obesity as an enemy of the public good, Dietz and Mokdad unveiled a series of "infographics" that represented the steady climb of obesity rates over the previous 15 years as an outbreak. In their images, "hot zones" appear across a set of maps of the United States: particular areas slowly turn deeper shades of blue until, dramatically, red states appear and then darken ominously, indicating the nefarious "spread" of obesity through social networks. Because the statistics Dietz and Mokdad revealed through these maps were already both widely available and acknowledged, their use and deployment can only be understood as a "redefinitional tactic," a distortion that, Lauren Berlant (2007) tells us, "aspires to make an environmental phenomenon appear suddenly as an event" (760). Rather than simply reproducing the numbers, then, the power of Dietz and Mokdad's maps consisted in their ability to reinscribe the data in more cogently spatial and visual terms. These maps have been widely disseminated, providing the foundation for subsequent efforts by many health professionals to map out the obesity issue. A 2010 article in *Newsweek* entitled, "Culture of Corpulence," underscores the sustained influence these images have had over public imaginings of the epidemic:

> Look around anywhere in America and the reality assaults you: we are simply too big. Nowhere is the evidence for this more striking than the Centers for Disease Control and Prevention's color-coded map. Between 1990 and 2008 the country morphs from a sea of pleasant blue, representing an obese population of less than 19 percent, to an alarming patchwork of tan, orange and maroon. (Kalb 2010, para. 1)

Not unlike the color-coded Homeland Security Advisory System that described the affective politics of a hyper-insularized, post-9/11 United States, Dietz's diagram of obesity "hot zones" continues to command a fear of fat's threat to a healthy public sphere.

In the developing stages of sociological methodology, "social contagion" gradually emerges from theoretical work that employs it as a convenient metaphor for collective behavior and begins to function as an increasingly literal and practical framework for grasping the mechanics of social organization (cf. Wald 2008). One of the many scientific models vying to explain the "spread" of obesity, social contagion problematizes contact with "overweight" and "obese" members of society on the basis of the assumption that, in a way, one "catches" obesity from one's social network. As it operates in obesity research, social contagion locates the "cause" of obesity in the sharing of norms and habits at the local level *and* in the effects of "exposure" to the visuality of "overweight" and "obese" co-workers, friends, relatives, and so on.

In a widely reported study, Nicholas Christakis and James Fowler (2007) address what they call "friendship effects" (377). One of their more provocative explanations for how obesity spreads through social contact is that having obese peers increases the individual's "tolerance" for fatness: meaning that as fatness becomes increasingly banal, it will begin to register as normal and its associated stigma—the healthy sense of its abnormality—erodes. It is worth quoting Christakis and Fowler at length, as my reading of the stigma of obesity in visual culture draws from their analysis:

> Whereas obesity has been stigmatized in the past, attitudes may be changing. To the extent that obesity is a product of voluntary choices or behaviors, the fact that people are embedded in social networks and are influenced by the evident appearance and behaviors of those around them suggests that weight gain in one person might influence weight gain in others. Having obese social contacts might change a person's tolerance for being obese or might influence his or her adoption of specific behaviors. (371)

What is too often displaced in the technocratic drive to map out and understand obesity is any discussion about the increased stereotyping of fat bodies. That said, Alexandra Brewis et al. (2011) point out that a "global diffusion of negative ideas about obesity" has become a reality of the epidemic (269). Through an analysis of survey participants' attitudes toward fat in ten culturally diverse nations, Brewis and her collaborators conclude that it is the collection of "moral attributions embedded in these now shared ideas about fat bodies"—things like the belief that fat bodies are socially undesirable, addicted, or frustrated, and that they make themselves so—that make it possible to condemn the supposed victims of the "obesity epidemic" (269).

READING SIDIBE'S PRECIOUS

Theories of social contagion express an implicit desire for a certain type of public, one built around a notion of freedom as a "negative right" (Roberts 1997, 309), and one that implicitly posits the types of bodies and communities we are meant to prefer and value. Reading *Precious* and its reception in relation to anti-obesity texts and interventions that use techniques of shock and disgust to convey the starkness of the societal drain represented by fat requires us to look at the regularizing function of "the public." Part of the perceived function of stigmatizing images is that they inspire disgust regarding fat. This sense of the utility of shame grows out of a social contagion thesis that connects obesity to the social transmission of "bad" lifestyles—an idea that has a racial history in sociology. The shaping power of the visual consists in its determination of what is tolerable and intolerable about the visible body of both self and other. The research hypothesis presupposing that exposure to fatness puts one at risk of miscalculating the objectionableness of obesity, of becoming oblivious to the relative normative size of one's own body, is not only openly hostile to fat people, but also belies the continuing structural inequality caused by fatphobia.

In turning now to the subject of *Precious*—a contemporary film that features Gabourey Sidibe in the eponymous role as a young person whose race, lack of education, illness, and obesity relegate her not just to the ranks of the "underclass," but more particularly to a cultural condemnation—I want to emphasize the way in which the visual field is saturated and contested by the fear of difference. In the face of arguments that stigmatizing stereotypes might be necessary as a means of social control, it becomes necessary to, in Butler's (2004) terms, read this visual field "aggressively" in order to further an alternative hegemony "over the visual field" (307).

How can the ideology of an obesity epidemic be said to influence possible readings of Precious, the character? Is there a gaze, a viewing of the film, which is not also already a presumptuous reading of the title character's girth? How does the prevalence of obesity epidemic discourse influence our ability to read Precious? Is our reading of Precious fatphobically schematized? How, I wonder, would an obesity scholar invested in understanding the effects of one's built environment speak to the meaning of the scene in which we see Precious rushing to her first day of class at an alternative school and stopping for fast food (which she steals, quickly consumes, and promptly throws back up)? Precious ostensibly lives in what nutritionists in obesity studies call a "food desert," wherein the only food available in one's immediate social environment is high in fat, relatively devoid of healthful nutritional content, and loaded with processed ingredients. Her choices are therefore conscripted, coerced.

Where in this formula can Precious's ability to react to her environment be imagined? If, on the one hand, fat embodiment is a question of social justice, then the issue here is not the abuse of Precious' body by her environment but, rather, the ways in which Precious' body mediates and determines the nature of her relationship to that environment. If, on the other hand, fat embodiment is understood in principally normative terms as an issue for public health, issues of identity, representation, and power tend to be jettisoned in favor of devising strategies of social control.

Despite her presumptuous sense that Precious's size and suffering will necessarily repulse viewers, in truth Hirschberg (2009) was right to raise the important question of whether the public is "ready for a movie about an obese Harlem girl." The tendency in reviews of the film not only to link the on-screen believability of Precious to Sidibe's size, but also to collapse the two into a subject that is wholly denied the capacity for intelligible speech, and thus subjectivity, or one whose ability to convey emotion is supposedly effaced by the fat that comprises her body, indicates that audiences were *not* ready—that widespread intolerance of fat bodies increasingly militates against one's ability, as a visual reader, to do justice to fat characters. It also confirms Sapphire's own anxieties about the possibility that, translated from her source text into the modality of the hyper-visible, the shape and scale of Precious' embodiment will cause her to be viciously misread. In a 2009 CBS News interview, Sapphire said that her biggest fear in clearing Daniels to adapt *Push* was that Precious might end up being viewed as part of a continuum of voiceless black "obese maids," and that the character might reinforce the notion that the stigmatized and disadvantaged cannot speak for themselves or articulate their own needs (Couric 2010).

Claims by fat advocates and obesity skeptics that the obesity epidemic has engendered pedagogies of healthiest individualism (in the form of viral video campaigns or public billboards) that implicitly shame the fat body are beginning to emerge as the fulcrum of a backlash against the still largely univocal debate regarding what must be done to curtail obesity rates. When, for example, the Disney corporation introduced its "Habit Heroes" attraction at one of its parks in February 2012, the show's characterization of stereotypically fattening lifestyle traits (inactivity, overeating, and so on) as embodied fat villains provoked the ire of fat-acceptance groups, concerned parents, and even obesity doctors. Facing a somehow unexpected public relations backlash, Disney quickly closed the show for "retooling" (Freedhoff 2012), but the effect of Habit Heroes—to conflate fat with an uncivil expression of individual freedom—had already taken place.

REFERENCES

1st Canadian Summit on Weight Bias and Discrimination a Success. (2011). http://www.obesitynetwork.ca/page.aspx?page=2483&app=182&cat1=457&tp=12&lk=no&menu=37 (accessed April 14, 2011).

Appadurai, A., Berlant, L., Breckenridge, C. A., and Diawara, M. (1994). On Thinking the Black Public Sphere. *Public Culture, 7*, xi–xiv.

Bauman, Z. (1999). *In Search of Politics*. Cambridge, MA: Polity Press.

Berlant, L. (2007). Slow Death (Sovereignty, Obesity, Lateral Agency). *Critical Inquiry, 33*, 754–780.

Boesveld, S. (2009, October 9). Thin's Not In. *The Globe and Mail*. http://www.theglobeandmail.com/life/were-having-a-fat-moment/article1319369/ (accessed January 9, 2011).

Brewis, A., Wutich, A., Falletta-Cowden, A., and Rodriguez Soto, I. (2011). Body Norms and Fat Stigma in Global Perspective. *Current Anthropology, 52*(2), 269–276.

Butler, J. (2004). *The Judith Butler Reader*. Malden, MA: Blackwell Publishing.

Christakis, N. and Fowler, J. (2007). The Spread of Obesity in a Large Social Network over 32 Years. *New England Journal of Medicine, 357*, 370–379.

Couric, K. (2010, September 21). *Interview with Sapphire*. http://www.cbsnews.com/video/watch/?id=5426254n&tag=cbsnewsSectionsArea.69 (accessed November 3, 2011).

Crawford, R. (2006). Health as a Meaningful Social Practice. *Health, 10*, 401–420.

Crawford, T. (2011, January 17). No More Fat Jokes. *The Toronto Star*. http://www.thestar.com/living/article/922259–no-more-fat-jokes (accessed April 10, 2011).

Critser, G. (2000). Let Them Eat Fat. *Harper's Magazine, 41*(9), 41–47.

Daniels, L. (Dir.) (2009). *Precious: Based on the Novel* Push *by Sapphire* [DVD]. Canada: Lionsgate.

Edelstein, D. (2009, November 1). When Push Comes to Shove. *New York Magazine*. http://nymag.com/movies/reviews/61750/ (accessed January 10, 2011).

Ferguson, L. (Dir.) (2011, April 4.). *Dead Fat*. Northern Ireland: BBC One.

Freedhoff, Y. (2012, February 23). Disney's Horrifying New Interactive Childhood Obesity Exhibit at Epcot. *Weighty Matters: Musings of an Obesity Medicine Doc and Certifiably Cynical Realist*. http://www.weightymatters.ca/2012/02/disneys-horrifying-new-interactive.html (accessed March 23, 2012).

Gard, M. (2011). *The End of the Obesity Epidemic*. New York: Routledge.

Greenstreet, S. (Dir.) (2008). *Killer At Large* [DVD]. USA: Disinformation Company.

Hancock, A.-M. (2004). *The Politics of Disgust: The Public Identity of the Welfare Queen*. New York: New York University.

Hirschberg, L. (2009, October 21). The Audacity of Precious. *New York Times*. http://www.nytimes.com/2009/10/25/magazine/25precious-t.html (accessed February 2, 2011).

Kalb, Ca. (2010, March 14). Culture of Corpulence. *Newsweek*. http://www.newsweek.com/2010/03/13/culture-of-corpulence.html (accessed March 10, 2011).

Kent, L. (2001). Fighting Abjection: Representing Fat Women. In J. Evans Braziel & K. LeBesco (Eds.), *Bodies Out Of Bounds: Fatness and Transgression* (pp. 130–145). Berkeley: University of California Press.

Kirkey, S. (2011, January 12). Toronto Summit to Weigh the Social Strains of Obesity Discrimination. http://www2.canada.com/topics/news/features/story.html?id=4102741 (accessed April 8, 2011).

Lane, A. (2009, November 9). Making Peace. *The New Yorker*. http://www.newyorker.com/arts/critics/cinema/2009/11/09/091109crci_cinema_lane (accessed February 2, 2011).

Moffat, T. (2010). The "Childhood Obesity Epidemic": Health Crisis or Social Construction? *Medical Anthropology Quarterly*, *24*(1), 1–21.

Ngai, S. (2005). *Ugly Feelings*. Cambridge, MA: Harvard University Press.

Rawlins, E. (2008). Citizenship, Health Education and the Obesity "Crisis." *ACME: An International E-Journal for Critical Geographies*, *7*(2), 135–151.

Rich, E. and Evans, J. (2005). "Fat Ethics"—The Obesity Discourse and Body Politics. *Social Theory & Health*, *3*, 341–358.

Roberts, D. (1997). *Killing the Black Body: Race, Reproduction, and the Meaning of Liberty*. New York: Pantheon.

Rose, N. (1999). *Powers of Freedom: Reframing Political Thought*. Cambridge, UK: Cambridge University Press.

Sapphire. (1996). *Push*. New York: Knopf.

Satel, S. (2007). In Praise of Stigma. In J. Henningfield, P. Santora & W. Bickel (Eds.), *Addiction Treatment: Science and Policy for the Twenty-first Century* (pp. 147–151). Baltimore: The Johns Hopkins University Press.

Scott, A. O. (2009, November 6). Howls of a Life, Buried Deep Within. *New York Times*. http://movies.nytimes.com/2009/11/06/movies/06precious.html (accessed February 2, 2011).

Sealey, G. (2003, September 30). Fat Kid in Class No More. ABC News. http://abcnews.go.com/Health/story?id=116682&page=1 (accessed February 10, 2011).

Sedgwick, E. K. and Moon, M. (1994). *Tendencies*. London: Routledge.

Sharkey, B. (2009, November 6). Precious Cuts Deep. *LA Times*. http://articles.latimes.com/2009/nov/06/entertainment/et-precious6 (accessed February 2, 2011).

Timson, J. (2011, February 24). We Live in a Food Nanny State. *The Globe and Mail*. http://www.theglobeandmail.com/life/relationships/news-and-views/judith-timson/we-live-in-a-food-nanny-state/article1919691/email/ (accessed March 10, 2011).

Wald, P. (2008). *Contagious: Cultures, Carriers, and the Outbreak Narrative*. Durham, NC: Duke University Press.

White, A. (2009, November 4). Pride and Precious. *New York Press*. http://www.nypress.com/article-20554-pride-precious.html (accessed February 3, 2011).

Afterword: The End of Contested Corporealities

Robert McRuer

As the title suggests, Tanya Titchkosky's article, which opens this special issue, is all about "The Ends of the Body." More specifically, the article critiques the ways in which disability, in particular, is always and everywhere made to *figure* "the end." "An array of cultural processes," Titchkosky insists, "make 'disability' represent limit without possibility. Disability is made to serve as a signifier of an end without appreciable difference and without future" (Titchkosky this issue, 82). Titchkosky brings forward the "eugenicist orientation" (87) of Peter Singer to exemplify these cultural processes, not only as that orientation is legible in Singer's well-known, highly-public questioning of the value of disabled lives (especially the lives of disabled infants, whom he suggests might be better off dead), but also in his 2008 *New York Times* obituary for Harriet McBryde Johnson, the disability activist and disability rights lawyer who repeatedly challenged his views, sometimes in an open debate. Titchkosky notes that Singer's obituary for Johnson focuses on an incident about which he "thought nothing"—a moment when Johnson asked for assistance at a dinner because her elbow had slipped out from under her and she needed help bringing it back to the table. Titchkosky argues that to "think nothing" of the moment was, for Singer, to do little more than reaffirm the "functionalist reduction" (87) that animates his oeuvre in general: disability signifies, conclusively, the end of "normal" or appropriate functionality; given that conclusion, disabled lives (or at least the lives of disabled infants) should perhaps be brought to an end; and that, for Singer, is the end of the issue. Given his consent to the myriad of cultural forces that mark the end of disability and disability as end, Singer is free—or, rather, able—to think nothing of what Titchkosky calls "differing conceptions of disability" (87), conceptions that might value intersubjectivity or trans-corporeality.[1]

Of course, via Audre Lorde and an array of other critical and theoretical commitments, Titchkosky writes beyond the end of disability or the end of the body marked by Singer, and I will return to her generative insights momentarily. Here, however, at the beginning of the end of this special issue, I want to flag Titchkosky's central, twinned critique: disability is made to figure the end (limit without possibility) and, *because of that figuration*, disability must be ended/eliminated. In other words, Titchkosky traces the movement from a figuration of disability-as-end to the ongoing eugenicist orientation of our culture back to disability-as-end: nothing more to think about. That dangerous and quotidian cultural movement can certainly be followed through the career of Peter Singer, but it is at work everywhere.

Indeed, that "everywhere" is on full display in this special issue; a remarkable number of the other articles collected in "Pedagogy, Image Practices, and Contested Corporealities" are *also* about the end of the body or, even more specifically, the end of disability. Nicole Markotić's critique of *Mar Adentro* (*The Sea Inside*) excavates the ways in which the figure of Ramón Sampedro (Javier Bardem) consistently presents death as "the only reasonable course of action" (Markotić this issue, 140) in his appeal to the Spanish state for the right to take his life, which he essentially believes has ended due to his disability. (For Markotić, the film itself visually underscores this "reasonable" argument in its repeated representation of Sampedro's rescue from the diving accident that disabled him as a mistake, or as an interruption of a desired end.) Scott Stoneman attends to anti-obesity campaigns (campaigns against an "obesity epidemic" that pundits and politicians believe must be stopped) and to cultural representations implicitly invested—in the name of health, wellness, and able-bodiedness—in the "end" of fatness or fat bodies. In "Why Do Dolls Die? The Power of Passivity and the Embodied Interplay Between Disability and Sex Dolls" Eunjung Kim, considering "the figure of the doll in these films as an embodiment of disability" (Kim this issue, 95), attempts to counter the ableist understanding of passivity and disability circulated by figures like Singer and argues that the filmic representation of doll bodies generally proves so disruptive to normative (active and able-bodied) logics that an end must be envisioned. Invariably, the dolls in the films Kim analyzes are depicted as having a "death" of sorts.

Several of the remaining articles in this special issue are concerned with both the representation of the end of bodies and the idea that bodies or body parts can be put to useful and new (and, usually, problematic and normative) ends. Katherine W. Sweaney's article begins with the end of a disabled figure, since its focus is on Project H.M., a virtual and interactive pedagogical experiment that allowed viewers to watch the dissection of "the most famous brain in the world": that of Henry Molaison, who underwent radical brain surgery in 1957 and was unable thereafter to form new conscious memories. After the end of Molaison's life, through Project H.M. and the virtual broadcast of the dissection, his brain is controversially put to scientific or pedagogical ends (ends that some participants resist through the space allowed them for contained criticism). The end of poor bodies, immigrant bodies, and, often, disabled bodies is also implicitly the subject of Donna McCormack's article, which traces filmic representations of the traffic in organs. These films conjure up the end of one body (or, in what—according to the logic of the films—roughly amounts to the same thing, the *disabling* of one body) so that another, more privileged, body, can have a healthy and able-bodied future. Even Michael Gill is writing here about a television series—the British reality show, *The Specials*—that quickly ends (or flops, or cannot be renewed). Gill argues that the representation of intellectual disability in the series is ultimately only articulated through ableist and homophobic norms. Implicitly, in Gill's analysis, disability and queerness as such (i.e., disability and queerness expansively generating ability trouble and gender trouble) must either be contained through hegemonic norms or end. Finally, as we turn to the question of disability potentially crossing the U.S.–Canadian border, my own conversation with Danielle Peers and Melisa Brittain is, in part, about the fear that disability might represent an end (to, say, resources) and the subsequent urgency of stopping or containing disability at the border through an explicit exclusion clause.

Yet, in the end, this special issue also puts forward "contested corporealities" and "image practices" that will not let these containments, exclusions, or eliminations stand. Contested corporealities, because they are by definition *never conclusive*, cannot simply reproduce the end of disability and disability-as-end, nor do they allow for bodies to be contained or disciplined in ways that serve only limited ends (the body as marketable for neoliberalism or as useful for securing extant gendered or racialized hierarchies). In short, this special issue, from Titchkosky's article to this Afterword, imagines other ends. Perhaps what is paradoxically emergent in this issue, with its array of contested corporealities, is the end of disability studies. In that sense, we might say that the end (purpose, aim, goal) of contested corporealities, and the end (purpose, aim, goal) of disability studies, is the end (termination or permanent transformation) of health, embodiment, visual culture, representation, and spatiality as we know—or think we know, or are compelled to know—them.[2]

Pursuing that end, to come back to Titchkosky, allows for "pedagogic possibility," "interpretations that could be (and sometimes are) otherwise" (this issue, 83), and the ongoing crip pursuit of "that intermeshed place where the meaning of the human is made, unmade, and remade" (this issue, 89). Titchkosky's "otherwise" implies that this un/making is a collaborative project and, in fact, some of the explicitly collaborative projects in this issue (which is itself the result of Sarah Brophy's and Janice Hladki's ongoing collaboration) seem particularly committed to the end of hegemonic conceptions of health, embodiment, visual culture, representation, and spatiality and to the construction of what I've elsewhere termed *convivial visual rhetorics of embodiment* (McRuer 2012, 234). Peers, Brittain, and I are focused in this issue on a crip excess that is articulated through what Peers describes as "diverse, interrelated, and transnational resistance strategies that have emerged and spilled over within and against common sites of containment" (Peers, Brittain, and McRuer this issue, 154)—strategies that are often especially evident in the image practices of filmmakers such as Brittain and Peers themselves. Ann Fudge Schormans and Adrienne Chambon, likewise, attend to the transformative tactics that people labeled intellectually disabled deploy to remake the spaces they have been compelled to inhabit. Focusing specifically on the "What's Wrong with this Picture?" project, in which people with intellectual disabilities literally redrew dominant and stigmatizing public representations (photographs, advertisements, and so on), Fudge Schormans and Chambon emphasize that collaborative and creative practices like this transform "spaces of pain, suffering, and a limited life ... into spaces of pleasure; and spaces of exclusion ... into relational spaces—spaces of belonging, of being with others, and of being-in-the-world" (this issue, 131). Finally, Katerie Gladdys and Deshae E. Lott explain how they intend their "interactive sonic art installation" (this issue, 107), *Augmented Spirit/Extreme Embodiment*, to "co-construct a polyphony" that would rescript both dominant able-bodied narratives and image practices (this issue, 108). *Augmented Spirit/Extreme Embodiment* recreates for viewers the spaces that Lott, who uses a range of health machinery to sustain her life, inhabits and navigates. Viewers are invited into a transcorporeal experience structured by the textures, images, and sounds of a vent-user's life. Through this installation, Gladdys and Lott "make us aware of overflowing, intersubjective ontologies," to borrow a conclusion from Kim's article (Kim this issue, 105), or of "the pleasures embedded in everyday physical yearnings and gratifications," to draw another from Markotić's (Markotić this issue, 145).

This special issue ultimately demonstrates how thoroughly unimaginative and univocal the array of cultural practices is that sustains the "functionalist reduction" of disability to and as the bitter end. The end of contested corporealities is to move beyond that bitter end, materializing—in the process—collaborative pedagogies, imaginative reading strategies, and expansive visual practices.

NOTES

1. Feminist disability studies (including, of course, Titchkosky's article) has long valued and theorized "intersubjectivity"; I pull the term *trans-corporeality* from Stacy Alaimo's important book *Bodily Natures: Science, Environment, and the Material Self* (2010). Alaimo uses *trans-corporeality* to reflect on the ways in which bodies are always located in complex discursive *and* material social, environmental, and scientific networks or systems.
2. In that sense, it might be generative to imagine this special issue as aligned with Jonathan M. Metzl and Anna Kirkland's recently published anthology, *Against Health: How Health Became the New Morality* (2010).

REFERENCES

Alaimo, S. (2010). *Bodily Natures: Science, Environment, and the Material Self.* Bloomington: Indiana University Press.

Fudge Schormans, A. and Chambon, A. (this issue). The Reworking of Spatial Attribution: People with Intellectual Disabilities and the Micropolitics of Dissensus. *The Review of Education, Pedagogy & Cultural Studies, 34*(3–4), 123–135.

Gladdys, K. and Lott, D. E. (this issue). Augmented Spirit/Extreme Embodiment: A Mapped Landscape of Vent Life. *The Review of Education, Pedagogy & Cultural Studies, 34*(3–4), 107–122.

Kim, E. (this issue). Why Do Dolls Die? The Power of Passivity and the Embodied Interplay Between Disability and Sex Dolls. *The Review of Education, Pedagogy & Cultural Studies, 34*(3–4), 94–106.

Markotić, N. (this issue). The Narrator Witness: Dis/Connections Between Disability and Death. *The Review of Education, Pedagogy & Cultural Studies, 34*(3–4), 136–147.

McRuer, R. (2012). Enfreakment; or, Aliens of Extraordinary Disability. In R. Dingo & J. Blake Scott (Eds.), *The Megarhetorics of Global Development* (pp. 233–252). Pittsburgh: University of Pittsburgh Press.

Metzl, J. M. and Kirkland, A. (Eds.). (2010). *Against Health: How Health Became the New Morality.* New York: NYU Press.

Peers, D., Brittain, M., and McRuer, R. (this issue). Crip Excess, Art, and Politics: A Conversation with Robert McRuer. *The Review of Education, Pedagogy & Cultural Studies, 34*(3–4), 148–155

Titchkosky, T. (this issue). The Ends of the Body as Pedagogic Possibility. *The Review of Education, Pedagogy & Cultural Studies, 34*(3–4), 82–93.

Index

ableism 90, 92
Aboriginals 3
accommodation 21
ACT UP 80
adolescent adiposity 128
adversaries 59
aesthetics of disability 23, 29
Agamben, Giorgio 99, 104
agonistic space of opposition 57–9
aheterosexuality 26
Ahmed, Sara 15–16, 105
AIDS 3, 76, 124
Air Doll 21, 26–30
Alexander, Jacqui 89–90
alienation 25
Alpers, Svetlana 119
ambiguity 10, 24, 84
Amenábar, Alejandro 62–3, 66
amnesiac brain 110–22
Andrejevic, Marc 82, 90
Annese, Dr. Jacopo 110–111, 116–18, 120
anthropomorphology 25
anti-obesity 123–33, 135
art and politics 74–81
art project documentation 45
articulation of bodies 12–15, 18
asexuality 92
Asperger syndrome 25
assisted suicide 62, 71
augmented spirit 33–48; art project documentation 45; aural and visual space 38–40; conclusion 46–7; day in the life of Deshae 37–8; description of the piece 41–2; impetus for the collaboration 35–6; mapping unrecognized space 38; movement in the piece 43–4; process 36–7; role of collaboration 40–41; size and scope 42–3; technology and materials 44
Augmented Spirit/Extreme Embodiment installation 33–48, 137
aural space of Deshae's house 38–40
autism 25
autonomy 20, 30, 70

"bare life" 99
Baudrillard, Jean 25
Bauman, Zygmunt 128
being open to the other 107–8
being in the way 15
Belmore, Rebecca 4
Bennett, Jane 29
Bennett, Jill 2
Berlant, Lauren 129
Bérubé, Michael 20
"better off dead" 11, 63, 67, 134
bioethics 10, 15, 20, 107–8
Bishop, Claire 59
blackness 15–18
Blair, Tony 125
blind photography 3
blindness 8–9, 16–17, 101
blurring the borders of gender 87
BMI *see* body mass index
body mass index 126–7, 129
body morphology 127
"body without organs" 30
Body Worlds exhibition 3, 115
Boesveld, Sarah 126, 128
Bourdieu, Pierre 49–50, 55–8
Brain Observatory 110–112, 115, 117–20
Brecht, Bertolt 113, 120–21
Brewis, Alexandra 130
bridging 14
Brophy, Sarah 136
Brown, Nik 105
bulimia 28
Bush, George 124
Butler, Judith 4, 86–7, 105, 131

cacophony 34
CADASIL 62–3
cancer 70
catatonia 26

"catching" the social 128–30
category shift 23–4, 28
causal attributions 126
centralization of the story 121
Chambon, Adrienne 136
chaos 38
Cheng, Anne Anlin 89–90
Chernobyl 114
Christakis, Nicholas 130
cinéma vérité 66
co-constructing a polyphony 34, 137
cognitive disability 17, 20, 63
Cohen, Ed 99
Cohen, Lawrence 104
Collins, Harry 111, 114
color blindness 17
compulsory able-bodiedness 64, 74–6
compulsory independence 70–71
configuration of power relations 50
contemporary film 96–109
cooptation 80
Corkin, Suzanne 117
counter-hegemonic intervention 59
The Count of Monte Cristo 71
Crawford, Robert 126
creative living 36
"crip excess" 5, 74–81
Crip Theory 74–7, 80
crisis of ethics 98, 106
critical space 114
Critser, Greg 129
cultural artifacts 15
cultural disqualification 17
culture of consensus 51
"Culture of Corpulence" 129–30
"A Cyborg Manifesto" 34

dangerous divides 9–10
Davey, Frank 63, 67–71
Davidson, Michael 30
Davis, Todd 66–8
day in the life of Deshae 37–8
De Certeau, Michel 57
Dead Fat 127
death of dolls 20–32; dollness and disability 25–6; ethics of passivity 30–31; on impassivity 24–5; magical thinking 21–4; sex doll deaths 26–30
death drive 69
death memoirs 67
debunking human–machine melds 33
defying intelligibility 30–31
degradation 10–11, 17–18, 31, 62, 125
deinstitutionalization 50
Deleuze, Gilles 24, 30
delusion 27
democracy as interrogation 1–7
departure from normalcy 10–14, 18
description of *Augmented Spirit* 41–2
desire 22, 86–9
deviance 39, 64, 72, 83, 88
dichotomous gendered thinking 85, 93
Dietz, William 129–30
Dirty Pretty Things 97, 103–7
dis-ease 37
dis/connections 62–73
"Disability Gulag" 11
disability and sex dolls 20–32
disability studies 8
disability-as-disqualification 17–18
dispositive 59
dissensus *see* micropolitics of dissensus
The Diving Bell and the Butterfly see Le Scaphandre et le papillon
doll-women 27
dollness and disability 25–7
donor histories 103–7
Down syndrome 11
drag 84–6, 92–3; and disability 92–3
dying to be told 71–2
dying to tell 62–3
dys-functionality 50

Edelstein, David 124
Egan, Susannah 67
Elle 65
embodied interplay 20–32
emptying of possibility 14
end of contested corporealities 134–7
The End of the Obesity Epidemic 129
ending fat stigma 123–33; "catching" the social 128–30; familiarizing fatness 123–8; reading Sidibe's Precious 130–32
ends of the body 8–19; dangerous divides 9–10; narrative beginnings 16–18; spaces between us 14–15; story of ends 10–14
Eng, David 85–6, 89
Erickson, Loree 75, 78
eroticization 84–5
erotophobia 22
ethical turn 66–7
ethics of organ transplantation 96–109
ethics of passivity 30–31
euthanasia 62, 66, 68–9
Evans, Robert 114
exclusion (disability) 8, 59
expunging the other 101–3
extreme embodiment 33–48
"Eye to Eye" 9, 16–17
The Eye 97, 101–3, 107

Facebook 110, 118
familiarizing fatness 123–8
Fantasy and Feather 84
"fat Kid in Class No More" 127
"fat moment" 123–33
fatphobia 124–6, 128–9, 131
Fausto-Sterling, Anne 87
feminism 22
fetishization 89–90
Feynman, Richard 114
First Contact 33
forensic autopsy 115
Foucault, Michel 6, 56, 58–9, 103
Fowler, James 130
freakishness 89
Frears, Stephen 97, 107
free speech 58
Freud, Sigmund 69, 89
friendship effects 130
"frozen moments" 37
Fudge Schormans, Ann 136
functionalist reduction 13, 134, 137

Gard, Michael 129
Garland-Thomson, Rosemarie 3
gender and sexuality 86–9
gender transgression 82–95
genitalia 86–7
geographies of desire 89–92
Gill, Michael 135–6
Giroux, Henry 111–13
Gladdys, Katerie 36–8, 40–41, 137
"global gays" 79
Globe 126
Gramsci, Antonio 80
Greenstreet, Steven 127–8
Greyson, John 4
Guattari, Félix 30
Guys and Dolls 25

Habit Heroes 132
habitus 56
Hallmark Hall of Fame 53–4
Hancock, Ange-Marie 124
Haraway, Donna J. 33–4, 37
Hardy, Michael 78–9
"headless stomach" 125
healthism 3, 126
hegemonic consensus 54–5, 58–9
hegemonic stability 69
heterological space 51, 56
heterotropic space 6
hierarchies 50
Hilgartner, Steven 113–14
Hirschberger, Lynn 123–4, 131
HIV/AIDS 3, 92
Hladki, Janice 136
hollowness 27
homophobia 90
homosexuality 26
How Linda Died 63, 66–7, 69–71
human organ transplantation 96–109
human rights 9–10
human verisimilitude 21–2, 65

I Can't Feel It Anyway 24–5
imagining trauma 1
immobility 26
imperialism 83
impetus for collaboration 35–6
inclusion (disability) 8
inflatable doll deaths 26–30
inoculation of fat 127
intellectual disabilities 49–61; keeping people "in their place" 49–52
intelligibility of sex 90
intercorporeal ontology 20–21, 23, 31
interdependency 35
International Year of Disabled Persons 1981 9
intersex 24–5
intersexuality 3
interview with Robert McRuer 74–81
intimate borders 96–109; bioethical matters 107–8; market economies 98–101; states of exception 103–7; wholesome bodies 101–3

Jasanoff, Shelia 114
jouissance 30

keeping people "in their place" 49–52
Kegley, Jacqueline Ann K. 36–7
Kessler, S. 87
Kim, Eunjung 135, 137
"kind of identification" 123–8
Kitchin, Rob 49–50

LA Times 123
labeling gender 87
labor of racism 16
Lacan, Jacques 103
Lady Boys of Bangkok 82–95
Lane, Anthony 124
Lars and the Real Girl 21, 26–30
Laslocky, Meghan 25
legal blindness 16, 18; *see also* blindness
"letting oneself go" 127
Levinas, Emmanuel 58
LGBT community 77–8
Limb Girdle Muscular Dystrophy 35
"location of culture" 8–9

Logue, Deidre 4
Lorde, Audre 9, 15–18, 134
loss of connection 30
Lott, Deshae E. 33–48, 137

McBryde Johnson, Harriet 9–16, 20, 31, 134
McClintock, Anne 83
McCormack, Donna 135
McDermott, John J. 34, 36
MacDorman, Karl 22
McKenna, W. 87
MacKinnon, Catharine 22–3
McRuer, Robert 3, 64, 70, 74–81; interview with 74–81
magical thinking 21–4
mapped landscape of vent life 33–48
mapping unrecognized space 38
Mar Adentro 62–8, 72, 135
marginality 25, 38, 55
market economies 98–101
Markoti , Nicole 26–8, 79, 135, 137
Means, Alex 6
mechanical body parts 98–101
medicalization 50, 57, 64, 72, 106
melancholic suspension 89
Michalko, Rod 17
micropolitics of dissensus 49–61
Million Dollar Baby 33
misogyny 22
Mitchell, Allyson 4
Mitchell, David 78
Mitchell, W. J. T. 23
Moffat, Tina 127
Mokdad, Ali 129
Molaison, Henry 110–111, 116–20, 135
Moon, Michael 126
morbidity 127
Moreau, David 97, 101
Mori, Masahiro 21–2
most famous brain in the world 110–22
Mouffe, Chantal 50–51, 58–9
movement in *Augmented Space* 43–4
Mulvey, Laura 64
Muñoz, José Esteban 88, 102
museum effect 119–20
mutual self-recognition 17

Nancy, Jean-Luc 107
narrative beginnings 16–18
narrator witness 62–73; dying to be told 71–2; dying to tell 62–3; how Linda died 69–71; norm in dis/ease 63–4; show-and-tell 68–9; telling/telling about 64–8
negative rights 125
Negri, Antonio 78–9
neoliberal consumption 29–30
.net 88
New Scientist 22
new subjectivities 59
New York Press 124
New York Times 12, 123–4, 134
New Yorker 124
Newsweek 129
Ngai, Sianne 126
non-impaired carnality 15
"norm of civility" 3, 126
norm in dis/ease 63–4
normalization of fat 128
normative heterosexuality 64, 91–2
Not Dead Yet movement 11–12

obesity 123–33
obituary 12–14
objecthood 31, 33
objectification of women 22
O'Brien, Kean 24–5, 30
on impassivity 24–5
oppression 31, 59
oral sex 24
"Organs without Bodies" 30
"other spaces" 56
Othered bodies 22
otherness of display 89–92
Ovid 33

parrhesia 58
passivity 20–32; ethics of 30–31
paternalism 34, 92
pedagogic possibility 8–19, 136
penetrative sex 24
people with intellectual disabilities 49–61
performance on an amnesiac brain 110–22; performative pedagogy 112–15; performing anatomies 115–16; performing identities 116–21
performative pedagogy 111–15
performing anatomies 115–16
performing identities 116–21
personhood 9–10, 20–21, 31
personscape 36–8
perverse sexual intimacy 100
perversion 22, 25
phallocentrism 64
Platonic ideals 115, 121
politics of disgust 124
Ponder, Stephen 127
pornography 22–3, 30, 75
post-9/11 United States 130
power of passivity 20–32
Precious 123–33
Price, Margaret 79

privileged narrative understanding 126, 128
"problem" bodies 26
proceeding with dangerous divides 9–10
process of collaboration 36–7
Project H.M. 110–22, 135
psychic perturbation 102
public photographic imagery 49–56
Puhl, Rebecca 125–6
Pygmalion 33

Queer Eye for the Straight Guy 77
queer liberalism 85–6
queer theory 8
queer-crip consciousness 78

racial melancholy 90
racialization 26
racialized religiosity 97–8
racist gaze 9, 16–17
racist-able-ism 18
Rancière, Jacques 6
Reading Sidibe's Precious 130–32
Reagan, Ronald 124
reification of otherness 84–6
relational arts approach 59
Repo Man 97–101, 105, 107
reworking spatial attribution 49–61; agonistic space of opposition 57–9; keeping people "in their place" 49–52; transformation of images 55–7; what's wrong with this picture? 52–5
rhetorical viruses 129
Rich, Adrienne 64
Riding the Bus With My Sister 53
right to die 62–73
"right to die" activism 67
Roberts, Dorothy 125
roboticism 21–2
role of collaboration 40–41
Rose, Nikolas 101, 126
Rossiter, Penelope 6
Rupp, Leila 84

The Safety of Objects 30
Said, Edward 83
Sapochnik, Miguel 97
SARS 125
Satel, Sally 127
Le Scaphandre et le papillon 63–6, 69, 71
schizoid personality disorder 25
Schnabel, Julian 63, 71–2
Scott, A. O. 124
Scrapes: Unruly Embodiments in Visual Art exhibition 4
Sealey, Geraldine 127
The Sea Inside see Mar Adentro
Sedgwick, Eve 126
self-care 126
self-consciousness 20
self-discovery 97
self-identification 86
self-preservation 22
self-representation 51
self-sufficiency 70
sense of place 50
sentience 20, 23
sex dolls 20–32
sexual transgression 82–95
sexualization of innocence 22
Sharkey, Betsy 123
Shildrick, Margrit 82, 90–92
show-and-tell 68–9
Sidibe, Gabourey 123–4, 131–2
Siebers, Tobin 23–4
Sinatra, Frank 83, 92–3
sinful idolatry 28
Singer, Peter 9–17, 20–21, 30–31, 134–5
sites of crisis 6
size and scope of *Augmented Space* 42–3
smashing intellectual disability 82–95; conclusion 92–3; gender, sexuality, desire 86–9; geographies of desire 89–92; reification of otherness 84–6
Snyder, Sharon 78
sociability 29
social contagion 126, 128–9
social positioning 49
Sotelo-Castro, Luis Carlos 58
space of opposition 57–9, 136
spaces between us 14–15
spatial attribution 49–61
The Specials 82–95
Spider-Man 2 33
Star Trek 33
states of exception 103–7
stereotypes 126, 132
sterility 28
stigma of fatness 123–33
stigma of queer 64
story of ends 10–14; an obituary 12–14
"stuff happens" 15
suicide 26, 28, 53, 62–3, 66, 68
"super-crips" 63
super-values 126
superstition 23
surrealism 24
surrogates 24–5, 28
Sweaney, Katherine W. 135
symbolic castration 64
symbolic power 57–9

symbolic violence 55
synecdoche 87

Taylor, Verta 84
technology/materials used in *Augmented Space* 44
telling/telling about 64–8
ten Brummelhuis, Han 85, 87
terrorism 97–8
Thai *kathoey* 83, 85, 87, 89; *see also* Lady Boys of Bangkok
"thing-power" 29
thingification 31
Timson, Judith 126–7
Titchkosky, Tanya 134–6
Too Late to Die Young 12–13
trafficking in women 22–3, 30
transcendence 14
transformation of images 55–7
transformative politics 59
transgender 24–5, 85, 92
transnational inequality 97
The Trouble With Normal 64
Twister game 43
Twitter 110, 118–19

uncanny valley 21–4
uncontaminated space 98
understanding intellectual disability 52–5
unrecognized space 38
"Unspeakable Conversations" 12–13

vent dependency 33–48, 137
virtual sex toys 22–3
visual culture 123–33
visual representations 49–52
visual space of Deshae's house 38–40
visual-democratic cartography 2
visuality and democracy 1–2
von Hagens, Gunther 115–16

war on obesity 125
Warner, Michael 64
Webster, Andrew 105
weirdness 21–2, 28, 30–31
What Do Pictures Want? 23
"What's Wrong with this Picture?" 51–5, 136
Wheelers Against Walkers movement 80
White, Armond 124
whiteness 102
Whitman Helfgot, Susan 97
WHO *see* World Health Organization
wholesome bodies 101–3
Winfrey, Oprah 123
Womack, Kenneth 66–8
World Health Organization 9
Wynne, Bryan 114, 120

Zimmermann, Patricia 1–2
Žižek, Slavoj 30